Principles
of

Real Estate Management

Nancye J. Kirk, Project Editor
Kathleen E. Coakley, Editorial Assistant
G. Patrick Charuhas, Production Assistant

Principles
of

Real Estate

Management

Twelfth Edition

James C. Downs Jr., CPM®

IREM **Institute of Real Estate Management**
of the **NATIONAL ASSOCIATION OF REALTORS®**
430 N. Michigan Avenue, Chicago, Illinois 60611

ACKNOWLEDGMENTS

Dollars and Cents of Shopping Centers. Copyright © 1978. *Shopping Center Development Handbook.* Copyright © 1977. Reprinted with permission from Urban Land Institute, 1200 18th Street, NW, Washington, D.C.

Standard Method of Floor Measurement for Office Buildings. Copyright © 1976. Reprinted with permission from Building Owners and Managers Association International, 1221 Massachusetts Avenue, NW, Washington, D.C.

Forms or other documents in this book are samples only; IREM does not endorse their use. Because of varying state and local laws, competent advice should be sought in the use of any document, form, or exhibit.

Throughout this publication, masculine pronouns occasionally are used to refer to individual property managers, leasing agents, tenants, and the like, regardless of whether they are men or women. This was done for the sake of convenience and does not imply that any or all of these persons are or should be men.

Foreword

THE INSTITUTE OF REAL ESTATE MANAGEMENT (IREM) of the NATIONAL ASSOCIATION OF REALTORS® is an organization of professional property managers who have distinguished themselves in the areas of education, experience, and ethical conduct. IREM offers an expansive program of education courses and materials. The 12th edition of *Principles of Real Estate Management* has been prepared as part of this professional program.

The objective of this text is to introduce property management as a specialized activity that offers services to property owners. To achieve this objective, the book is arranged in four parts: Part I focuses on the relationship between property management and real estate itself; Part II considers the techniques that must be mastered by the professional property manager; Part III applies these techniques to the management of individual property types; and Part IV outlines the administrative skills and entrepreneurial attitudes that are essential to success in the property management business.

About the Author

James C. Downs Jr., holder of the number one CPM® key, was instrumental in establishing the Institute of Real Estate Management. A recognized authority on real estate economics, Downs currently is author of the *National Market Letter,* published by Real Estate Research Corporation, Chicago, of which he was founder and chairman of the board.

The author has an unusually broad scope of experience. He was cofounder of Downs, Mohl & Company, one of the first firms established exclusively for property management; chairman of the board of the First National Bank of Oakbrook, Illinois; director of the Republic Realty & Mortgage Company, National Homes Corporation, Christiana Oil Corporation, and the J. M. Foster Construction Company; past president of IREM; and an editor of IREM's *Journal of Property Management*. He has been a consultant to many government agencies, both in the United States and abroad, and has served two Chicago mayors as housing and development coordinator.

Heeding his own advice to participate in civic activity, Downs is a life trustee of the University of Chicago. He has served as president of the Chicago Community Fund, the Economic Club of Chicago, and the famed Hull House and director of the Chicago Association of Commerce. Downs holds an honorary doctorate from the University of Florida for academic contributions to real estate.

Acknowledgments

Preparing a comprehensive, up-to-date textbook on property management required participation from many professionals in the real estate industry. Persons who reviewed the manuscript and offered important contributions were:

CHARLES ACHILLES, staff vice president, Services and Legislative Affairs Divisions, Institute of Real Estate Management of the NATIONAL ASSOCIATION OF REALTORS®, Chicago, Illinois

FLOYD M. ADASHEK, CPM®, faculty member, Waukesha County Technical Institute, Milwaukee, Wisconsin

ERIC ALEXANDER, CPM®, retired, Oceanside, California

JOHN R. BAKER, CPM®, senior vice president, Molton, Allen & Williams Realty Company, Inc., Birmingham, Alabama

BODIE J. BEARD JR., CPM®, president, Associated Real Estate Appraisers, Inc., a division of Bodie Beard Interests, Inc., Hattiesburg, Mississippi

A. ALEXANDER BUL, CPM®, executive vice president, Henry S. Miller Management Corporation, Dallas, Texas

WALLACE H. CAMPBELL, CPM®, chairman of the board, Wallace H. Campbell & Company, Inc., Baltimore, Maryland

GEORGE J. CRAWFORD, CPM®, assistant vice president, Morton G. Thalhimer, Inc., Richmond, Virginia

LINDLEY C. DEARDORFF, CPM®, vice president, Oxford Development of Minnesota, Minneapolis, Minnesota

DAVID O. DIERCOFF, CPM®, CSM, RPA, executive vice president, Vantage Management Company, Dallas, Texas

W. MICHAEL DORAMUS, CPM®, executive vice president, Brentwood Properties, Dallas, Texas

JULES GALANTER, CPM®, marketing/management supervisor, Illinois Housing Development Authority, Chicago, Illinois

C. RICHARD GRIFFITH JR., CPM®, real estate director, Rosso & Mastracco, Inc., Norfolk, Virginia

RAYMOND P. GUERNEY, CPM®, assistant vice president/property manager, People's Savings Bank, Bridgeport, Connecticut

WINSTON S. HEY, CPM®, property management consultant and instructor, Consolidated Realty Management, San Antonio, Texas

H. ELLSWORTH JONES, CPM®, president, Jones & Jones, Inc., Lombard, Illinois

GARY LANGENDOEN, CPM®, vice president, Wilshire Mortgage Corporation, Glendale, California

J. CLAIR LANNING, CPM®, president, J. Clair Lanning, St. Petersburg, Florida

ROBERT M. LATTIMORE, CPM®, buildings manager, Corporation Properties Division, Hilton Hotels Corporation, Denver, Colorado

GEORGE A. LEEAH, CPM®, partner, Investment Realty Company, San Antonio, Texas

LAWRENCE I. LEVY, CPM®, president, Levy-Leventhal-Nettleton Realty Services, Inc., Orange, Connecticut

ROBERT J. LOFTON, CPM®, vice president, Boyle Investment Company, Memphis, Tennessee

RICHARD F. MUHLEBACH, CPM®, CSM, vice president, Tishman West Management Corporation, Orange, California

DAVID C. NILGES, CPM®, vice president, The T. W. Grogan Company, Cleveland, Ohio

WALTER L. OTSTOT, CPM®, proprietor, Otstot Real Estate, Cherry Hill, New Jersey

RODMAR H. PULLEY, CPM®, executive director, Santa Cruz County Housing Authority, Santa Cruz, California

JAMES W. RAY, CPM®, SRA, chief, Finance and Mortgage Credit, U.S. Department of Housing and Urban Development, Nashville, Tennessee

THOMAS A. SCAPILLATO, CPM®, vice president, Balcor Property Management, Inc., Skokie, Illinois

WILLIAM M. SHENKEL, CPM®, professor, Department of Real Estate and Legal Studies, College of Business Administration, University of Georgia, Athens, Georgia

EDWARD S. SNYDER, CPM®, ASA, president, Edward S. Snyder Real Estate, Inc., Philadelphia, Pennsylvania

RICHARD J. STAMPAHAR, CPM®, brokerage manager, Oliver Realty Inc., Pittsburgh, Pennsylvania

LEOTA MASSA STEWART, CPM®, president, Riddle Property Management, Inc., Houston, Texas

WILLIAM WALTERS JR., CPM®, president, William Walters Company, Los Angeles, California

THOMAS J. WILHITE, CPM®, sole proprietor, Wilhite Associates, Clayton, Missouri

ELTON F. YOUNG JR., CPM®, assistant director/property management, Community Realty Company, Inc., Washington, D.C.

Many of the property management forms that appear in this text were adapted from *Forms for Apartment Management* (Chicago: Institute of Real Estate Management, 1978). Additional illustrations were provided by these property managers:

FRANK H. LIVINGSTON, CPM®, senior vice president, Draper and Kramer, Inc., Chicago, Illinois

ROBERT MOYER, CPM®, Independent Order of Foresters, Solana Beach, California

MICHAEL R. NEILL, CPM®, vice president, property management, IDM Corporation, Long Beach, California

DAVID C. NILGES, CPM®, vice president, The T. W. Grogan Company, Cleveland, Ohio

Contents

xi

Author's Preface

THE FIRST EDITION of *Principles of Real Estate Management* was published in 1947, when the nation was emerging from its five-year involvement in World War II. Since that time, dramatic changes have been made in the structure of American society.

Between 1947 and 1979, the population of the United States grew from 144.7 million to 219.5 million, a gain of more than 50 percent. Just as significant as the change in population size have been the changes in the mores and lifestyles of that population. The introduction of new ideas and new attitudes has affected virtually every phase of business and society. Real estate has been no exception, as seen by the modifications in its nature, design, and structure.

Real property, as will be noted throughout this text, reflects the society it houses. In an effort to match the population's postwar growth, massive construction of all types of properties—residential, commercial, industrial, and governmental—was undertaken. By accommodating contemporary lifestyles and standards, real estate adjusted to the nation's social, financial, economic, and political condition.

The 1970s proved again that housing patterns correspond to society's needs. An analysis of the trends and events of the period will illustrate.

Throughout the 1970s the birth rate decreased substantially, introducing a much smaller average American household. This trend has been accompanied by a declining marriage rate, an increasing divorce rate, and the establishment of less conventional households

1

(i.e., single-person households, unwed couples). The result has been a widespread change in the nature of American housing. The obvious impact has been on the size of dwelling units. Smaller units are needed to accommodate the smaller, modern household, a factor in the growing popularity of condominium ownership. Even locational criteria have been affected. Proximity to schools is not important to childless families; rather, their concern is convenience to entertainment and shopping. In addition to this, childless families have fewer roots than families with children and, therefore, are likely to change residences more frequently.

Mobility is one of the most influential trends of the 1970s. The registration of more than 120 million private passenger automobiles and the construction of an extensive interstate highway system have been largely responsible for the tendency toward urban decentralization. These developments revolutionized the retail trade habits of consumers and consequently the locational preferences of merchants. Evidence of retail trade decentralization is seen throughout the nation, especially in the construction of large regional shopping centers.

It is interesting to note that in the office building industry, and especially in major cities, the recent trend has been toward recentralization. Rentals for new office space in prime downtown locations have reached $15, $25, and even more per square foot. In some cases, large mixed-use developments that combine several interdependent property types within one planned project have been key factors in revitalizing stagnant central business districts.

This does not imply that office buildings have not been constructed in outlying locations. Suburban construction has been strong, especially near regional shopping centers and airports.

Industrial construction never achieved government expectations, and in 1979 it became obvious that plant development and expansion would be needed to increase productivity. Social consciousness also has influenced the industrial scene. The trend has been toward upgrading atmosphere and surroundings with an awareness (often forced on industry by government) for the environment.

Certainly, no discussion of the real estate industry during the 1970s would be complete without specific mention of the nation's economy, and particularly the impact of inflation. In the period between 1974 and 1979, the Gross National Product rose from $1,412.9 billion to $2,391.5 billion, and the average weekly wage in private, nonagricultural industry increased from $154.76 to $212.50. The rate of inflation crept into double-digit levels, and virtually all of the recognized standards relating to income and the cost of housing became obsolete. As property prices (especially for single-family homes) surpassed the rate of inflation, real estate was glorified as an inflationary hedge that attracted not only users but speculators, too.

Another economic trend was the increasing use of credit, which enabled consumers to make purchases without paying immediately. The level of consumer installment credit rose from nearly $175 million in 1974 to more than $300 million in 1979. The combination of record earnings, largely due to inflation, plus credit set buying power at record levels.

Innovations in the capitalist system benefited consumers not only by providing credit. The system also enabled many more people to invest in real estate through syndicates, limited partnerships, trusts, and, to a limited extent, corporations.

Economic and financial developments had an undeniable effect on real estate trends. Although the residential housing market still was dominated by the single-family home, the last months of 1979 witnessed a decrease in the volume of new houses, the result of record-high financing costs. The rental housing sector never recovered fully from the depression it experienced in 1974; as construction costs rose higher and financing become more costly, profitability was restricted even further. At the same time, converting apartments to condominium ownership absorbed thousands of rental units. New condominium projects (especially in resort areas) provided substantial additions to the housing market. All of these units were taken as people sought protection from occupancy loss and increasing rents.

Although largely attributable to inflation, the nation's economy expanded, and the total real estate inventory kept apace. New hotels were erected in large numbers, with room rates often as high as $100 per night and more. Recreational properties prospered. Topping the list were eating and drinking establishments, especially the fast-food restaurants that made eating out practical for the general public. Miniwarehouses were developed for consumers who accumulated more goods than their households could store.

Whatever the trends in real estate, its economics always have been interrelated with government activity. When he adopted the economic theories of John Maynard Keynes and proposed the New Deal, Franklin D. Roosevelt convinced the American electorate that the depression could be remedied and the nation's financial ills eliminated by a managed economy. Although Roosevelt never really restored prosperity (since it was the outbreak of World War II that actually saved the United States economy), the American people firmly believed in the use of political power to achieve economic stability. Their belief became stronger when several postwar recessions were curbed through this power.

Succeeding administrations adopted this same policy. In the mid-1970s, however, many problems arose. Continuous federal deficits were recorded because of these policies. The result has been inflation, a revaluation of the United States currency, and a marked decline in the value of the dollar on world markets. While the concept of a free and open real estate market has prevailed, the future of real estate (and the currency in which its value is expressed) depends on the nation's lawmakers.

Despite the developments that have occurred since 1947, it is interesting that the principles of managing real estate have remained relatively constant. Marketing techniques, personnel management, management plans, tenant and public relations, the solicitation and treatment of clients—in fact, the entire professional bearing of the property manager and the skills that must be mastered—remain much the same. The change has been in the application of these skills to the various property types that have developed. While condominiums were unknown in 1947, they represent a profitable opportunity to today's manager. Regional shopping centers did not exist in 1947, but today dot the suburban landscape and require professional management. Potential in the field of property management has increased greatly, and, likewise, the opportunity it affords.

Dimensions of
Real Estate and
Its Management

Real Estate Management: Industry and Profession

PROFESSIONAL REAL ESTATE MANAGEMENT is the administrative operation and maintenance of property according to the objectives of ownership. Basic to this definition is the concept of property rights. Indeed, only within a legal system such as that adopted by the United States can private property ownership have any real meaning. In the absence of a legal system that discourages infringements on the property rights of others, the institution of private property, and its management, could not exist. Since the practice of real estate management is so closely connected to the institution of private real property, a familiarity with these basic rights is necessary to an understanding of property management.

Historical Perspective of Real Property

In a historical sense, the year of the Norman Conquests, 1066, marked the beginning of American property law. Before this, a system of private ownership had been developing in England, but, with the ascendancy of William the Conqueror, a new system of landholding—*feudalism*—was introduced.

Medieval Legal System

Under the feudal system, neither complete private ownership nor the free transfer of title to real property was possible. The king assumed supreme right over the land and had sole determination of its transfer or forfeiture to the Crown.

The land was divided among lords, who then redistributed their property to vassals for expected services. The tenants owed allegiance to the lord, and the lord owed service to the Crown. In this way, the Crown ensured itself of continued military support. Feudal society was organized with the king at the top, the serfs at the bottom, and the middle strata occupied by lords of varying degrees of importance. Rights in land flowed downward, while services and obligations moved upward: the chain that bound it all together was tenure.

Feudal land tenure involved much more than the use of land: it also presented a hierarchy of social and political rights and obligations. The lord of the manor assumed control of the area's economy and legal jurisdiction over tenants. Because the quality of justice depended on the temperament of the individual lord and his customs, there was no consistency throughout the country with respect to the law.

The accession to the throne of Henry II in the year 1154, however, marked the beginning of a new legal system that eventually dominated England and reached the New World. In order to curb the growing power of the land barons, the new king established a system of royal courts presided over by circuit judges. What is known today as English *common law*—law common to all men, geographically and socially—was created in these courts. Thus, the inconsistencies of local law were broken down. The majority of early common law developed from general customs, traditions, and decisions of actual trials conducted in the royal courts. As the number of decided cases grew, the common law became more established and, therefore, more predictable.

Meanwhile, the Crown began to find new ways to support its armies (e.g. professional soldiers), and a breakdown in the feudal system resulted. Private landholding known as the *allodial system* emerged. The transformation from the feudal to the allodial system was gradual, beginning in the thirteenth century and surviving more than 400 years. Not until the passage of the English Property Act of 1925 were the last traces of feudalism erased.

American Colonial Era

Allodial tenure gives the title holder free and full ownership of property; that is, the owner is not subject to proprietary control by a sovereign. Under English common law, this meant that the landlord owned not only the surface of the land but all that was built upon it, everything below it to the center of the earth, and above it to the sky. Early American colonists attempted to transplant both feudalism and English common law, but only common law survived. Although the colonists established some new rules of law adapted specially to their needs, they actually developed a legal system structured very closely with the English model. Feudalism failed largely because of the vastness of the country; a few English-patterned manors were established, but the American Revolution ended whatever tenurial relationships might have existed between England and America. The allodial system formed the basis of real estate law in the United States.

At the time of the Revolutionary War, America was more than 90 percent rural. Land ownership determined social conditions, national growth, and the country's political life. It is no wonder that property ownership was the most significant internal economic factor of the nation's early years.

A major cause of friction between England and the colonies was the change in policy regarding western land. The Proclamation of 1763, issued by the British government, forbade colonial governors from warranting surveys or granting land west of the Atlantic seaboard. This enraged two special-interest groups: frontier settlers who wanted to move westward and speculators who realized that gambling on land was an easy way to quick wealth.

The resentment deepened in 1774 when the Crown issued additional regulations. One of these was the Quebec Act, which declared that only the Crown (proclaimed owner of the land) could grant land in the western territories. This interference with westward movement enraged the colonists and precipitated the Revolutionary War. The Declaration of Independence asserted that the King of England stifled the normal growth and development of the country by imposing unreasonable conditions on acquiring new land.

It is not surprising that the United States Constitution, framed by representatives of the commercial, financial, creditor, and speculating classes, was concerned primarily with bolstering the rights of private property owners. The first ten amendments (the Bill of Rights) guaranteed both fundamental human and property rights. It is generally agreed that, in the Constitution's reference to "life, liberty and property," the term "property" denotes the right to hold title to and possess property, make legal use of it, and pledge, mortgage, sell, or transfer it. It is an important point that the Constitution was drafted during a revolutionary period by people fleeing their homelands in the hope of finding a new country free from oppressive government. They envisaged a "hands-off" government under which private rights, including property rights, would be guaranteed.

Evolution of Property Management

After the Revolutionary War, cities began to grow in size and number, and this created new investment opportunities. Wealthy capitalists considered real estate an alternative investment for surplus funds, but they did not want the burden of managing it. A few people found this a profitable opportunity, marking the beginning of property management as a service industry. Still, most real estate activity centered around brokerage.

After the Civil War, the population grew rapidly and construction boomed. Downtown areas attracted offices and large hotels, and these properties required management. Most residential properties were single-family and small, owner-occupied multifamily residences; large, multifamily dwellings were as yet uncommon. Neighborhood businesses, primarily owner-tenanted, were still unimportant sources of management income.

Early Urban Trends

Shortly after 1890, several major trends affected urban real estate. First, and most important to property management, was the gradual shift of residential property from the single-family home and two- and three-family dwelling to the larger, multifamily apartment building. Residential construction of this type reached a peak in the mid-twenties. As living standards rose, residential conditions and equipment also were upgraded. Central heating, air conditioning, iceless refrigeration, additional bathrooms, better fenestration, and other improvements were standard features in many new buildings. At the same time, smaller units, such as studio apartments, became popular. For these smaller quarters, built-in furniture (e.g., in-a-door beds and other space-saving devices) combined the uses of several rooms into one.

Advances in structural engineering generated a second urban real estate trend: the tall steel-frame building, popularly known as the *skyscraper*. This technological feat, and the perfection of passenger elevators, provided almost unlimited possibilities for vertical growth. It also introduced the need for special skills in the leasing of high-rise office space.

The decentralization of retail business activity, from the traditional downtown shopping district to important, outlying sub-centers, initiated a third trend: the development of suburbia. Invention of the automobile and the widespread use of electricity were responsible for this dramatic change in living patterns throughout the country.

As these trends took a firm hold on the building activity of most American cities, the need for broad-scale property management became evident. Most buildings constructed in these early years were sold to individuals retiring from other lines of business. These buildings provided an attractive medium of investment, and their management was an interesting post-retirement occupation. Except for a brief period during World War I, residential occupancy was high, rental demand was strong, and the problem of building management had not become complex.

Twenties Boom

The primary cause of the breakdown of owner management was the great rental boom of 1920 to 1922. Many retired businessmen had bought real estate believing it would provide a modest living, and suddenly these investors found that their incomes had skyrocketed to unheard-of levels. They were rich beyond expectation. Their increased incomes opened new vistas, and old yearnings became possibilities. The most important of these was the opportunity to travel, which resulted in extended absences from their real estate investments.

Faced with the problem of managing their buildings while spending winters at far-off resorts, owners went to the best-known local real estate agents and asked them to collect rents, pay the janitor, order the required fuel, pay the utilities bills, and forward the net proceeds. No expenditures were made without an owner's specific instruction, and, usually, the owner planned to be in the city during the leasing season.

In most cases, the local real estate agent entered into this new relationship strictly as an accommodation to a potential sales customer. A clerk was assigned to collect rents, and a bookkeeper sent the owner a simple statement of receipts and disbursements at the end of each month. However, in neighborhoods where rents were highest and multifamily buildings most common, the volume of this business became significant. Real estate agents recognized that management was a profitable field by itself. The greatest amount of management business would belong to the firm or individual who paid closest attention to clients' properties and tried to do a better-than-average job.

Before 1929, the nation's buildings were owned principally by rugged, opinionated individuals who had made their money in specialized fields and imposed their business ideas and practices on their real estate ventures. Property managers were limited in the use of their meager and newly acquired knowledge by owners who insisted that their buildings be managed according to individual dictates. Except in a few isolated instances, the managers and management companies were a brand of "office boy" who had as many policies as they had clients. Properties were operated intelligently for intelligent owners, carelessly for careless ones. Groping for an answer to the problem of efficiency, the agents did not have sufficient freedom to try different management methods or were afraid of losing the newly found business. They lacked courage to defy clients' orders, even when the orders were mistaken or unsatisfactory.

During the twenties, financing was readily available, a condition that greatly influenced income property and its management. One financing trend was *split mortgages,* which broke loans into small denomination bonds for sale to the investing public through investment bankers. Due to a limited knowledge of real estate investments, plus the competition for loans, overlending became widespread. In the reorganization following mass foreclosures, these properties presented a significant income potential for property managers.

Unparalleled urban prosperity characterized the twenties. Building construction was high and was financed primarily by private sources, i.e., insurance companies, building and loan associations, and trustee bonds. Industrial and manufacturing efficiency increased, principally through the use of power machinery, mass production techniques, standardization of parts and processes, and the electrification of industry. Just as production expanded, so did corporate profits and personal income. Due to the security produced by abundant credit, installment purchases became popular, and the economy developed at an unprecedented rate. Not surprisingly, innovations were made in retail business as well, including the emergence of coast-to-coast networks of chain stores. The most prominent were the Great Atlantic and Pacific Tea Company (A & P), F. W. Woolworth, Piggly Wiggly, and Kroger.

Great Depression

Just as the economy was spiraling upward at a record pace and everyone was spending freely, the Great Depression struck. The depression of the thirties (which for the income real estate field actually began in 1928) brought about a wholesale liquidation of the individual owner. Most of the country's income real estate (especially multi-family and commercial buildings built from 1920 to 1929) defaulted to banks, insurance companies, savings societies, trust companies, and investment protective committees. In this fiasco, modern property management had its true origin since, for the first time, a large volume of property was gathered under one ownership, one policy, and one common perspective.

Early in the depression, the lenders-turned-owners studied the existing property management organizations and often concluded that their interests could be served best by creating their own management departments. Not being familiar with the complexities of building management, they believed that the operation of real estate was limited to collecting rents and maintaining the physical structures. Many of those forming these new management departments were builders, architects, and contractors whose work was supplemented by routine collectors and, perhaps, a law graduate. Merchandising, analysis, and real estate economics were overlooked frequently because they were unknown to most of the executives, and also because property management had not been important or advanced enough to demand training in such disciplines.

After the first years of the depression—years of trial and error as management's experience broadened—other views were accepted by the executives responsible for the operation of real estate. The need for adequate analysis, market research, and scientific administration was widely recognized, and many organizations were filling this need.

Recovery and World War II

The concentration of property ownership due to mass foreclosures from 1929 to 1933 was redistributed during the recovery years. Once again, real estate provided a profitable opportunity for investors. Individuals and partnerships—sometimes called *syndicates*—purchased property from banks, insurance companies, and reorganization committees that were reducing their real estate portfolios to resume their predepression responsibilities. Many times, property managers were retained to ensure that properties were put to their highest and best use.

The recovery period of 1934 to 1939 created an upsurge in occupancy, rental rates, and property values. When the United States entered World War II in 1941, urban property was in such demand that the need for professional property management diminished considerably. From the time of Pearl Harbor to the end of 1957, rental market conditions were so favorable for the owner that there was little need for professional management. In the first place, leasing space was no problem because there were more consumers than accommodations. During, and in some cases after, the war years, residential property was subject to federal rent control, so rents could not be increased. Tenants were so happy to find space that it was possible for landlords to neglect interior maintenance almost entirely, lower services, and ignore the whole merchandising process.

Post-War Period through the Seventies

The wartime demand for space was satisfied by large-scale construction that took place from 1946 to 1956. By the end of this period, the number of new units introduced to the market exceeded the demand. Much of this construction occurred in newly developed suburbs, which became more numerous with increased automobile ownership. In early 1957, vacancies appeared; by the end of 1963, local markets assumed more normal characteristics. With ample space, rental rates stabilized and occupancy levels fell, and property owners once again sought professional management.

The postwar period saw greater changes in American attitudes and lifestyles than had been noted in any previous period. Because real estate is a part of society, it too underwent changes in form and structure.

In the first place, the nature of housing changed to reflect the radical differences in the basic family structure brought about by an increased divorce rate, a marked drop in the birth rate, an increased proportion of women in the labor force, greater average longevity, and unprecedented mobility. To accommodate the needs of the new households, a greater percentage of new housing units were found in high-rise multifamily structures that offer greater density and a lower average unit size.

Similar changes were noted in commercial, industrial, and institutional buildings and in their locations. Society's consumer capability and habits, its recreational patterns, its mobility, and its living standards led to the development of shopping centers, fast-food restaurants, skating rinks, golf courses, and widely distributed industrial parks—all comparatively new in concept and design.

The postwar period also was characterized by an enormous demand for office space. Several factors were responsible. More people were employed in government, retailing, and services—

occupations based in office buildings. Also, during this inflationary period, businesses prospered and outgrew their existing quarters. Simultaneously, the need for office space accelerated with the increasing complexity of operations; special rooms for computers, libraries, and seminars were necessary for many office users. Opportunities for professional management increased dramatically.

During the sixties and seventies two important developments affected the burgeoning field of property management. Condominiums were the first. Most were primary homes, but some were second homes in resort and recreation areas and, to a limited extent, commercial properties. For most of the larger multiowned properties, professional management was a necessity. Residential condominiums became even more popular as inflation spread and home ownership was sought as protection. Property management professionals and management firms thrived.

A sharp increase in the mortgage money supply also affected the property management industry by permitting the development of a number of large income properties. A significant mortgage money source was *real estate investment trusts (REITs)*. REITs of both the equity and mortgage variety were offered by investment bankers, real estate firms, and commercial banks at a time when the public was convinced that these securities were desirable forms of investment. In less than a decade, hundreds of millions of dollars in certificates of beneficial interest were marketed to eager customers. During the money crunch of 1974 to 1975, these trusts became suspect because of imprudent loans to developers and builders. Their troubles proved to be a windfall for property managers, who were asked to sustain the properties financed by the failing trusts.

Strangely enough, the problems of the REITs occurred when the real estate industry prospered most. With inflation the chief incentive, many people looked on real property as a hedge against a dwindling dollar—an expectation turned fact for owners of single-family homes, farms, ranges, groves, and land. But, this did not hold true for income property. Such was the situation from 1976 to 1980, a time when various types of investment properties reacted like gold on world markets.

Property Management and Professionalism

Just as the practice of property management evolved from changes in the real estate industry, so did the profession of property management evolve from changes in society's definition of professionalism.

Professionalism grows along with society and the challenges of life, with professions being created on an ad hoc basis as problems occur. The first professions were established in response to the most basic of human needs, i.e., the medical profession was created to care for physical ills and the legal profession to settle interpersonal disputes. The professionalism associated with these occupations developed from the skills and knowledge acquired by their practitioners and were then passed on by educators. Basic needs being satisfied, newer professions are created by people interested in developing a specific field for their own benefit and competitive advantage.

In modern professional organizations (e.g., certified life underwriters, certified financial analysts, and certified public accountants) two factors prevail: first, to establish a corps of tested, capable, and honest individuals in the given field from which prospective clients can choose, and, second, to provide an advantage for those sufficiently skilled to be certified over their unaccredited competitors. In most cases, the original members of a commercial art are self-selected, simply declaring themselves certified under grandfather clauses. These ad hoc professionals establish both a body of knowledge in the field and educational requirements for future candidates.

Founding the Institute of Real Estate Management

During the depression, thousands of income-property mortgages were foreclosed; afterwards, there was a pressing demand for skilled managers to operate these buildings. Although few people or firms had management experience, the new owners needed help.

To relieve this situation, a group of individuals gathered in 1933 to establish an organization of responsible real estate managers. The result was a group of 100 property management firms forming the Institute of Real Estate Management (IREM), an affiliate of the National Association of Real Estate Boards (today the NATIONAL ASSOCIATION OF REALTORS®). Each firm was required to pledge itself to certain practices: (1) The firm would set up separate bank accounts for its own funds and the funds of its clients. Under no circumstances would the funds be commingled. (2) The firm would carry a fidelity bond on all applicable employees. (3) The firm would in no way benefit financially from a client's funds, without full disclosure to and permission from the property owner.

Although the original organization of the Institute of Real Estate Management was simply an adoption of specific ethical standards practiced by a group of private firms, it was the first step ever taken by property managers to determine principles of qualification.

In 1938, a few founders of IREM recognized a need for stronger professional standards. They agreed that only an individual—and not a firm—could qualify for accreditation. John Jones & Company, for example, might be qualified to manage property so long as John Jones was its administrative head, but when John Jones retired, died, or sold the firm, the character of its management might change completely. Obviously, the individual rather than the firm should be certified for property management. Agreeing on this principle, the members of IREM reorganized into a truly professional society, whose membership was restricted to individuals.

Currently, 6,500 individuals have been certified by the Institute of Real Estate Management, and more than 4,300 actively practice as CERTIFIED PROPERTY MANAGERS® (CPMs®). These professionals manage more than $194 billion of the nation's real estate assets. Although most of their time is spent in property management, CPMs® also are involved in brokerage, syndication, counseling, and appraising. There is a great need for professional training in this field, since CPMs® must manage a wide variety of property types— office buildings, shopping centers, mobile home parks, apartments, and condominiums.

Property Management Skills

An effective property manager demonstrates a variety of skills. Diplomacy is essential, since the manager negotiates many delicate matters that arise between landlord and tenant. Expertise in advertising and business promotion is valuable, since the typical building is not large enough to warrant the specialized services of an advertising agency. The manager also should be familiar with economics, statistics, and appraising, because a property's economic life must be considered. Realistic rents must be set, not only for the present, but for the foreseeable future as well.

Education is a vital qualification for the professional property manager. Generally, the educated property manager copes better with the specialized problems presented by diverse properties. For this reason, most states have continuing education requirements for the relicensing of property managers. Today's professional property manager must anticipate and deal effectively with economic, social, and political change. Through education, flexibility and foresight are attained.

There is no doubt that property management is big business today, but it remains essentially a personal service profession, assisting both property owners and the public. A conscientious property manager is aware of the responsibilities for self-improvement and adherence to a strict code of ethics.

Property Management Firms

The advantages of association have been recognized in nearly every field of human activity. The need for specialization has resulted in groups of technicians uniting to provide broader services to clients. Law firms staff specialists in tax law, corporate law, and probate law; medical practitioners form clinics; and property managers establish firms. The objectives of such alliances are sound and worthy of professional recognition.

The Institute of Real Estate Management, although a society of individual professional property managers, is aware of the advantages gained by organization. It realizes that the building-owning public benefits from a single agency that offers specialized services in the many areas of real estate management. As a professional society that testifies to the character and ability of its members, IREM recognizes its responsibility in certifying firms to manage property.

In 1945, the Institute set standards under which certain firms could be recognized as ACCREDITED MANAGEMENT ORGANIZATIONs® (AMO®). Holders of the AMO® designation have met IREM's standards in the areas of education, experience, integrity, and fiscal stability. A firm cannot receive this designation unless it manages property in which it holds no financial interest for a fee and unless it employs at least one CPM® in a supervisory role.

On-Site Management

As properties became larger and operations more complex, professional real estate managers recognized the need for specially trained on-site assistants to handle the day-to-day problems faced by both building owners and occupants. Although initially assigned caretaker duties, the responsibilities of these on-site employees soon rose to sophisticated levels. They became managers in the truest sense, developing skills in purchasing, salesmanship, human relations, insurance, and budgeting.

The Institute of Real Estate Management created the ACCREDITED RESIDENT MANAGER™ (ARM®) designation for the on-site manager who successfully completes a prescribed educational program, meets an experience requirement, and subscribes to IREM's ethical code and rules and regulations. The accreditation denotes the on-site manager's ability as an assistant to the property manager.

Changing Nature of Property Management

Professional real estate management is growing steadily because of three significant trends. First, the simultaneous growth of the population and its requirements for space have increased the total number of all types of buildings. Second, a higher percentage of real estate can be considered investment property. Third, there is a wide acceptance of the fact that property management requires special training and education.

Real estate management may be regarded as a growth profession. Although people have been overseeing real property for most of recorded history, the first managers were concerned chiefly with agriculture and increasing the productivity of the land. Soon, shelters were being constructed for homes and a wide range of human activities.

The real estate industry reflects the demands of an ever-changing society, demands that must lie within the bounds of what is possible and profitable. Society's growth and the distribution, structure, and lifestyles of the population; its economic, cultural, and social evolution; and technological capabilities have altered the form and functions of real estate. This almost continuous progress has produced a definite need for the knowledge and skills that are the subject of this text.

As society expands and changes, the management profession responds to the diverse and complex problems of real properties. Management today requires the services of more professionals; some may be property owners or direct employees of owners, but most professional property managers are self-employed or employees of management agencies.

Real estate in its broadest sense refers to land and the improvements (if any) on it. Farms, mines (with buried mineral content), golf courses, forests, even deserts are considered real estate. However, the classic definition often is limited to nonagricultural property which accommodates individuals, families, commerce, industry, professions, and other institutions. This text, then, shall discuss urban land and its use, with emphasis on income property and its management.

Summary

The professional property manager's role is to oversee the operation and maintenance of real property according to the objectives of the property's owner. Inherent in this definition is the concept of private property, without which individual ownership and use of real estate would not be possible. So important were private property rights to the American colonists that they were guaranteed in the Bill of Rights.

The development of property management within the real estate industry results from a number of factors. The initial demand for management expertise came in the 1930s. After foreclosing on hundreds of mortgages, lenders discovered that the management of these properties required specialized skills. Since that time, the need for property management has been heightened by absentee ownership of real estate, ownership by groups of investors through syndicates and by corporations, and increased urbanization and its accompanying trends.

Recognizing the need for management specialists, a group of property managers gathered during the depression and founded the Institute of Real Estate Management, an affiliate of the NATIONAL ASSOCIATION OF REALTORS®. The Institute awards three designations: the CERTIFIED PROPERTY MANAGER® to qualified individual managers; the ACCREDITED MANAGEMENT ORGANIZATION® to qualified management firms; and the AC-CREDITED RESIDENT MANAGER™ to qualified on-site apartment managers. Through the educational programs offered by the Institute of Real Estate Management and on-the-job experience, property managers are becoming better prepared to provide the management skills that are beyond the scope of most property owners.

REVIEW QUESTIONS

1. Define *real estate management.*
2. What is the difference between the *feudal* system and the *allodial* system? From which did the American system of private property rights evolve?
3. Describe three urban trends that developed during the nineteenth century, and explain what effect they had on the real estate industry.

4. What occurred during the depression of the 1930s that created a need for specialized property management skills?
5. Why was there little demand for property management during the recovery period of 1934 to 1939?
6. What was the condition of the office building industry in the post-World War II period? Why?
7. What was the condition of the mortgage money supply in the 1960s and early 1970s, and what impact did it have on property management?
8. When and how was property management professionalized?
9. What is the Institute of Real Estate Management? What designations does it offer, and to whom?
10. Define *real estate* as it is used in the text.

Chapter Two

Economics of Real Estate

THE PROFESSIONAL PROPERTY MANAGER must understand real estate economics if clients' properties are to be administered successfully.

Real estate represents the largest single segment of the nation's wealth. It has been estimated that two-thirds of the country's wealth is composed of land, land improvements, and land resources (e.g. coal and oil); and it is this wealth that attracts investors.

Real estate is not only important in and of itself but is a major influence in the total economy. In addition to the real estate business (i.e., the sale, management, development, and appraisal of real property), it has an overwhelming influence on the mortgage banking and savings and loan industries, life insurance and construction industries, and the building trades. Further, the property manager must be aware of the influence of the real estate construction industry on the nation's economy. If this construction industry experiences a recession, the economy as a whole will falter. When housing starts decrease, the sale of consumer goods (carpeting, television sets, furniture, and appliances) to furnish these houses also decreases. The result is a national economic slowdown.

Equally important, real estate is the tax basis of local governments. It provides funds for police and fire protection, primary and secondary education, health services, and other social agencies. The value of real estate theoretically backs all municipal bonds, which is indicated by their tax immunity.

Because of its versatility, real estate is recognized by economists and business leaders as a key force in assuring national prosperity.

During slack times, real estate can stimulate the national economy. When business is moving too rapidly, real estate controls are employed to slow down the economy, i.e., through a tight money market and higher interest rates.

Real Estate Market

A *market* is best defined as a meeting of people for the purpose of trading through private purchase or sale, and success in any business requires familiarity with the market in that particular field. The successful property manager, then, must understand the nature of the real estate market, be able to recognize market trends, and know what makes a market strong or weak.

A direct relationship exists between the real estate market and the operation of income property. No property manager can justify an unfamiliarity with the real estate market on the assumption that property managers are not involved in the sale of property. On the contrary, buildings are real estate, just as land and its natural resources are. Renting is selling, just as land brokerage is selling. Since the property manager's "sale" (i.e., renting or leasing) generally does not involve title transfer to a new owner, and because space must be resold as it becomes available, the property manager's interest in the real estate market is actually greater than the real estate broker's.

Although real estate may be purchased either for use or investment, the occupants of a property—as opposed to its owner—are the ultimate users. Economically, then, real estate may be classified as a consumer good rather than a capital good. The economic wellbeing of the real estate industry depends more on consumer conditions than on capital markets.

Because people use buildings, people determine real estate values. This relationship depends not only on the number of people but also on their purchasing power, state of mind, social status, and, in some cases, why they are present at the location of the property. A multistory building would have no value in the center of the Sahara Desert, little value in a small Iowa town, a fair value in a small city, but it would be worth a fortune on New York's Park Avenue. The value would differ not because of the land under the building but because of the effect of people on the earning power of the land. Consequently, since the value of real estate depends on its location, value must be considered principally on a local level.

Real estate markets are subject to 11 factors. Six of these may be termed factors of cause, and the other five factors of effect. The factors of cause are more important, because they bring about major developments in the real estate market. Factors of effect are lesser, but still valuable, indicators of the same economic conditions. Complete knowledge of these factors is essential to an appraisal of real estate conditions and the trends they may produce. Information concerning all of these factors should be compiled on a regular basis. Five factors of cause and four factors of effect depend on local data; only two are national in scope.

Factors of Cause

The six influences on the real estate market are supply and value of money, occupancy, rental price level, local eviction suits, employment level, and family formation.

Supply and Value of Money. The purchasing power of the dollar and its availability for real estate transactions is important in setting the tone of property markets. The influences of cost, availability, and value of money are sufficiently important to the price, value, and earning power of real estate to require a detailed discussion of money later in this chapter.

Occupancy. The law of supply and demand operates as surely in the real estate industry as in any other commodity market. Therefore, the total number of units available for occupancy (*supply*) and the number of tenants who are able to pay the current rent level for these units (*demand*) must be considered in a study of the real estate market.

One fallacy concerning real estate is that there is a normal vacancy level for each property type. It once was believed that real estate, on the average, would be unoccupied ten percent of the time. Recently, the normal vacancy level was set at five percent. However, vacancy is in a constant state of flux, as shown by the graph in figure 2.1, which depicts levels of residential occupancy in the United States between 1914 and 1979. There is no recurring pattern from one decade to the next, so the concept of normal vacancy level is suspect.

In applying the law of supply and demand to real property, managers must recognize that there are two distinct types of oversupply that may result in increased vacancies: *technical oversupply* and *economic oversupply*. Technical oversupply arises when there are more property units in a given community than there are consumers for them. Interestingly, in the case of residential property, there has never been a time when the number of housing units in major United States cities exceeded the number of families to occupy them. It seems that technical oversupply exists only in isolated communities in which a declining population produces the condition.

Economic oversupply, on the other hand, is caused entirely by the inability to pay current rents. This condition occurred during the depression. The country's population expanded, yet, as a result of unemployment and business and banking failures, many potential housing customers simply lacked the necessary money.

Within this context, the term "shortage" can also be explained. *Technical shortage* exists when there are more consumers than units. *Economic shortage* exists when there are more able-to-buy consumers than units. An economic shortage, then, is predicated on the existence of a technical shortage.

Since the turn of the century, there have been only four periods that might be considered real estate booms, namely, the periods between 1922 and 1929, 1946 and 1957, 1964 and 1969, and 1975 and 1979. The most recent boom was caused by inflation, and only certain types of property were involved. Before the inflation of the late 1970s, only war periods presented the necessary circumstances to create an actual real estate boom. During wartimes, it is essential to restrict construction and limit production to those goods vital to the war effort.

FIGURE 2.1

CHART SHOWING OCCUPANCY FROM 1914 TO 1979

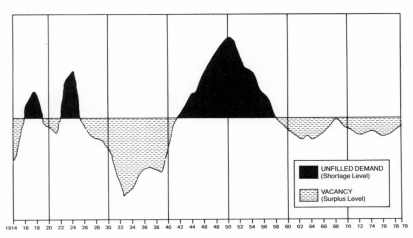

UNFILLED DEMAND (Shortage Level)

VACANCY (Surplus Level)

1914 16 18 20 22 24 26 28 30 32 34 36 38 40 42 44 46 48 50 52 54 56 58 60 62 64 66 68 70 72 74 76 78 79

Consequently, wars are preludes to boom periods: with demobilization and the return of many people to the civilian sector, pent-up housing demands produce consumer pressure.

The real estate boom of the 1975 to 1979 period was not sparked by a war but rather by the steadily worsening of inflation which caused an epidemic distrust of the dollar. As house, farm, grove, and ranch prices soared, the motivation to get off the dollar and into real estate accelerated. Real estate prices—as well as the price of gold—were pushed even higher. Activity in real estate (sales and mortgage lending) set new records.

Since the real estate market is affected by the number of applicable units available, an inventory study should be given substantial weight in analyzing the market. However, the property manager's knowledge of occupancy should be based on a study of occupancy trends rather than current status. Occupancy levels are never stationary: they fluctuate up or down. Which way and how fast they move have a direct bearing on the property manager's planning and merchandising policies.

Unoccupied space is excess inventory and a weight on the real estate market. On the other hand, very high occupancy levels indicate a probable space shortage, and perhaps rent increases are justified. Occupancy levels and their movement are a significant concern of management. An upward trend indicates a strong market, while a downward trend indicates weakness. In any case, the public—not the manager—sets the tone of the market. In periods of high vacancy, the public is alerted to market weakness by increased media advertising and numerous "for rent" signs. Noting these indications, consumers resist rent increases or make greater demands for services at renewal time (decorating and equipment). Property managers and owners must cope with the situation the best they can. In periods of high occupancy, on the other hand, when rental space is hard to find, there is little advertising and few "for rent" signs. During these times, managers raise rents, tighten negotiations, and reduce optional services.

These conditions present two rules. One is that rental market decline is directly proportional to the renting public's awareness of increasing vacancy. A corollary rule is that in periods of increasing occupancy, rent reductions due to high vacancy are terminated when the public becomes conscious of the changing trend.

While the emphasis here is on residential property, these theories apply to all types of properties, commercial and industrial as well. In other words, high occupancy always implies market strength, and low occupancy suggests weakness.

Occupancy data is of fundamental importance to market analysis, and the manager must maintain a systematic record of its trend on a quarterly basis at least. Several sources of data are available in studying the local housing situation. The decennial housing census is a complete list of all urban properties. It includes statistics that reveal the actual vacancy level of residential properties at the time the census was taken. Between census periods, the U.S. Department of Commerce issues a report which lists vacancies by region for both homes owned and rental accommodations. Statistics on vacancy are given for areas inside and outside standard metropolitan areas. While these figures are symptomatic and may be used in a general reference for the overall trends of occupancy, they do not have specific application in any one locale.

Data on office building occupancy is provided annually by the Building Owners and Managers Association (BOMA). Store occupancy is relatively easy to estimate, since vacancies are so obvious.

Other sources of data include local power companies, which can provide the ratio of idle meters to total units; the local postmaster, who can have mail carriers report vacancies on their routes and relate that to the total number of active mail recipients; county planning commissions, which have data on vacancies and new units; and a property manager's own vacancy statistics, which indicate the kind and trend of occupancy. Often a number of property managers combine statistics into a larger and more representative sample of the operating experience in their area.

Rental Level.   While occupancy shows the relationship between supply and demand at the current rental level, rental price level shows the economic strength of the existing real estate situation.

It is essential that the student of real estate economics understand one peculiarity of the rental price structure: rental price cannot be controlled. It moves upward and downward in response to supply and demand.

Although rent controls have, on occasion, been imposed, the rental market has continued to mount in spite of them. For example, when rent control was imposed during World War II, premium rents charged by landlords operating illegally, bonuses, and other devices resulted in higher rental rates, despite the controls. (Rent control is discussed in more detail in chapter 3.)

There are two types of rent raises—*nuisance raises* and *economic raises*. A nuisance raise is an adjustment based on the property manager's appraisal of the amount a tenant will pay to avoid the expense, discomfort, and inconvenience of moving. The amount is in no sense proportionate to the tenant's rent nor subject to generalization. Rather, it is an estimate based on familiarity with local conditions. The use of the term "nuisance" does not indicate that the motive for raising rents is based on a desire either to annoy or take advantage of tenants. Instead, it is presumed that increases in operating expenses and taxes require an upward adjustment, the manager being in the position of determining the fairness of the actual increase.

An economic rent raise is based on the existence of shortage and requires exploration of two questions: (1) When does the market reach the point of shortage required for economic rent raises? (2) How is the level of rents to be related to consumer income?

The points involved may be illustrated by citing a representative example. By definition, a residential space shortage exists when an able-to-buy family cannot find suitable accommodations. In most cities, this occurs when the residential occupancy factor is at 98.5 percent or higher. Consider a family with a monthly income of $1,500 currently living in a unit that commands $240 a month, or 16 percent of the family income. Suppose, too, that the current level of occupancy is 99 percent, and, at the earliest moment, the rent is increased by 35 percent to $325 monthly, or almost 22 percent of the family income. The family's first reaction probably will be to tell the landlord that the proposed rent increase is not acceptable and search for a comparable place to live. However, in a nearly saturated real estate market, the search will reveal that any move—in addition to its inconvenience—would force the family either to pay an even higher rent or accept a lower standard of housing. Consequently, the family will agree to the $325 monthly rent. Naturally, the outcome suggested assumes that the higher rent is based on a correct judgment about the state of the market.

Another lesson can be learned; that is, there is no fixed relationship between the level of residential rents and family income. Rent is essentially an independent factor, governed by its own law of supply and demand and fluctuating with occupancy trends. Only if there were a continuing correlation between family income and the status of the real estate market would a fixed relationship make sense. While it is clear that there is a point beyond which the family budget cannot

be strained, it is at this point that the family accepts a lower standard
of housing. The fact remains that the scale of rentals may be raised
(maybe 25 to 40 percent of family income) whenever shortages appear.

The same principles hold true for other categories of real estate,
with the strength of the specific market established by the level of
occupancy. This is the basis on which rental price is determined, more
or less automatically. At this time, reference should be made to *lease
escalation clauses,* often used for office buildings and retail properties.
These clauses (described more fully in subsequent chapters) guarantee automatic rent adjustments for increased operating expenses.
However, such provisions serve only as palliatives, since real rents still
depend on the occupancy trend.

Property managers can identify nation-wide housing trends and
trends in related areas by using the statistics on rental rates paid by
occupants for residential quarters collected by the decennial Census
of Housing. Between census periods, the Bureau of Labor Statistics
includes residential rental rates of 20 metropolitan areas in its consumer price index.

Other sources of data, though far from exact, also may be useful
in spotting trends. For instance, the manager periodically may study
properties under management to determine the average monthly
rent per room or per square foot. These individual statistics may be
combined with those provided by other managers to get a broader
perspective. Managers also might analyze rental rates given in classified advertisements. While these methods leave something to be desired in their statistical validity, they do provide the property
manager some knowledge of rental trends.

Local Eviction Suits.   Tenant credit is important in market analysis
because, when tenants become delinquent in their rent payments,
they do so in relation to current economic conditions. Most tenants
pay rents promptly, except when economic conditions produce layoffs
and rising prices.

A monthly check on eviction suits filed by landlords because of
tenants' failure to pay rent is a reliable indication of tenant credit.
Ordinarily, rent suits are not filed against paying tenants. In times
of vacancy, an increase in such suits signifies weaker economic conditions among tenant groups.

The property manager should be aware, however, that eviction
suits may increase sharply for reasons other than failure to pay rent.
When there is little vacancy and employment is high, for instance,
home ownership transfers will increase through the purchase of

homes for use by those seeking housing. The lack of an alternate residence may force the present occupant's eviction by court action. Thus, the number of eviction suits measures the intensity of a housing shortage rather than a weakness in tenant credit. Because the conditions that cause these situations are entirely dissimilar, there is little chance of confusing their respective meanings.

Statistics on eviction suits are maintained by the local courts in which these suits are filed. The property manager need not know the outcome of these cases, since the number filed indicates the level of legal action taken. The number of cases should be recorded monthly, since this is a reliable indicator of local tenant credit. Eviction suits fluctuate seasonally: most occur during the summer when vacations take place or during the winter when Christmas spending upsets family budgets. It is, therefore, important for the property manager to study the monthly level of suits for a period of years, so that seasonal norms can be established and accurate computations performed.

Employment Level. A market analysis should incorporate those statistics that identify trends of consumer spending. The real estate analyst must answer at least three questions: (1) How many consumers are in the able-to-buy category? (2) What is the trend of their earnings? (3) How do they feel about spending versus saving?

Monthly statistics issued by the U.S. Department of Labor are most important in answering the first question. These statistics disclose (by geographical distribution) the total number of people available for work, the number of persons currently employed, and the ratio of the unemployed to the total labor force. By comparing these data with the latest census data, a manager may determine the number of housing units per employed person and draw accurate inferences about housing demand. Also, information about the number of people collecting unemployment insurance and other forms of public assistance indicate consumer strength or weakness.

In answer to the second question: while it is seldom possible to determine exactly how much money particular consumers possess, their gross purchasing power can be estimated from trends in consumer income. Statistics on average weekly earnings and gross personal income, and the relationship of these factors to the consumer price index, are revealing.

Consumer savings are another indication of consumer attitudes. In times of declining public confidence, consumers save more and spend less as protection against an uncertain future. These actions are reflected in all rental markets, including commercial, industrial, and residential.

This systematic compilation of statistics about the labor force may seem an academic exercise. But the record proves that the professional who gathers and utilizes these data will be ahead of competitors on market information and will earn respect from both clients and colleagues.

Appropriate data may be obtained from local employment offices of the U.S. Department of Labor, whose analysts will provide current statistics on local and regional employment. Information regarding public assistance programs is available from municipal, county, and state welfare agencies and from the U.S. Department of Health and Human Services (which, prior to 1980, was part of the U.S. Department of Health, Education, and Welfare).

Family Formation.   The sixth factor of cause concerns the social revolution that is changing basic lifestyles in the United States.

Formerly, the number of marriage licenses indicated the formation of family units of some permanence, predictable as to size, growth, and composition. No longer is this necessarily the case, and no longer is the family the only measure of housing demand.

In recent years, the Bureau of the Census has applied the term *household* to all persons who occupy a *housing unit,* that is, an apartment, a group of rooms, or a room that constitutes "separate living quarters." A household includes related family members and all unrelated persons, if any, such as lodgers, foster children, wards, or employees who share the housing unit. A person living alone or a group of unrelated persons sharing the same housing unit also is considered a household.

It was announced by the Census Bureau in 1979 that there were more than 1,500,000 unmarried couples who had established households, and there are increasing numbers of childless married couples, single adults, and senior citizens. With these smaller households, the average residential unit also will be smaller in the future.

Factors of Effect
The five factors of effect—foreclosures, mortgage volume, building activity, real estate sales, and real estate securities—are widely accepted indices of real estate conditions.

Two views emerge on measuring the strength or weakness of the real estate market. One states that the level of activity in real estate is the key to understanding the fluctuations in its values. The other view claims activity in itself is unimportant and that other factors (those of effect) must be considered for a broader perspective.

Foreclosures.   An increase in the number of mortgage forclosures indicates an inability of real estate to pay its debts. Mortgage holders file suit against debtors only when interest and principal payments are delinquent, usually because the mortgaged property or the owner cannot earn sufficient money to make payment. A study of foreclosures, then, will confirm trends already observed from studying the factors of cause. In other words, when occupancy and rental levels decrease and the purchasing power of the dollar increases, when there are fewer marriages and more tenants are evicted, it is clear that real estate is losing its earning power. This loss of earning power leads first to unpaid debts, then to creditors taking legal action, i.e., foreclosures. Statistics on the number or dollar volume of foreclosures are not universally available. This information may be obtained, however, from the courts, possibly a local agency (e.g., a title agency), or legal journals.

The student of real estate should remember that the absence of foreclosures in itself does not guarantee prosperity. The lack only shows that real estate is paying its debts, if there are debts. During the Great Depression, real estate debts were liquidated to such an extent that foreclosures (after rising to unprecedented peaks) simply disappeared, but there was definitely no real estate prosperity during this period.

Mortgage Volume.   Most loans reflect the lender's confidence in the borrower, in the security offered as collateral, or both. Loans made on real estate are no exception. Lenders must believe that the real estate is sound, that it will retain or increase its value, and that it can earn enough to ensure repayment of the loan. Increases in mortgage lending indicate confidence in the safety and desirability of real estate, but they do not create improved real estate conditions. When the trend is downward and the factors of cause are unfavorable, mortgage volume will be lower, fewer lenders having the confidence to make loans. Mortgage lending is adversely affected by rising interest rates; this was apparent in 1974 and again in 1979. (There will be a more detailed discussion of this situation later in the chapter.)

In most counties, statistics are gathered on the number and dollar value of the monthly trust deed entries. If this information is not released by public authorities, it may be compiled and made available by savings and loan associations and mortgage bankers.

Building Activity.　In spite of the emphasis placed on construction as a factor in real estate prosperity, it cannot be considered a cause. Rather, it is a measure of the financial potential of vacant land.

Large-scale building depresses the real estate market by introducing new supply and reducing the scarcity factor; this is true for both commercial and residential space. A high volume of building, therefore, may precede slack periods unless it is matched by a corresponding increase in demand. In 1973 to 1975 and again in 1978 to 1979 (when building was at high levels), housing construction dropped sharply because of high money costs without reference to demand.

Since the construction business is one of the country's largest industries and housing starts are an important index of economic wellbeing, it would miss the point to discount the influence of building volume on the local economy. However, when surplus space increases so much that private construction is curtailed seriously, the resulting cutbacks actually reduce the number of consumers for such space. For example, if 1,000 carpenters are laid off because of reduced local construction, a number of them may move on to other areas or be forced to limit their spending.

Virtually all communities issue statistics on the current volume of new construction, types of construction, and the total dollar volume. These are available through local building departments.

Real Estate Sales.　Whenever the question, "How's business?" is posed, the reply reflects the attitude of the salesman or developer. When real estate enjoys a volume turnover of ownership, with frequent sales at high prices, then the answer is that the real estate business, meaning its condition, is good. The real estate analyst, however, considers brisk sales significant only because they indicate the possibility of successful liquidation. This condition reflects a need for and confidence in real estate but in no sense improves conditions.

There is no precise method of reporting real estate prices similar to the systematic and specific quotation of stock prices. Most real estate owners quote values that combine incomplete information with wishful thinking. Recorders of deeds issue statistics on real estate transfers; however, not all transfers can be counted as sales (e.g., inheritances, divorce settlements).

Real Estate Securities. A *security* is an evidence of debt or ownership either given, deposited, or pledged in fulfillment of an obligation. While evidences of debt secured by real property are termed *mortgages,* real estate securities refer to common or preferred stocks in corporations owning real property, bonds secured by real estate, certificates of beneficial interest in real estate investment trusts, or other paper instruments concerning real estate ownership or debt. Securities are considered personal rather than real property, even though they may be secured by real property.

In most instances, real estate securities are not listed on major stock exchanges but are handled over-the-counter by dealers specializing in such securities. Real estate investment trust shares, which are listed on major exchanges, are an exception.

Virtually all real estate investment securities are backed by large residential properties; recently, however, single-family house mortgages are being pooled in "pass-through" funds, against which securities are issued. Pools may be created by cities, and thus the income is tax free, or by the Government National Mortgage Association (Ginnie Mae) and banks, the income of which does not have tax-free status.

The marketability and price fluctuation of securities are more changeable than the property behind them. In adverse times, the market for these securities drops to lower levels than does the real estate they are issued against; at favorable times, they rebound rapidly. While real estate security prices do not cause property values to rise and fall, their price level does reflect changes in real estate value.

Real Estate Cycles

Roy Wenzlick, a well-known real estate economist of the early 1930s, wrote a book entitled *The Coming Boom in Real Estate.* Wenzlick theorized that real estate activity experiences peak-and-valley cycles every 17 to 20 years. He supported the claim with years of research.

The fallacy of Wenzlick's forecast lay in the fact that, in the history of its peaks and valleys, the nation had operated on a classic *laissez-faire* (i.e., government "hands off") economic policy. Yet the theory was proposed when the political and economic climate was changing from this philosophy to the managed-economy philosophy of the New Deal.

Real estate still operates in cycles. The statistics of real estate sales, mortgage lending, and new construction disclose periods of high activity followed by years in which it is markedly lower. But with government control, these cycles are shorter and the amplitude greater.

The traditional graph of long-range business performance depicts a normal horizontal line, above and below which a series of waves represent rises above normal activity and drops below it. (See figure 2.2.) One *cycle* is completed when the wave moves up from the

FIGURE 2.2
CHARACTERISTICS OF CYCLES

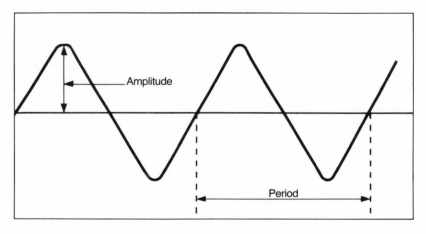

normal line to its peak, down to its lowest reach, and back to normal. The distance between the height of the wave and the depth of the dip is known as the *amplitude*. The number of cycles in a given period of time is the *frequency*.

Why do the lines wave and what do the waves mean? When on the down side, real estate is in trouble: unemployment is on the rise, vacancy is increasing, rental and mortgage delinquency are edging up, real estate sales are off in number as well as price, new building is down, the number and dollar volume of mortgage lending are down, and family formation is on the wane. The reverse is true during recovery; two of the first indications are increasing employment and higher occupancy levels.

The development of the *dynamic cycle* resulted in the gradual upward movement of the normal horizontal line. Research has shown that the amplitude of each succeeding cycle is higher than that of the preceding cycle, as wages and costs of building and land reach new heights. Likewise, the amplitude of each succeeding cycle's dip is not as great, because prices do not drop as far in succeeding down-turns as they did in previous cycles. In this situation, the normal line rises with each cycle.

These changes in the operation, frequency, and levels of recent cycles do not mean that real estate trends and factors will move continually upward. Deflation is not an obsolete concept. Dips in the economy certainly will reappear, and, when they do, it will be as important as ever to recognize them.

Real Estate and Money

Money—its availability, cost, and value—is a deciding factor in the desirability of real estate as an investment. The monetary influences on real estate markets are so important that the property manager must have a basic knowledge of the history, nature, and function of money.

History of Money

Money was widely used in early Phoenician and Egyptian times and in the Golden Age of the Mediterranean, but the Dark Ages produced a society and economy in which its use dwindled. With the development of merchant and craft guilds and the specialized manufacture of particular types of goods, the need for a universal medium of exchange arose again. Indeed, any universally valued commodity used as a medium of exchange can be described as *money* as long as it is durable, scarce, and available. Gold met these requirements admirably.

During the Industrial Revolution with its greater mobility and broader supply of goods, the problem of transporting gold arose. As a solution, goldsmiths stored this metal then issued receipts, or *chits,* for it. Chits issued by reputable goldsmiths were accepted as legal tender in lieu of the actual gold. As trade and travel expanded, the problem of standardizing the chits arose. The logical solution was for the government to standardize and distribute them. Since trade was international, however, it was necessary to establish a world-wide unit of value against which individual currencies could be measured. In 1816, England established the *gold standard,* which meant that the government guaranteed that for each currency unit issued, a certain weight of actual gold had been stored in its vaults, so that on demand the holder of the currency could redeem paper money for gold.

In colonial times, the English-speaking people called the Spanish peso the *dollar*. Thus it was that the dollar was adopted officially as the name of the United States monetary unit. The Coinage Act of 1792 specified that dollars were valued at either 24.75 ounces of fine gold or 371.15 of fine silver. The first coins were minted in 1794. In 1837, and until the passage of the Gold Reserve Act of 1934, the standard was changed to one thirty-fifth of a troy ounce of gold. Under the Gold Reserve Act, citizens were prohibited from owning gold money, and the nation's currency was no longer redeemable in the precious metal. At that time, both the United States and England abandoned the gold standard.

Governments, like people, sometimes yield to temptation. Even before the United States and Great Britain disclaimed the gold standard, a number of countries (including Russia, France, and Germany) had devalued their currencies by failing to maintain specified reserves. Instead, they printed *fiat money* (money not backed by gold or silver), which resulted in inflation.

Political pressure on Great Britain and the United States to increase their money supplies resulted from the theories of John Maynard Keynes, an English economist. According to Keynes, government could reverse the downward trend of its economy through spending programs. This spending would revive industry and commerce, restore general prosperity, and relieve unemployment. Keynes's followers believed that, once prosperity had been restored, government could gain its investment by increasing taxes on the accelerated volume of business and trade. Franklin Roosevelt adopted this theory in his economic policies.

Although implementing this theory lifted the economy from the bottom of the depression, it did not restore general prosperity. The Roosevelt administration's free spending caused the 73rd Congress to cut back funds in 1937, which produced another financial downturn in 1938 and 1939. Concomitant with this, national unemployment, which in 1933 was at an incredible rate of 25.2 percent and had dropped to 14.3 percent in 1937, rose to 19.1 percent in 1938, and still higher in the early months of 1939. The outbreak of World War II and the high production it required led to decreased unemployment; the level was 9.9 percent even before the attack on Pearl Harbor.

During the war period, fiscal caution was abandoned in an

effort to achieve victory. Between 1942 and 1946, the federal deficit totaled $176.3 billion. In spite of this enormous expenditure, the United States dollar at the close of the war was the strongest monetary unit in the world. Indeed, the United States was the most powerful and dominant nation in history—financially, politically, militarily, industrially, and commercially. Out of this came the unprecedented largess of the Marshall Plan, which provided massive aid to the recently defeated enemy as well as other foreign assistance programs. However, the ensuing 30 years have seen vast changes in the underpinnings of this strength. The dollar's desirability in world markets has fallen sharply because of a negative balance of trade, chiefly attributable to the import of petroleum. Domestic inflation also threatens the strength of the economy; the government has consistently spent more money than it had, and the federal debt has risen to record levels. Furthermore, the United States is no longer the sole possessor of atomic weapons, as it was immediately after World War II.

Inflation

The terms *inflation* and *deflation* describe the relationship between money and goods. Inflation occurs when the money supply increases in relation to goods, and deflation occurs when money declines in quantity and goods are comparatively scarce.

In the late 1970s, the supply of money rose much faster than the supply of goods for two reasons. First, the nation could not produce enough oil at home to meet its needs and was forced to import large quantities. With oil in great demand, its price on the world market soared. This led to a continuing deficit in the balance of payments.

Second, the government (local, state, and national) was spending money faster than it was being collected through tax revenues. Political pressure for welfare, education, health care, and disaster relief caused the government to create credit and currency in large amounts, further undermining confidence in the dollar.

The consequence was inflation, and it reached an annual rate of more than 13 percent by 1979. Although the government introduced measures to decrease inflation, it condoned the deficits and preserved a free market in oil, which further aggravated the situation.

Real Estate as an Investment

People acquire real estate for one of two reasons: (1) for use and occupancy (a home, a place of business, for agriculture or recreation), or

(2) as an investment (an income-producing apartment complex, office building, or shopping center). The focus here is on real estate as an investment.

Considered as an investment, real estate is one vehicle for preserving wealth and providing an ongoing return. In making an investment decision, a variety of investments must be examined which compete with real estate in their ability to produce comparable or higher yields on the capital invested or greater profits from appreciation. These alternatives include bonds, stocks, commodities, annuities, and other investment options.

One of the most vexing problems in the management of wealth is whether it should be stored in money or in property. And if in property, what kind? In the inflationary late 1970s, Americans had to decide whether to get "on" or "off" the dollar. Obviously, it is best to get "on" the dollar when it is cheap and "off" when it is dear. The problem is that dollars today are never in a deflationary state; they only grow cheaper. Until inflation is defeated, the best method of preserving wealth is to store it in property, either real or personal (gold, jewels, art works, or antiques); in other words, to get "off" the dollar.

The price and value of income property is controlled by the operation of money markets. For example, if the net operating income from an income property is $50,000 a year, and the yield in the money market increases from six to nine percent, the capitalized value of that property drops by 50 percent. On the other hand, if the yield in the money market increases by an equal amount, the property's value gains by the same percentage. Monetary criteria, rather than real estate factors, control the value of income property.

For this reason, the impact of inflation must be weighed in making an investment decision. The ability of income property to capitalize on long-term debt is a strong incentive in inflationary periods. Apartments are good examples. Barring rent controls and long-term leases, their rental rates are subject to regular revision, yet the financing is almost always long term. Assume an apartment complex cost $3 million to build and was financed on a $2.6 million mortgage when one-bedroom unit rates were $150. Ten years later, its one-bedroom units were renting for $275. If all operating ratios remain the same, the debt is reduced proportionately by inflation alone.

It is not clear at this time whether inflation can be curbed. Economists cannot agree on the subject. Much depends on political factors, and there will be no easy solution. The author believes that so long as values are based on money, the impact of inflation on real estate activity will be great.

Based on these conditions, the investor should consider four questions:

1. What are the trends of money values?
2. What will it cost to borrow money (i.e., interest rates)?
3. What percentage of the purchase price can be borrowed (i.e., leverage)?
4. How long should the loan be extended?

A closer look at these questions will provide the best answers.

Money Value Trends. Month-to-month changes in money values can be observed in government statistical reports covering consumer prices, producer prices for finished goods, prices received and paid by farmers, the money supply, and fluctuations in the interest rate. It is extremely difficult, however, to project these statistics into the longer-term future trends, chiefly because of the government's intervention in economic affairs. Since the 1930s, legislation has been passed to create a wide variety of social programs designed to guarantee citizens economic benefits that previously were left to the natural movements of a laissez-faire system. The costs of these programs have resulted in deficit spending and increased the government's debt from $16.2 billion in 1930 to $780 billion in 1978. From 1970 to 1978 alone, the accumulated deficit amounted to $279.3 billion, and there is no indication that a balanced budget can be attained in the near future.

While the outlook for financial stability might seem bleak, inflation of even greater magnitude has racked other nations over even longer periods without their economic collapse. Between 1973 and 1976, the United States experienced a similar surge of prices plus a recession that was checked briefly only to rise again in 1977 to 1979. Even in that short period, prices—especially in certain categories of real estate—rose dramatically.

Two predictions may affect money values. The first is that inflation can be brought under reasonable control by the government, despite complications presented by the energy crisis. Even so, most economists forecast a recession of unknown intensity and duration. The second prediction is that inflation will continue to worsen until there is a monetary crisis. At that time, the government will issue a new, hard currency under which cash and cash equivalents, as well as debts, will be established at whatever level is necessary. France and

Germany chose this course not too long ago. Those people who own real or personal property, free and clear of debt, will continue to own it, but its value will be determined by the market in relation to the new currency.

There is no sure means for knowing how money values will be affected in either case, but it may be more apparent to the well-informed property manager after a close study of interim values.

Money Cost Trends. An economics student at a major university concluded in a thesis on interest rates that no one could predict fluctuations accurately. This conclusion seems justifiable, as there is no agreement whether interest rates will rise or fall from current levels. Even experienced economists differ on the matter, some believing that the recession which began in 1979 will drive interest rates down, and others claiming that further inflation will keep money rates at high levels. The property manager should be familiar with the arguments supporting each view in order to make informed decisions when problems arise.

Economists who predict lower interest rates argue that the pending recession will result from consumer fears over the energy situation, the squeeze of mounting prices, and rising unemployment, all of which have a deflationary effect. Those who believe that interest rates will increase claim that facts do not support a deflationary trend. Three reasons are cited: (1) the attainment of a balanced budget is unlikely with present political conditions; (2) the balance-of-payments problem created by oil imports cannot be solved overnight (or, perhaps, in less than a decade); and (3) the recession will cause more government spending for relief measures, which will speed inflation.

The supply of and the demand for money actually determine interest rates. Another influencing factor is the amount of confidence that the public has in the future purchasing power of the money to be loaned. The length of the money lease, therefore, also affects the interest rate. The experts do agree on at least one point: high interest rates discourage real estate activity.

Liberality of Lenders. Lending terms have become more liberal in recent years. There have been gradual increases in the loan-to-value relationships as well as longer repayment periods. This trend stems from the widespread use of credit by merchants and dealers in a competitive attempt to increase market activity. Surprisingly, the trend developed during an inflationary period when one would have expected lenders to prefer earlier repayment of loans.

Since the early 1930s, loans for single-family houses have been affected by loan insurance (e.g., FHA and VA insurance) because of government policy to encourage home ownership. These loans were made for much longer terms than were available before their issuance. Initially, they were offered at lower-than-normal interest rates, but these are no longer in effect because of economic conditions.

The amount and terms of loans are determined by existing financial conditions and the real estate market. During prosperity, with money in ample supply and real estate markets strong, lending terms are liberal, especially when competition among lenders is keen. On the other hand, during periods of above-normal vacancy, increasing foreclosures, and falling rent, lenders are conservative.

The highest volume of loans was reached when both the real estate industry and the general economy prospered. This occurred in the early 1970s, when banks, insurance companies, mortgage bankers, and securities dealers overexpanded real estate credit to disastrous levels. In 1974 to 1975, these loans (especially those made by real estate investment trusts) produced a recession in the income-property field, even though housing demand was strong. Single-family homes were bought quickly as inflation hedges, despite rising prices. At the same time, lending terms tightened considerably as economic conditions worsened.

Before arranging financing, the real estate manager should be aware of current economic conditions, remembering that the higher the loan-to-value ratio, the greater the potential profit to a borrower in an inflationary period.

Length of Term. The average American is not well informed on the subject of loans and debt service payments. The person who buys a moderately-priced automobile on time payments over a four- or five-year period pays more than someone who purchases a luxury model for cash. The purchaser of a house for $35,000 with $5,000 down and the balance in a 25-year, 9½-percent-interest mortgage pays $78,633 in accumulated monthly installments, raising the total cost to $83,633. Nothing tangible is received for the interest that has been paid—no land, no additional improvements, no added space.

True, the deductibility of mortgage interest and property tax payments has been a factor in offsetting the high cost of money. However, the point that interest is a waste is still valid. In late 1979, as fears of a coming recession mounted, the rate of gain in real estate prices slackened, even though inflation remained high. The owner of a home has only the benefits of occupancy and a possible profit at the time of sale.

When mortgage interest rates were low, there was an advantage in making the lowest possible downpayment and carrying the highest possible mortgage. However, with a mortgage interest rate in double figures and monthly payment requirements in amortization, there is little likelihood of benefiting from long-term debt. On interest-only loans (no amortization required and the entire principal due at maturity), at least a gamble on further inflation is being taken.

Real Estate Money Supply

Some economists believe that forecasting business conditions requires close scrutiny of the nation's *money supply* (defined as the total amount of currency outstanding plus the total number of demand deposits in all of the nation's banks). These economists theorize that decreases in the money supply depress business activity. The total money supply of the nation has increased substantially through the years—sometimes at a higher rate, sometimes at a slower rate, but rarely has it decreased. The Federal Reserve Bank controls the money supply and thus is an important factor in the national economy.

Real estate activity also is influenced by its own money supply, i.e., money available (especially from the mortgage money market) for the financing of sales, new construction, land development, and acquisition. Real estate activity is stimulated when funds are available at reasonable rates; it is curbed by a reduction in the money supply or an increase in mortgage rates to higher than conventional rates.

A number of sources supply money for real estate. The principal ones are discussed here.

Savings and Loan Associations. Savings and loan associations are a major source of real estate capital. Traditionally, their loans were confined to single-family homes (often still true), but some have expanded into the field of income property and, through service corporations, can allocate a limited portion of their capital to investment activities.

Because they rely almost entirely on the savings of the American people for the source of their funds, savings and loan associations respond to changes in savings habits. Also, they are affected by the competitive situation in the savings market. When rates offered by other institutions are higher than those legally possible for the savings and loan associations, problems can be anticipated. This situation occurred when United States Treasury bills cut into their savings during the 1978 to 1979 inflationary period. To help them out, the government permitted the savings and loan associations to issue special certificates linked to Treasury bill rates. This permitted them a fairy constant hold on their assets.

Banks and Bank Holding Companies. Commercial banks traditionally have operated mortgage loan departments in conjunction with their savings departments, so they could offer mortgages to savers and retain their business. In addition, these banks make construction loans on income property once other lenders have committed to providing permanent financing. These loans also are made to commercial customers for business and investment purposes.

In the mid-1960s, bank holding companies were established through which banks could expand into a limited number of non-banking enterprises. The mortgage banking field was an important acquisition. In the following ten years, most of the leading mortgage banking firms were bought by the numerous bank holding companies. There was a distinct advantage to these purchases, arising from the fact that bank holding companies can issue *commercial paper* (i.e., short-term negotiable instruments) and use the proceeds to finance projects in the real estate field. The increase in the real estate money supply, from these sources, totaled countless millions of dollars.

Mortgage Banking Firms. Certain firms are in business as mortgage brokers, principally for life and other insurance companies that have large investments in real estate mortgages. Since these firms can place funds in long-term loans (20 years, for example), they are important sources of home and income-property loans.

With the accelerating inflation of recent years, many life insurance companies protect themselves against loss of real capital from fixed-dollar loans through a practice known as "a piece of the action," i.e., participation in the ownership of the properties on which they are making loans. Another protective measure is the outright ownership of investment property which is not affected by inflation. In most cases, insurance companies have refrained from granting loans on single-family homes in favor of loans on large income properties.

Real Estate Investment Trusts. The Real Estate Investment Trust Act resulted in the establishment of many real estate investment trusts (REITs) in the 1960s. These trusts could operate for their beneficiaries, and pay no income tax, if they distributed at least 90 percent of their ordinarily taxable income to their shareholders annually.

Public experience with REITs was disastrous, as had been the case with real estate bonds a generation earlier. The same problems arose with both forms of real estate securities—unrestrained lending, high underwriting profits, and exaggerated estimates of earnings. While the REIT is a sound form of investment, public confidence must be restored first.

Corporate Conglomerates. In the late 1960s and early 1970s, corporations in the industrial, commercial, and financial fields expanded their operations into real estate. Because lack of experience made such involvement impractical, these efforts were largely unsuccessful, and many corporations withdrew from their ventures into real property. Until this occurred, however, corporations were a major source of capital.

Syndicates and Limited Partnerships. Tax shelters for individuals have become popular protection from federal income taxes. Real estate ownership (especially residential types) offers many advantages to the investor. Financial and real estate experts quickly discovered that partnerships and syndicates, which act as conduits to pass tax benefits through to individual investors, could be extremely profitable. These measures offered much higher after-tax yields than other forms of investment. The added funds increased the already large new money supply available to developers and promoters.

Pension Funds. Just starting to have an impact on the real estate money supply are pension funds, which hold assets for the payment of pensions to corporate and government employees and members of unions and other groups. These assets can be invested in long-term holdings. Most pension fund investments are quite conservative, i.e., blue-chip stocks and high-grade bonds. However, largely as a result of a disappointing stock market, these institutions have begun to consider real estate. As yet, pension funds have not had a major influence on the money supply, and any involvement usually is limited to conservative real estate investments, such as high-grade, occupied commercial properties.

Government. In one way or another, the government has been responsible for the broad fluctuations in the mortgage money supply since the early 1930s. Because of the expanding role of government in stimulating real estate activity (not only through control of the money supply but also through housing programs), the subject is discussed in detail in the next chapter.

Summary

The property manager should not underestimate the importance of understanding the real estate market, the real estate cycle, and the effect of money on real estate conditions.

Ongoing analysis of the real estate market, with emphasis on local trends, is fundamental to successful property management. The real estate market is analyzed by weighing the factors of cause and effect. The six factors of cause, which are responsible for activity in the real estate market, are: (1) supply and value of money, (2) occupancy, (3) rental price level, (4) local eviction suits, (5) employment level, and (6) family formation. The five factors of effect, which are indices of market activity, are: (1) foreclosures, (2) mortgage volume, (3) building activity, (4) real estate sales, and (5) real estate securities.

The analysis of the factors of cause and effect should indicate to the property manager the trend of real estate activity. The real estate industry, like business in general, operates in cycles. These cycles are characterized by alternate periods of expansion and contraction.

Theoretically, the periods of expansion are characterized by inflation, and the periods of contraction are characterized by deflation. Inflation is an increase in the general price level because of an increased money supply relative to the supply of goods. Deflation is a decrease in the general price level because of a decrease in the money supply relative to the supply of goods. In reality, there has been no deflation since the 1930s, although there have been declines in overall economic activity.

Of all the factors of cause and effect, probably the most significant is the supply and value of money. The value of income property is controlled by the operation of the money markets. In offering advice on an investment decision, the property manager must examine four factors: (1) money value trends, (2) money cost trends (i.e., interest rates), (3) liberality of lenders, and (4) loan term.

The real estate money supply (the money available to finance sales, construction, development, and acquisition) also influences real estate activity. The principal sources of mortgage money are savings and loan associations, banks, bank holding companies, mortgage bankers acting for life insurance companies and other lenders, real estate investment trusts, corporations, syndicates, limited partnerships, and the government.

1. What are the factors that reflect real estate conditions? Explain each briefly.
2. What are the factors of cause? What is the impact of each on local real estate?
3. How can local trends that influence real estate be measured?
4. Who sets real estate values?
5. In what respect can real estate be described as a consumer good rather than a capital investment?
6. Explain the difference between *technical oversupply* and *economic oversupply*.
7. How does United States involvement in a major war affect the country's housing market?
8. Under what conditions can rents be raised? Describe the two types of rent increases and give examples of each.
9. What is meant by a *household* in the real estate industry?
10. Define *cycle* in the real estate field. Draw a graph showing a full cycle in residential real estate.
11. Is the normal period in a real estate cycle always the same? Why or why not?
12. How can cycle theory be used to forecast real estate trends?
13. What was the theory espoused by John Maynard Keynes? What impact has the implementation of this theory had on the real estate cycle?
14. How did the establishment of the *gold standard* come about? When and by whom was it first established? When did the United States go off the gold standard, and why?
15. What should a property manager know about the purchasing power of a dollar, and why?
16. Where can the property manager find factual help on interpreting money trends?
17. Define *inflation* and *deflation*. What two conditions led to the double-digit inflation of the 1970s?
18. What is meant by the real estate money supply? What are the principal sources of money for real estate? Why should a property manager be familiar with these sources?

Chapter Three

Government Involvement
in Real Estate Activity

THE UNITED STATES Declaration of Independence, written in 1776, asserts that governments derive "their just powers from the consent of the governed" and are instituted to secure for all citizens "certain unalienable rights," such as "life, liberty, and the pursuit of happiness." From this document, the rule of law and responsible government developed, as it has to some extent almost everywhere in the free world.

The need for government seldom will be contested (anarchists excepted), especially where there is a trend toward democratic government for and by the people. Still, there is a growing belief that modern government has departed from the original intent, that it has become too big and complicated to respond to the needs of the population. Change often occurs so gradually that it can be noticed only by professional observers, and today government has extended its power far beyond the original provisions.

There are several reasons for this trend. One of these is the dramatic population growth and the accompanying urbanization that occurred during the first half of the twentieth century. Faced with a suddenly huge population, the central government found it necessary to intervene to maintain order and provide needed services. Social injustices in housing, education, and employment, and dislocations caused by wars and threats of wars, are two other factors that have contributed to government's growth. Since individuals cannot cope with these problems, government at all levels has assumed this responsibility. Yet with the population and the size of government and its bureaucracies increasing, many individuals feel insignificant and powerless.

Government has extended its role into most activities, and real estate is no exception. This rise in power has been rapid, sometimes misguided, and often misunderstood. Nevertheless, the government is a major factor in the real estate industry, and the belief that it will reduce its influence is not realistic. For this reason, the property manager, to be truly effective, must be aware of all governmental policies affecting real estate.

Many government policies are directed toward controlling the money market and consequently have an impact on the real estate industry. Those policies were the focus of chapter 2. The emphasis of this chapter is on the government's direct involvement in administering land usage and providing housing.

Local Government Intervention

For many years the government did not interfere with property owners or their rights and privileges. The property owner could use the land for any purpose. It could be improved in any way or left vacant as a forest of weeds.

Local governments, acting under *police powers* which entailed them to pass any statutes or ordinances necessary to safeguard the health, morals, and safety of citizens, were the first to interfere with real property rights that had been absolute. Legislation was enacted, usually to promote the health and safety of occupants, and regulatory codes were established to control occupancy standards, implement fire regulations, and guarantee the reliability of construction materials.

Zoning

As early as 1905, *zoning* codes were adopted by many cities to limit the uses of real estate. These arbitrary regulations often radically changed the value of the properties involved. Still, since they were imposed by official local governments, the ordinances were accepted by the public, which assumed they were for the common good.

Zoning ordinances were designed to protect the character of individual parcels of land, assure the continued desirability for local areas, keep land developments in line with planned objectives, assure compatibility of land use, and control population densities. As has happened many other times, the people, through democratic means, employed government powers to protect their common interest.

Since their original passage, zoning regulations have been strengthened by more rigid ordinances, public awareness of the benefits from controlled land use, and court rulings. As might be expected, stronger zoning controls have stiffer penalties for either their violation or repudiation.

Since the value of urban land usually increases with the intensity of its usage, zoning has an impact on real estate values. Land that may be worth $500 per acre when zoned for agricultural purposes can bring many times that amount when zoned for single-family residences at a density of three or four families per acre. If this same land is zoned for townhouses or garden apartments with a density of 15 to 25 families per acre, its value is still higher. Zoning for a multi-family apartment building (with an even higher density per acre) will, of course, produce still greater value. If this same land is zoned for industrial use (assuming it is economically suitable), the value may reach levels exceeding $50,000 per acre. And if zoned for commercial purposes, the land value may rise to astronomical levels, with amounts no longer computed by acreage but in dollars per square foot.

In a dynamic economy, it is not always desirable to freeze the pattern of land use. Sometimes it is prudent to amend zoning ordinances and bring them into line with current planning objectives. On the other hand, instead of changing the zoning ordinance itself, changing only the use of a given parcel may be considered. This practice is *spot zoning*. It is objected to because it permits a property to be used in a manner that is inconsistent with the area's zoning classification and because it usually favors the owner of the property. Safeguards against spot zoning are contained in most local zoning procedures; should such zoning be permitted, it likely would be invalidated by the courts if incompatible with the city's overall plan.

Because conversion of property from a lower to a higher zoning category can be profitable and favor individual owners, honest officials make amendments to zoning ordinances only for serious and sound reasons. Property managers often are asked to prepare studies to be used for expert testimony before zoning boards of appeals and the courts. Before supporting a zoning change, the property manager must be sure that the client's objective is in accord with the common good. For instance, the property manager should beware of any zoning actions that would be destructive, arbitrary, racially motivated, or purely profit motivated.

Land-Use Planning

Land-use planning includes more activities than does zoning. While zoning is concerned with specific subdivisions of a municipality, land-use planning deals with property in a wide geographic area, sometimes even on a state-wide basis, and with more far-reaching implications and policies. Although land-use planning was unknown before the twentieth century, the need arose as cities expanded and, especially, with the development of the skyscraper.

Land-use planning is viewed as a logical outcome of government's involvement in real estate matters. Plans may be formed to eliminate slums and unsafe areas, handle urban transportation problems, decide the placement of airports and sanitary facilities, provide low-cost housing, and for similar reasons.

Government's Role in Housing

With few exceptions, real estate regulation was a matter only for local governments until the 1930s, when the depression stimulated the federal government's concern with the problems of its citizens as well as their rights. During the Hoover administration, a national conference was convened to consider ways to alleviate the problems being encountered during the early years of the depression.

The main challenge was to rebuild the economy, particularly through correcting the deficiencies in home financing. As a result of this conference, the federal government issued administrative regulations and took legislative actions that led to its active participation in the field of housing.

One of the first programs was the Home Owner's Loan Corporation (HOLC), designed to aid the thousands of families who were threatened by foreclosure of their home mortgages. This agency assisted by providing long-term, self-amortizing emergency loans.

Since this change in government policy, its agencies have taken one of four approaches in their real estate involvement. These may be termed indirect influences, direct financial influences, direct housing subsidies, and community-related programs.

Indirect influences affect housing as the result of monetary, fiscal, and credit policies designed to maintain prosperity by combating inflation. A key example of an indirect influence is the federal government's tax laws, which offer special tax benefits to real estate owners that encourage both investment in housing and ownership of homes for personal use.

Direct financial influences increase the housing supply through credit and institutional arrangements, exclusive of providing direct financial aid. Examples of these influences are: the Federal Housing Administration (FHA), which issues mortgage insurance; the Federal National Mortgage Corporation (FNMC) and the Government National Mortgage Association (GNMA), which provide secondary markets in mortgages; and the Farmers Home Administration (FmHA), which is a direct lender in rural areas.

Direct housing subsidies increase the supply of housing available to low-income households. Although the government's original aim was to stimulate construction during the depression, in later periods its emphasis shifted to social improvements. This was shown by its position on Sections 235 and 236 of the National Housing Act, as well as its rent supplement programs.

Community-related programs attempt to influence the structure of urban areas and public attitudes toward newly developed communities. Examples include the interstate housing and urban renewal programs.

Evolution of a Federal Housing Policy

Government involvement in real estate has centered on the housing needs of it citizens. The nation's philosophy was best expressed in the preamble to the Housing Act of 1949, which began:

> The Congress hereby declares that the general welfare and security of the Nation and the health and living standards of its people require housing production and related community development sufficient to remedy the serious housing shortage, the elimination of substandard and other inadequate housing through the clearance of slums and blighted areas, and the realization as soon as feasible of the goal of a decent home and a suitable living environment for every American family, thus contributing to the development and redevelopment of communities and to the advancement of the growth, wealth, and security of the Nation.

Every president since Hoover has been active in the development of a United States housing policy. The agencies that supervise government housing programs, and the programs they administer, are determined by a series of acts passed by Congress. Housing legislation is passed almost every year. However, five acts can be singled out as significant.

The first notable housing legislation was the National Housing Act of 1934. This act created the FHA, which was given the authority to insure long-term mortgage loans made by private lending institutions on individual homes. By providing a home-financing system through federal mortgage insurance, the FHA encouraged improvement in housing conditions and relieved unemployment by stimulating construction.

While this Act was noteworthy, it did nothing to reach lower-income families. To meet the needs of this group, the United States Housing Act of 1937 was passed. This legislation established the public housing program to be administered by the United States Public Housing Authority. The Public Housing Authority was authorized to provide loans and annual contributions to local public housing agencies for low-rent public housing and slum-clearance projects.

The third significant housing act was the Housing Act of 1949, which was passed in response to the flight of the middle class to the suburbs and consequent urban decline. This act provided for: federal assistance to localities for slum clearance and urban redevelopment; construction of low-rent public housing; research into reducing construction and maintenance costs; and new programs for rural housing through FmHA.

Also worthy of special attention is the Housing and Urban Development Act of 1965, which created the U.S. Department of Housing and Urban Development. By creating HUD, cabinet-level recognition was given to the nation's housing problems. HUD became the successor of a number of federal housing agencies that gradually evolved out of the effort that began in the depression to stimulate housing development.

Fifth is the Housing and Community Development Act of 1974, which represented a new turn in the government's housing philosophy. The Act authorized the Section 8 program of housing assistance and the community development block grant program (both of which are discussed in detail later in this chapter). These two programs form the core of current federal housing assistance.

As new housing programs are authorized by legislation, they often are in the form of amendments to one of these basic acts and referred to by their numbers in the amended act. For example, Section 201 of the Housing and Community Development Act of 1974 amended the Housing Act of 1937 to create Section 8 of the 1937 Act. This program now is known as Section 8, rather than Section 201. If new provisions do not correspond with an earlier act, the section number of the act that creates them is used. This numbering system can be confusing, yet it must be understood by the property manager involved in government-assisted housing.

While government involvement in housing initially was to pass temporary measures until problems were eliminated, current belief is that it will be permanent. The need for housing assistance is a reflection of three seemingly permanent and pervasive conditions:

1. There are many poor people in this country who cannot afford adequate housing. Current figures indicate that almost 15 percent of the population is below the poverty income level.
2. The relatively high-quality standards for new buildings make buying difficult for those with low budgets.
3. In spite of the trend toward integrated housing, middle- and upper-income families still wish poor people to remain in other neighborhoods.

Added to these trends are the adverse effects of inflation and the high cost of borrowing money whenever inflation exists. Government, then, will be active in the housing market for a long time to come, and the property manager must be familiar with the key programs aimed to encourage community development and provide housing.

Community Planning and Development

Recognizing the close association between housing and living conditions, the federal government provides substantial assistance to improve local communities throughout the nation. In order to interpret the federal government's current policies, the property manager must understand the impact of urbanization and the concept of urban redevelopment.

In rural areas, one doesn't speak of "real estate"; one speaks of "land." "Real estate," then, is an urban term, and real estate management is an urban profession. The property management student who is familiar with the history of urban society will be able to more fully understand government intervention in the housing market.

Urbanization in the United States (and in other advanced nations as well) has been a growing trend. For example, in the year 1850, when the population was 23,192,000, only 15.3 percent of the population lived in cities. In 1900, with a total population of 75,995,000, the number of urban dwellers was 39.7 percent. By the year 1970, only 20 percent of the more than 203 million persons lived in nonurban

communities. In fact, 1970 may have been the peak year for urbanization in the United States, since, in the period from 1970 to 1975, the
Standard Metropolitan Statistical Area (SMSA) increased by only
four percent, while nonmetropolitan areas increased by six percent.

Traditionally, Americans have regarded the ownership of private property—especially land—as a sacred right. Millions of people
immigrated to this nation believing that the ordinary person could
acquire property to use without interference from authorities.

In a society as dynamic as that of the United States, where population growth and the rise of the individual's living standard was
phenomenal, society began to dislike anything old—the Old World,
old goods, old houses. As immigrants arrived and later prospered,
they moved to more impressive dwellings away from their original
homes, while more newly arrived immigrants took their places. During this process, living standards rose as well and the older houses
became obsolete rapidly. Eventually, the immigrants took over the
older, very large homes, but not as originally designed single-family
residences. Rather, these houses were converted to multiple-tenant
occupancy. The process of creating slums had begun.

The two principal characteristics of slums (overcrowding and
deterioration) are evident in the centers of most major cities. Other
characteristics include poor original construction, lack of facilities,
deferred maintenance, inadequate city services, and unplanned
development.

Urban Renewal.   Almost immediately after his first election, President Dwight D. Eisenhower formed the President's Advisory Committee on Government Housing Policies and Programs. This committee, representing the housing industry, labor unions, citizens'
organizations, and the financial community, recognized the need for
a comprehensive approach to revitalizing the nation's cities.

Principal concern was with accommodating public objections
to the razing of slum areas, which then remained vacant for long
periods because of setbacks in starting redevelopment. The Eisenhower Committee recommended a redirection and broadening of the
scope of urban redevelopment projects. The term *urban renewal* was
coined to describe the new, complete program.

The philosophy of urban renewal recognized two basic ways of
treating urban blight: (1) slum clearance followed by immediate redevelopment; and (2) neighborhood conservation and rehabilitation.
This philosophy continues to be applicable to today's programs.

Slum clearance occurs when urban real estate, having deteriorated to a point beyond which it cannot be salvaged, is razed for redevelopment. Local governments typically condemn properties in slum areas, and the federal government subsidizes private developers who construct new projects on the sites.

Government's initial involvement in the control, financing, and creation of real property met with formidable and continuing opposition, both ideologically and practically. While some of these objections were founded on self-interest, many people and organizations were genuinely concerned over what they described as "creeping socialism."

Some facts, however, were obvious after analysis. One was that the best remedy for severe urban blight was through large-scale slum clearance and redevelopment of these areas with new structures. If healthy, livable neighborhoods were to be reestablished, sizable projects had to be developed. These new developments could not be limited to residential use but, depending on the needs of the community, also might serve industrial, commercial, private, and public institutional purposes. Because slum properties were still valuable to their owners, it was not economically feasible for developers to acquire slum buildings (even when condemnation rights were extended for this purpose), demolish them, and redevelop the cleared land. Government assistance was required to write off the residual value of the slum buildings that were a plague to urban society.

Slum clearance alone is not a solution to the urban problem. Measures are needed to protect the physical integrity of neighboring properties, provide homes for displaced families, and replace slums with new projects. Without such measures, slum clearance only leads to the creation of new slums elsewhere.

Much less expensive and less radical a physical change is the kind of urban renewal known as *rehabilitation* and *conservation*. These two programs are linked to preventing the spread of urban blight by improving, rather than razing, existing neighborhoods.

Rehabilitation refers to the repair or structural alteration of buildings, usually required as the result of past neglect of property maintenance. Conservation is concerned with neighborhoods rather than buildings. It refers to a large-scale plan to improve the characteristics of a neighborhood, including not only its buildings but also its services, job opportunities, and general economic condition.

To understand the role of neighborhood conservation, the five general types of urban neighborhood are described:

1. In the *developing neighborhood,* the existing buildings are of recent construction, growth is occurring, and more land is available for further improvement.
2. Most of the land in the *established, healthy, dynamic neighborhood* has been improved. Continuing residential desirability creates self-redevelopment through conversion of land use (for example, the demolition of single-family homes and replacement with apartment buildings) and through rehabilitation, modernization, and upgrading of existing structures.
3. In the *sound, aging neighborhood,* most of the land is improved, and the average age of structures is between one and ten decades old. Housing units are used as originally designed (not cut up or converted); educational, cultural, and spiritual institutions are strong and active; family composition is normal and healthy.
4. The *changing, deteriorating, obsolescent neighborhood* is an area similar to the one just described in age and degree of development. However, here, many of the buildings have been cut up and converted; a large proportion of the dwelling units are overcrowded; there are more transient tenants; the vitality of local institutions has been weakened; and much property is in disrepair or complete dilapidation.
5. The *slum neighborhood,* as defined in the Illinois Blighted Areas Redevelopment Act of 1947, is "any area of not less in the aggregate than two acres located within the territorial limits of a municipality where buildings or improvements by reason of dilapidation, obsolescence, over-crowding, faulty arrangement or design, lack of ventilation, light and sanitary facilities, excessive land coverage, deleterious land use or layout or any combination of these factors, are detrimental to the public safety, health, morals, or welfare."

The government focused initially on those neighborhoods classified as changing, deteriorating, and obsolescent and those considered as slum. More recent focus is on preventing the decline of sound neighborhoods and arresting the blight in those already deteriorating. Housing rehabilitation and neighborhood conservation are designed to achieve this objective.

Community Development Block Grants.   A comprehensive Community Development Block Grant program was formed by Title I of the

Housing and Community Development Act of 1974 to solve some of the nation's housing problems by improving neighborhoods and cities. The *block grant* program, as it commonly is known, replaced seven programs under which communities applied for funds: (1) urban renewal; (2) neighborhood development; (3) open space, urban beautification, and historic preservation; (4) public facility loans; (5) water and sewer facilities; (6) neighborhood facilities; and (7) Model Cities.

The block grant program is a flexible-purpose, revenue-sharing program that makes direct grants to fund local governments in developing viable urban communities. Generally, local governments have total discretion as to how and where block grants will be spent; there is no project-by-project approval as there was in the past.

The block grant program has seven objectives:

1. To eliminate slums and prevent blight.
2. To eliminate conditions harmful to health, safety, and the public welfare.
3. To conserve and expand the nation's housing supply, especially for low- and moderate-income households.
4. To expand and improve community services.
5. To use land and other national resources intelligently.
6. To reduce the isolation of income groups within communities and encourage demographic diversity.
7. To preserve properties with special historical, architectural, or aesthetic value.

Property managers, more than any other professional group, should be interested in maintaining the desirability of cities through this and similar programs. Their livelihoods depend on an adequate supply of sound income structures, especially in the residential field. The manager's first concern should be that of a citizen anxious to improve the community welfare. A dedicated manager should be among the first to stimulate citizens and public officials into improving their cities. The high standards of the American way of life will meet a great challenge in cities, where the majority of citizens live and work. Living standards in these cities must be improved, and the block grant program can and should play a dominant role.

Community development programs require much expertise in the real estate field. Areas for urban renewal and redevelopment first must be identified. Trained to perform property and neighborhood analyses, the manager is uniquely qualified to conduct surveys and advise authorities. Appraisals of the properties and land to be acquired and projections that indicate what type of property is best suited for the reuse of the land must be prepared. Later, these buildings must be financed, constructed, and managed.

In the important work of conservation, rehabilitation, and rejuvenation that will determine the overall success of urban redevelopment, the property manager will find many opportunities for entrepreneurial as well as professional skills. While government, financial, and legal aid is necessary in initiating action, urban renewal is really a private enterprise program. The goal is the restoration and preservation of sound, privately owned, and privately operated structures.

Housing Programs

The principal housing programs now operative share two characteristics. First, they are designed to increase the supply of housing units for low- and moderate-income families. Second, they are subsidy programs with the subsidy tied both to the dwelling unit and to the family. The programs affect both rental and home ownership units in urban and rural areas and permit profit-motivated as well as nonprofit developers and sponsors a role. Characteristics of the major (but by no means all) housing programs are summarized here. However, the property manager should be aware that housing legislation is enacted frequently, and the programs may be subject to change.

Low-Income Public Housing. The *public housing* program is the principal form of federal housing assistance for low-income families. Public housing, though federally financed, is operated locally by public housing agencies (PHAs). There are more than 3,000 locally autonomous authorities throughout the United States.

HUD provides assistance in planning, developing, and managing the projects and gives two kinds of financial assistance: (1) preliminary loans for planning; and (2) annual contributions to pay the debt service of PHA obligations, assure low rents, and maintain adequate services and reserve funds. Rents are based on residents' ability to pay and are applied toward the cost of managing and operating the housing.

Low-income public housing is the most controversial federal housing program. It has been criticized because of the deteriorating living conditions found in many public housing projects. Most of these projects are located in urban settings, and many of the problems are tied to urban environments. In too many cases, public housing has become the "housing of last resort" for the nation's poorest citizens.

Adding to the unfavorable image of public housing is the fact that the federal subsidies often are not enough to supply the difference between spiraling expenses and tenant rental payments. Some housing projects further deteriorate, then, because of deferred maintenance and a fixed or falling rental base.

Rent Supplement. Although no new rent supplement contracts have been available since the program was suspended in 1973, the program was highly popular after introduction in the 1960s. The rent supplement program provides subsidies through a contract in which the government makes monthly rent payments to private owners of multifamily housing on tenants' behalf. The payment makes up the difference between 25 percent of a tenant's adjusted income and the fair market rent determined by HUD. However, the subsidy may not exceed 70 percent of the HUD-approved rent for the unit.

The rent supplement program assists certain disadvantaged low-income persons, including the elderly, handicapped, displaced, and present members or veterans of the military. To be eligible, the individual or family must earn less than what the local law allows for admission to public housing.

Section 202. Section 202 is a direct-loan program that encourages housing development for the elderly and handicapped. This is achieved through long-term loans to eligible, private, nonprofit sponsors to finance rental or cooperative housing facilities. The interest rate on these loans is based on the average rent paid on federal obligations during the preceding year.

Section 235. Section 235 encourages home ownership by assisting low- and moderate-income home buyers. The program operates by federally insuring mortgages on HUD-approved single-family homes and condominium units and through a subsidy. The subsidy is a direct cash payment to the lender on behalf of the family.

The home owner must contribute 20 percent of adjusted income to monthly mortgage payments and must make a down payment of three percent of the cost of acquisition. There are dollar limits on loans and the prices of the dwelling units.

Section 236.   In another attempt to solve the nation's housing problems, Section 236 was implemented to supersede the Section 221(d)(3) program. Section 236 offers operating subsidies to reduce rents and mortgage interest rate subsidies to project owners who provide multi-family housing to lower-income households. It also provides FHA mortgage insurance, which encourages private lenders to participate by reducing their risk.

Tenants contribute 25 percent of adjusted income or the basic rent, whichever is greater. HUD subsidizes the difference between the tenants' contribution and the actual costs of operating the project.

The housing subsidy moratorium of 1973 suspended the Section 236 program. Consequently, current activity consists mainly of servicing Section 236 projects developed before that time.

Section 8.   The federal government's role in housing and urban development was changed significantly by the Housing and Community Development Act of 1974. Since the Act's passage, Section 8 has become the federal government's principal medium for housing assistance.

There are three major Section 8 programs: (1) the existing housing program; (2) the new construction program; and (3) the substantial rehabilitation program.

Designed as a cooperative project between government and industry, the *existing housing program* was developed to relieve the displeasure expressed with the interest rate subsidies offered by earlier programs and to give families more choice in the housing market.

Through this program, eligible families find existing units in the private market. The units are inspected by PHAs, which supervise the program, to be certain they are of standard quality. Upon approval, the PHA makes rental payments to the owner on the family's behalf. A subsidy paid by HUD makes up the difference between what a lower-income household can afford and the fair market rent for an adequate housing unit. No eligible tenant need pay more than 25 percent of adjusted income toward rent.

The Section 8 existing housing program has achieved some success. It is innovative in at least one respect: it permits participating families to choose units freely in the marketplace. Also, it can be managed by virtually any local administrative unit, often a local housing authority that manages conventional public housing as well. The Section 8 program also benefits the landlord, because the federal government's financial participation assures that a known portion of each rental will be paid. Drawbacks are the heavy paperwork required and the unrealistic basis of some fair market rents. Also, there is concern that Section 8 programs may be more costly to the federal government than other government-assisted housing for low-income families.

Under the Section 8 *new construction program,* HUD guarantees private developers of new housing projects, before their construction, that eligible tenants who apply directly to the owner will be subsidized. The *substantial rehabilitation program* of Section 8 operates similarly but assists in the renovation of existing structures. As more emphasis is placed on improving the existing inventory of urban housing, this function of Section 8 probably will expand, especially if the rehabilitation program remains tied to neighborhood revitalization programs.

Section 515.   The Section 515 multifamily subsidy program, regulated by the FmHA, finances new or rehabilitated structures in rural communities. This housing is primarily for low- and moderate-income families and the elderly.

FmHA becomes a direct lender to eligible private and public sponsors. Under Section 515, interest credits then reduce the effective interest rates on loans. The credits are based on individual tenant income: if a tenant's income is low enough, the government subsidizes the interest rate down to one percent on loans made to limited-profit corporations and nonprofit organizations. Under Section 515, the tenant pays less, the owner's debt service is lowered, and the government pays the additional interest to the mortgage holder.

State Housing Finance Programs

Although federal programs provide most housing assistance, in recent years, state governments have become a notable force in the housing field. In reaction to the housing programs established in the 1960s, most states have created their own housing finance and development agencies. The overall goal of these agencies is to aid in the planning, construction, and management of housing.

Housing finance agencies (HFAs) provide financial assistance to a wide range of income groups. Most raise the needed funds by issuing tax-exempt bonds. They are authorized to make construction loans, as well as permanent mortgages, to cover entire projects. Although lending practices vary, most HFAs offer lower-cost loans to developers.

Although the degree of activity differs among the states that have agencies, most HFAs have a broad range of authority. The main programs they are involved in are the following: construction and permanent financing for multifamily projects; direct mortgages for single-family homes; seed money loans; insurance; and housing programs for special groups (i.e., veterans and the handicapped). Some HFAs are empowered to act as developers; however, most work with private developers, with the agency participating in site selection and acquisition, design review, and determining the size and number of units in the project.

Trends in Urban America

People have moved to cities to take advantage of job opportunities and what they have considered more attractive lifestyles offered by urban environments. However, they have not always found what they were seeking. In the late 1970s, both the nation's largest city, New York, and its tenth largest, Cleveland, narrowly averted bankruptcy. Acting with foresight, in late 1975, Congress passed the Municipal Bankruptcy Act which can be invoked in these situations; only through this Act and the efforts of the states of New York and Ohio were these cities saved from financial disaster.

Many other cities were and are similarly threatened. Factors such as inflation, organization of public workers, additional demands for public services by low-income workers, and more welfare cases have increased the costs of city government enormously. With no monies of their own to inflate, these cities, too, run the risk of falling into deficit.

In addition to the financial difficulties of the 1970s, three major challenges appeared that could be met only by more government intervention. The first, and the most serious, was the energy crisis; the second, and closely linked to the energy crisis, was the environmental problem; and the third was the protection of consumers.

Energy and the Environment

All of these were—and continue to be—important concerns of the property manager. For instance, a shortage of petroleum products may have an enormous effect on real estate utility and value. Residential, commercial, and industrial properties, whose access depends on a cheap and available supply of gasoline for cars, may decrease in value during an oil shortage. Properties whose initial values are based on air-conditioning, abundant heating fuel, and other energy-using facilities also will decrease in value during an energy crisis.

Beginning with the oil embargo of October 1973, and continuing throughout the seventies, government action has been directed toward energy conservation policies. One example of government intervention is the approval of financial incentives (i.e., federal income tax credits) for the installation of energy-saving devices. Also, the 1979 call for temperatures in public buildings to be kept within established minimum and maximum levels is further evidence of government concern for the energy problem. With higher fuel bills and a national goal of energy independence, such involvement likely will continue.

The federal government's response to environmental concerns also could change land-use patterns entirely. Expanding land usage, which resulted from private and public development in the three decades following World War II, has been marked by environmental deterioration. The effects have been both emotionally and physically disastrous.

The enthusiasm of the environmentalists, and the virtue of the majority of their proposals, has provided an effective rallying ground for citizens groups pressing for government controls. This has resulted in many questions concerning land use and pollution, and, unsurprisingly, much government activity that has had the effect (if not the intent) of thwarting the objectives of developers.

On the federal level, the Environmental Protection Agency (EPA) was authorized by presidential order in 1970 to develop environmental review procedures. An environmental impact statement represents a detailed analysis of the effects a proposed development will have on its immediate and more distant environment. In many cases, environmental impact statements must be drafted and approved before construction may proceed. On all levels of government, special departments have been set up for regulating air and water pollution, noise abatement, and waste treatment.

Some states have enacted coastal protection laws and regulations that restrict residential, commercial, and industrial development within specified distances of coastal boundaries. The availability and treatment of water have been discussed extensively, and hundreds of communities have cut back expansion plans until a greater utilities capacity can be provided. All newly proposed land developments and redevelopments are considered from the consequences they may have on the environment before permits are granted to proceed.

Many of the measures that have been proposed are too extreme to be implemented. Some call for "no-growth" measures which either are impossible or undesirable to effect. Remembering the saying that "one man's medicine may be another man's poison," it is clear that value judgments are involved in defining terms such as "undesirable," "impossible," and "impractical."

Decisions are made finally by what people want and are willing to pay in extra costs. The hope is, of course, that politics will not affect the operations and rulings of the EPA. This agency must balance man's tendency to pollute the environment against man's desire to see nature preserved entirely.

Environmental issues affect not only proposals for new land use but also existing use. Consider an apartment building that loses comparative value because an interstate highway, constructed after the building, is a noise nuisance. In this case, the apartment building is not the problem, nor would constructing additional residential spaces in the vicinity present an environmental problem. Noise pollution, created by the highway, has, however, substantially decreased the desirability of the residential units. This situation should concern the property manager and owner alike. Perhaps, they will conclude that, while the highway creates noise, it also produces accessibility. Still, the pros and cons must be evaluated for the present and the future.

The problems of energy and the environment are closely linked. With an oil shortage, the EPA may be pressured to relax regulations on the burning of high-sulfur coal, even though its adverse effect on air quality is well known. Or, it may be encouraged to devote renewed interest in nuclear or other forms of energy. Energy and environmental problems also are linked in the sense that either or both can be solved as soon as the public provides funds for research and development.

Finally, it may be added that the energy problem has two sides. Assuredly, present shortages—not only of petroleum products but of natural gas and other energy sources as well—affect the use of existing properties. However, they also seriously limit future building and redevelopment plans. This concerns the property manager because properties must be constructed before they can be managed.

Consumerism and Rent Control

Consumerism, the third noteworthy trend, could change business practices radically. With increased interest in protecting the rights of the average consumer (and a tenant is a consumer), more government action along these lines can be anticipated.

Rent controls are evidence of the consumer movement. Although chiefly found in the residential rental housing market, there is a trend toward establishing controls in the commercial real estate sector as well.

Rent controls first were implemented during wartimes as emergency measures to keep rental rates from soaring during severe housing shortages. In the late 1970s, they became popular to consumer advocate groups as a solution to inflation. Although the promised result was to provide comfortable housing at a fixed rent, the controls actually have had adverse side effects. According to a study prepared by the Institute of Real Estate Management in 1978, rent control causes:

- Deferred maintenance that results in housing deterioration: landlords simply are unable to charge rents sufficient to cover operating expenses.
- Eventual abandonment and demolition of unprofitable multi-family projects.
- No mobility for low-income families and a reduction in housing choices for all renters.
- The halt of new rental housing construction.
- Excessive condominium conversions.
- An increased property tax burden for the single-family home owner.

Each of these trends—energy, environmental concern, and consumerism—has involved huge expenditures and pervasive regulations that could influence the entire economy. Societies and their structures, their politics, and their lifestyles are constantly in flux. The alert property manager evaluates social, political, and economic trends as closely and comprehensively as possible in order to prepare for the future.

Government interest in real estate matters has greatly expanded the opportunities in the property management field as well as in the larger area of general real estate. With its wholesale acquisition of property and its wide variety of holdings in real property, the government has relied increasingly on professional management. For instance, HUD now requires managers of public housing projects containing more than 75 units to be certified as to minimum competence in managerial skills.

The designations of CERTIFIED PROPERTY MANAGER® and ACCREDITED MANAGEMENT ORGANIZATION® have become more meaningful, especially when efficiency and economical operation are essential. Indeed, the supply of qualified management personnel is not adequate to meet current demands in the field, even though the management of subsidized housing presents a special challenge to socially responsible property managers.

Summary

Throughout most of the nation's history, there was little government involvement in the real estate industry. The earliest change to this hands-off philosophy came on a local level in the forms of zoning ordinances designed to control land usage and more broad-scale land-use planning.

The role of the federal government in real estate originated in the collapse of the housing economy during the depression of the 1930s. The government's original intent was to provide temporary solutions until the economy could get back on its feet. Yet, since that time, scarcely a year has passed without some new form of housing legislation being enacted. What has emerged is a complex collection of programs being carried out to a large extent by the U.S. Department of Housing and Urban Development but also to a significant extent by state, local, and other federal agencies.

The key housing programs to be noted by the property manager are these:

- Low-Income Public Housing. This program of federal aid to local public housing agencies is aimed at providing decent shelter for low-income tenants at rents they can afford.
- Rent Supplement. The rent supplement program offers federal payments to reduce rents for certain disadvantaged low-income persons.
- Section 202. This program is designed to provide housing for the elderly and handicapped.
- Section 235. The Section 235 program provides mortgage insursurance to increase home ownership opportunities for low- and moderate-income families, especially those displaced by urban renewal.
- Section 236. This housing program provides mortgage insurance and interest reduction and operating subsidies to reduce rents for lower-income households.

- Section 8. Section 8 has become the federal government's principal answer to housing assistance through three major programs: (1) the existing housing program; (2) the new construction program; and (3) the substantial rehabilitation program.
- Section 515. This multifamily subsidy program for low- and moderate-income families and the elderly in rural areas is administered by the FmHA.

Also displayed by the federal government has been concern for community growth and development. This came about principally as a result of middle-class families moving from the cities and the consequent urban blight. The most all-encompassing response was urban renewal. Under urban renewal there are two methods of treating the problem: (1) slum clearance and subsequent redevelopment, which deals with advanced urban decay; and (2) neighborhood conservation and rehabilitation, which focuses on preventing urban decay altogether. Now forming the core of government involvement is the community development block grant program, which allocates funds for local projects on the basis of a federal funding formula.

In addition to the unsolved housing problem, other problems attending urbanization also are coming to the fore. Chief among these are the energy crisis, the concern for the environment, and consumerism (primarily as evidenced by the rent control movement). All present great challenges—and great opportunities—to the property manager.

REVIEW QUESTIONS
1. At what level did the government first intervene in the real estate industry? Why?
2. What is meant by *creeping socialism?* What is the concern of those in the real estate industry who have this fear?
3. Define *police powers* and *zoning.* What is the relationship between the two?
4. What was the impetus for the federal government's involvement in housing?
5. Write an essay about the pros and cons of: (1) slum clearance; (2) urban renewal; and (3) government-assisted housing. Conclude with recommendations for eliminating defects and minimizing problems in the future.
6. Name the five principal housing acts. Through library research and personal experience, compare their intent with their outcome.

7. Define *neighborhood conservation* and *housing rehabilitation.* How do these differ from slum clearance and redevelopment?
8. What impact does, and will, the community development block grant program have on the property management profession?
9. Define *public housing* and *subsidized housing.* In detail, explain the difference.
10. What are the three programs embodied in Section 8? Explain in detail. What impact will these programs have on property management?
11. Define *housing finance agency.* What is the role of an HFA?
12. Explain the interrelationship between the energy crisis and the environmental problem and the impact of both on real estate trends.
13. A property manager is faced with the possibility of rent control in a community. What action can be taken, what arguments can be raised, to work against the enactment of such control? What arguments will the supporters of rent control use?
14. Characterize the housing legislation (if any) that has been enacted since the publication of this text.

Part
Two

Techniques of
Real Estate
Management

The Management Plan

THE MOST IMPORTANT DOCUMENT in the supervision of real property is the *management plan*. It outlines the property's physical and fiscal management and is directed toward achieving the goals of the property's ownership.

It should be remembered that different owners may have widely different reasons for owning a real estate investment. (These goals are discussed in detail in chapter 5.) Furthermore, these goals may change during the term of the investment. For instance, during the initial term of the investment, an owner may be interested in a tax shelter (as achieved through depreciation and mortgage interest) and may want to make high mortgage payments plus high capital improvements. During the latter term of the investment and in anticipation of retirement, the owner may be more interested in cash flow and lower mortgage payments on the remaining debt.

The strategy expressed in the management plan should reflect the goals of the owner, and, on implementation, the plan should produce the greatest yield as compared with all other strategies considered. Although property managers, for the most part, are compensated for their services in proportion to their ability to produce gross revenue, their continued employment is based on the ability to produce the highest net revenue over a period of years.

A management plan is the formal result of gathering, analyzing, and interpreting all information pertaining to a given property. This is true regardless of the type of property or its specific design or character. Whether it is old or new, residential, commercial, or industrial, the same basic procedure must be adopted. A recommended format for a management plan is given in figure 4.1. An explanation of the components follows.

FIGURE 4.1
MANAGEMENT PLAN OUTLINE

    I. Regional Analysis
    II. Neighborhood Analysis
    III. Property Analysis (Present Status)
        A. Physical
        B. Fiscal
        C. Operations
            1. Policies
            2. Personnel
            3. Procedures
    IV. Market Analysis
    V. Analysis of Alternates
    VI. Property Analysis (Proposed)
        A. Physical
        B. Implementation and Timing
        C. Fiscal
        D. Operations
    VII. Financing (Proposed)
    VIII. After-Tax Financial Analysis
    IX. Valuation (Present Status vs. Proposed)
    X. Conclusion and Recommendation

Regional Analysis

Although the order of the activities undertaken in preparing a management plan may vary, the first step most managers take is to perform an in-depth study of the region in which the property is located.

There is no specific definition of a *region*, other than that it encompasses the city or metropolitan area that has a direct economic impact on the property to be managed. The *regional analysis* identifies the general economic and demographic conditions and physical aspects of the area surrounding the property and determines the trends that affect the property.

Since people create value in real estate, the numbers and nature of the region's population are an important topic. Growth factors and statistical data should be collected for business and industry, tourism and recreation, public improvements and facilities, public transportation and traffic conditions, education, and economic stability (industrial ingress and egress, corporate headquarters, and government installation). The region's political, governmental, and social climate and the condition of the real estate market also should be analyzed.

Most regional analyses are performed by using secondary data; i.e., data that is readily available through typical sources. This may include information published by the federal government (U.S. Census Bureau, U.S. Department of Labor, and U.S. Department of Housing and Urban Development) and trade associations (Institute of Real Estate Management, Building Owners and Managers Association, and International Council of Shopping Centers). State and local governments, local industries and utility companies, and banks and savings and loan associations also may perform studies and make the results available to the property manager.

Neighborhood Analysis

After analyzing the region in which the property is located, an in-depth study of the immediate neighborhood follows. The manager should compare the neighborhood with the broader economic and geographical area of which it is a part to determine why individuals and businesses are attracted to it.

A *neighborhood analysis* is not a recollection of a part of town with which the property manager is generally familiar. The science of property management does not permit the substitution of vague impressions for accurate, reliable data. Unless the manager has recently analyzed the neighborhood in which the building is located, the exacting process of gathering all the required information cannot be eliminated.

From the property manager's point of view, a *neighborhood* is an area within which there are common characteristics of population and land use. In rural areas, a neighborhood may comprise many square miles; in densely populated metropolitan areas, a neighborhood may consist of a few square blocks or the vicinity of intersecting major streets.

While the analytical processes are the same for all types of income property, the focus differs from residential properties to office buildings and shopping centers. The neighborhood is emphasized in evaluating a residential property's qualities, while location suitability is stressed for commercial or industrial properties.

Analyzing a neighborhood first requires defining its boundaries. Often, the boundaries are geographical or man-made barriers (rivers, lakes, ravines, railroad tracks, parks, and streets), with obvious differences in population and land usage on either side of them. In many cases, neighborhood limits are not discernible visually. The manager, then, can obtain information from United States census data, newspaper research offices, city libraries, city planning departments, school boards, welfare agencies, and statisticians. Aided by these sources, the manager will be able to circumscribe the neighborhood in which a property is located.

After the neighborhood limits have been defined, the second step in analyzing it is gathering information concerning the population and its trends. It is important to note that an increasing population is not necessarily a favorable trend. In a well-developed area, a population rise may indicate a change from single-family occupancy to rooming-house tenancy, which is not an improvement. Thus, if a developed area increases in population without simultaneous new construction, other factors must be analyzed to evaluate the trend. But, if a partially developed neighborhood's population increases and there is building activity, the new growth suggests higher values and greater public acceptance. This can be determined by studying the amount of vacant land available and its zoning. While generalizations are dangerous, it is usually safe to conclude that a decreasing population is an unfavorable trend. In any case, the neighborhood's life cycle stage should be noted.

In addition to studying population trends, other aspects of the population should be considered. In a residential neighborhood analysis, for example, a matter of concern is the family unit. Given information on the age and size of the typical family, some assumptions can be made about the stability of the neighborhood's population.

Similarly, the economic level of the population must be evaluated before computing the rent potential of a particular property. There is no better method of evaluating economic level than by determining average rentals or purchase prices within an area. The average rental level (for residential units or commercial space) indicates the type of facilities that the residential neighborhood or business location supports and the amount it contributes to its own maintenance and enhancing the desirability of its population. A significant factor in performing this analysis is the current employment situation. Whether the condition is stable, improving, or declining has a direct bearing on tenants' ability to pay rents.

A physical inspection of the neighborhood also is necessary. In performing this inspection, attention should be given to the level of maintenance exercised on the properties. Are the buildings and grounds well maintained, only in fair condition, or even poor? Are these conditions stable, improving, or declining? Efforts must be made to determine this trend. Evidence of changes in property use within the neighborhood also should be noted. Is there new construction within the area? If so, is it compatible with existing land uses? Is competing space being developed, and, if so, how much? A study of recent land purchases and building permits will reveal if new competition should be anticipated.

Change is an essential characteristic of a free-enterprise society and the communities within it. As the result of new area developments, old area redevelopments, population changes, obsolescence, and shifts in circulation patterns, some neighborhoods gain in desirability, while others decline. For this reason, the property manager should study neighborhood trends as well as existing neighborhood conditions.

The final phase of the neighborhood analysis is the study of the relationship between the neighborhood in general and the specific location of the property in question. Is this location considered desirable, or are there conditions within the area which work to the disadvantage of this property? Consideration must be given to access to transportation (public transit or highway system) and neighborhood amenities (parking, street lighting, shopping, schools, hospitals, and employment). It should be remembered that in spite of the characteristics of the property under consideration, the surrounding neighborhood can set certain limitations on its productivity.

Property Analysis

The next step in forming a management plan is to become familiar with the property itself. This is accomplished by preparing a complete description of the building and physically walking through the property to inspect its accommodations, basic architectural design, and overall physical condition. Specific questions should come to mind during the inspection, with the kinds of questions varying from one property type to another. In every case, an inspection of the structure and condition of a property is not complete until these questions have been answered:

- How many living units or rentable square feet does the building contain? If it is an apartment building, what are the sizes of the units (room size, number of rooms)?
- How desirable is the property (visual impression, age, style, layout, approaches, public space, character of tenancy)?
- How attractive is the rentable space (layout, exposure, view, equipment, fixtures, overall modernity)?
- What is the physical condition of the building (roof, masonry, elevators, heating plant, mechanical equipment, windows and trim, hardware) structurally and in regard to maintenance? Has maintenance been deferred? Can obsolescence be cured? Are there functional inadequacies that can be corrected? Is a structural engineer needed to assay problems?
- What is the condition of the marketable areas (decoration, floors or floor coverings, shades or blinds, entrance halls, stairways, lockers and laundries, public spaces)?
- What amenities are provided, and what is their physical condition and appearance?
- What is the relationship of land to building (e.g., parking facilities, zoning regulations)? Can building and land be used more efficiently?
- What are the standards of the building's current management? What policies and procedures are in effect involving tenant selection, purchasing controls, hiring and training, rent collection, maintenance, and administration?
- What are the existing occupancy level and tenant composition?
- How is the property currently staffed? What are personnel's attitudes, capabilities, training, and goals?
- What financial information is available concerning debts, insurance coverage, property and income taxes, and operating history?

The inspection of the entire property, along with observing all pertinent items and carefully recording the findings, is the *property analysis*. In this examination of the property, and each of its rental areas or units, the manager becomes familiar with the facilities to be marketed to the public and the physical structure to be maintained for the client. While performing this analysis, the property manager is mindful that the main objective is to outline a program through which the owner can achieve the greatest return and the property can be put to its highest and best use.

In the case of existing buildings, most property managers inquire about the present rent roll to determine the vacancy and occupancy, expense ratios, and cash-flow position. This information is useful; however, previous rental history should not be given undue importance when the management plan is formed and, especially, when the rental schedule is established. The truly professional manager is not influenced by rents that another manager established. Any decision on rents reached by a manager at the end of the first visit to a property would be premature, since the property analysis is only the first step in accurately estimating rental value.

Market Analysis

Although a general real estate market does exist, the property manager must identify many smaller markets in order to design a management plan for a specific property. These individual markets include commercial space markets, retail store markets, apartment markets, and single-family residence markets. When forming a management plan, the manager first must place the property in its correct submarket and then evaluate the property by the standards of that market. This process is *market analysis*.

Measurement of Market

Individual real estate markets are easy to identify but difficult to analyze. There are three reasons for this. First, there is no exact unit of measurement in real estate. In the grain market, for example, measurements are in terms of bushels, with each bushel equal to every other bushel. Or, in the stock market, a share of stock in a given issue is identical with every other share in the same issue. But in real estate, this is not the case. One apartment may differ greatly from another. Even within the commercial space market, with its various measuring devices (rentable square foot, usable square foot) and types of measurements (New York method, BOMA method), no universal standard exists.

The second problem in analyzing a real estate submarket is that there is no trading center. In the grain market, there are the boards of trade; in the stock market, trades are made on central exchanges. However, rentals are not made at a central location but are made in real estate management offices and landlords' homes throughout the nation.

This scattered trading results in the third major difference between income real estate markets and other markets: there is no systematic recording and reporting of sales, i.e., rents. When a bushel of corn is sold at the Chicago Board of Trade, the sale is recorded immediately and relayed internationally. When a share of stock is sold, the transaction immediately is transmitted on the ticker tape. In the real estate market, however, there is no complete recording of rental rates by an organized agency, and transactions are considered the confidential business of the individual lessor and lessee. Even recording the deeds of sale often does not require disclosure of the exact consideration in transactions.

While the process of analyzing the market is complicated by these three factors, it is possible. An examination of the residential real estate market illustrates the working technique. It must be realized that there are virtually scores of submarkets even within this market; the major categories are the multistory apartment, the walk-up apartment, the garden apartment, the duplex, the row and townhouse, and the single-family dwelling. Also, these submarkets vary from neighborhood to neighborhood. A manager with a specific property to supervise must decide into which category the property's space belongs.

With the general classification made, the market analyst must further define the submarket by size and character. For example, if an apartment building contains one-, two-, and three-bedroom apartments, the submarkets for each of these classifications must be analyzed individually, since each will have a separate supply-and-demand factor and a different price range. The following questions pertain to each market:

- How many units are available within the area?
- What is the average age and character of the buildings in which they are located?
- What is the average unit in this specific market (regarding layout, equipment, size, and amenities)?
- Based on facts obtained from the neighborhood analysis, is there an increase or decrease in the number of families within the area who are prospective consumers of this particular unit type?
- What is the current price of the average unit, both monthly and per square foot?

FIGURE 4.2

MARKET SURVEY WORKSHEET

	Subject		Area Competitors								
Name of Property											
Location Rating											
Age											
Percentage of Occupancy											
Overall Condition and Appeal											
Amount of Security Deposit											
Minimum Length of Lease											
Children Allowed											
Pets Allowed											
Unit Rents	Rate	Per Sq Ft	Rate	Per Sq Ft	Rate	Per Sq Ft	Rate	Per Sq Ft	Rate	Per Sq Ft	
Efficiency											
One-Bedroom											
Two-Bedroom											
Appliances											
Furnished											
Unfurnished											
Utilities Included											
Parking											
Recreational Facilities											
Clubhouse											
Pool											
Tennis Courts											
Sauna											
Exercise Facilities											
Other Inclusions											

- What is the occupancy level of all units of this type—above, below, and corresponding to the average?
- What was the price and occupancy level a year ago? What is the trend of each?
- How do these trends compare with real estate market trends in general?
- How do vacant units in the area compare for size, age, condition, amenities, and price?

FIGURE 4.3

FACTORS OF LOCATION ANALYSIS

I. Transportation (public)
   A. Distance to points of departure of various media
   B. Frequency of departure from those points
   C. Comforts of relative transportation facilities
   D. Type of passengers apt to be encountered on typical trip
   E. Time required to travel to main objectives
   F. Cost of travel to main objectives
II. Transportation (private)
   A. Distance to main traffic arteries
   B. Ease of driving to main objectives
   C. Time required to travel to main objectives
   D. Fare of taxicabs to main objectives
   E. Environment through which one must travel
   F. Parking facilities
III. Convenience
   A. To shopping areas
      1. Distance to necessary facilities
      2. Ability of local area to supply wants
      3. Facilities of local shops (delivery, service, prices)
   B. To recreational facilities
      1. Theaters (type of entertainment, price of admission)
      2. Sports centers
      3. Parks and public recreational facilities
   C. To educational facilities
      1. Kinds of schools (public, private, and parochial; elementary, junior
         high, senior high, junior college, and four-year college or university)
      2. Distance and type of transportation
      3. Hazards (or lack of) enroute for children
   D. To churches (denominations, services, and social values)
IV. Social Advantages
   A. Reputation and social acceptance of neighborhood
   B. Existence of social organizations within the area, membership require-
      ments, relative activity and availability, and cost
V. Personal and Property Safety
   A. Relative local record for crimes against persons
   B. Current statistics on crimes against property

While these questions concern residential property, the same
kinds of questions can be applied to an analysis of commercial and
other types of income real estate.

Analysis of Comparables

The study of the neighborhood in which a property is located is not
an end in itself; it provides the property manager with the informa-

tion to study that particular building's relationship to the neighborhood and, especially, other buildings. Once familiar with the neighborhood buildings, including their character, age, and desirability, the manager can compare a particular building to others in the neighborhood and note qualities that rank it above or below the average.

A *market survey* is a process of gathering information about specific, comparable properties and comparing it to data concerning the subject property. Through the survey, the property manager learns what the other buildings offer, and then evaluates the subject property's advantages and disadvantages accordingly. A worksheet, such as the one in figure 4.2 designed for residential properties, should be completed for this survey.

Most important, the analysis of the property location must relate both to competing buildings within the neighborhood and to the larger metropolitan area in which the neighborhood itself is located. All of these factors are needed to form a sound management plan.

In the real estate profession, no term is more significant than *location,* yet it is difficult to define in relation to a specific property. Location has one meaning for industrial property, another for commercial property, and still another for residential property. To generalize, however, location refers to the comparative advantages of one site in consideration of the factors listed in figure 4.3. Although some factors (such as convenience to educational facilities) are specific to the locational analysis of residential real estate, all of the concepts are either directly applicable or adaptable to analyzing retail, commercial, or industrial real estate.

With all this information, the manager now is ready to analyze alternate ways in which the property could be managed, then select the one that maximizes the owner's objectives.

Analysis of Alternates

A property's management ideally begins when the improvements are new. Most properties, however, have been supervised by others before they are managed professionally. The procedures just outlined are undertaken with the assumption that the building will be operated on an "as is" basis. That is, the original design will be retained, and the owner can expect a good return from the building in its present form and condition. But if it is discovered that the building no longer fulfills the requirements of its location, it may be profitable to alter its accommodations to meet current market trends and obtain the highest possible net return for the owner. This is what is meant by *analysis of alternates.*

If the building, in its present condition, is not producing the maximum yield consistent with the owner's objectives, two alternatives should be considered: (1) rehabilitation and modernization, or (2) alteration.

Rehabilitation is the process of renewing the equipment, surfaces, or materials within a building; it means correcting deferred maintenance without changing the building's basic plan, form, or style. The manager will *modernize* the building as it is rehabilitated. Original equipment will be replaced with similar features of modern design, since it is not feasible to merchandise a property with equipment or facilities that are below acceptable standards.

Rehabilitation and modernization lengthen a building's economic life within its present design. However, it might be desirable to change the function of the property, in which case *alteration,* or converting the structure's use, would be necessary.

If the property analysis or market analysis indicates that improvements are needed, the decision should be based solely on economic feasibility (if not ruled out by physical limitations). The funds must be allocated, a budget of income and expenses created, proper amortization of debt service computed, and the probable cash flow (net return) established. If the proposed project is profitable financially, the management plan should reflect this.

Consider a building with three- and four-bedroom units in a neighborhood composed of single adults and couples without children. The market analysis should indicate to the property manager a possible need to convert the apartments to smaller units. A complete financial analysis would be required to determine if the conversion would increase the owner's profit. This type of alteration involves property that is functionally obsolete.

A second type of alteration is intended to increase the earnings of a building, whether functional alteration is necessary or not. To illustrate, assume: (1) that a building contains one-, two-, and three-bedroom apartments in an area in which this unit mix is the highest and best use; (2) that the main floor of this property contains a spacious Spanish-motif lobby and three stores; (3) that the apartments in the building are presented to prospects in the most attractive condition; and (4) that the values of the units have been increased to their maximum.

In this case, management could not raise rents without losing tenants to more desirable buildings. By spending $10,000, however, management could reduce the size of the lobby and install two more stores in the inefficiently used space and, at the same time, increase its visual desirability. This alteration would require complete plans and specifications of the work to be performed. Competitive estimates then could be obtained for the total cost of the necessary work, plus amounts to be spent for furnishings and decorations. The property manager would analyze the income possibilities afforded by the new stores, as well as estimate the increased rental schedule attributed to the improved lobby. Also, there should be a determination of the extent to which the changed structure would affect the property's operating expenses.

When these procedures have been performed, the manager's decision to proceed will be based on one of two assumptions: (1) that the expense of the change could be completely amortized (i.e., written off) within a stated period; or (2) that the increased value of the property after alteration would justify the expense.

For the first premise, assume that the manager represents an owner who has no thought of selling the property. In this case, complete amortization within a stated period (during which an adequate return is produced) would be advisable. However, if the owner's objective is to raise the selling price of the property, the decision to alter depends on the equity that will result from the expenditure.

A growing trend is the *conversion* of rental projects to the condominium form of ownership. The manager of a rental property considers condominium conversion as an alternative when the rental market is weak, when high financing costs create negative cash flows, or when rent controls restrict the ability to raise rents in order to meet rising operating expenses.

In analyzing the conversion of an existing rental building into a condominium, the property manager must conduct a formal appraisal of the project and a feasibility study of the conversion. The value of the property as a rental project is compared with its value as a condominium. If this comparison reveals that the property would yield a higher net return if the units were sold individually than if sold as a rental project in one piece, the conversion should be pursued. This would require arranging financing commitments, adopting a plan for marketing the units, and obtaining legal counsel to draft the documents that legally create and subsequently govern the condominium.

Proposed Property Analysis

Having analyzed all possible courses of action and scientifically selected the one most compatible with the owner's objectives, the property manager formalizes the conclusions in the management plan. Some conclusions may be in narrative form, but the projection of operations should be presented as a detailed statement.

The manager determines an operational policy after examining the physical condition of the property, its location, and the value of its space in the current market. This policy then is stated explicitly in the income and expense budget for the coming year and supplemented by long-term projections. Since the income portion of a rental property's budget is based on its rental income potential, the property manager must first establish a rental schedule.

Rental Schedule

There is no rental schedule for any kind of property that reflects exact rental prices in a free supply-and-demand market. All rental schedules are estimates of a true price and judgments of the person in control. The accuracy of these estimates is determined only by tenant reaction and occupancy records.

The larger a building, the easier it is to set a realistic rental schedule. Increasing the rental of a single unit in a larger building (even to the extent of not finding a tenant) is one way to test the market with small potential loss to the total income. But, if the same experiment is performed in a smaller building, the manager risks a high vacancy level. For example, if one unit in a 200-unit apartment building is vacant because of high rent, the vacancy rate is only one-half of one percent. But, if one unit is vacant in a 20-unit apartment building, the vacancy rate is five percent.

While there is no exact means to establish rental rates, there is one relatively accurate method, which is termed the *base-unit-rate approach*. With this method, a base unit within a specific submarket is defined and becomes the standard against which all similar units may be measured. For example, a base unit in the one-bedroom apartment submarket might consist of a living-dining combination, bedroom, bath, kitchen with all appliances, carpeting, draperies, and air conditioning. The square footage of the base unit also must be established. This base unit is assigned a rental price, which is determined from the data compiled in the market survey.

The property manager then compares each unit in the subject building with the proper base unit and adjusts the base rate to reflect

FIGURE 4.4

FACTORS OF VALUE COMPARISON

I. Exterior Appearance
   A. Architectural character
   B. Maintenance of streets and walks
   C. Condition of lawns and shrubs
   D. Sightliness of signs and lawn fences
   E. Cleanliness of basement or main floor windows
   F. Taste and standardization of window treatment (shades, blinds, etc.)
   G. Condition of sash and trim
   H. Absence of evidences of slovenliness in tenancy (i.e., clothes lines, milk bottles on sills)
   I. Cleanliness of service areas, rear porches, courts, and stairways
   J. Indication of good tenant deportment (i.e., absence of children playing boisterously where tenant disturbance would result)
   K. Absence of bicycles, sleds, baby strollers, etc., in places where nuisance or unsightliness would result
II. Public Spaces
   A. Appearance of entrance doors and halls: kickplates and handrails; hardware and door checks; mail boxes and information signs; cleanliness of floors or carpets; and condition of walls, handrails, spindles
   B. Character of building as reflected by the physical atmosphere of the rental office (convenience, orderliness, and decorative taste)
   C. Appearance of lobbies and corridors
   D. Cleanliness and pleasant atmosphere of laundries, storerooms, and basement space
III. Reaction of Prospect to Building Personnel
   A. Courtesy of receptionist
   B. Treatment of tenants as revealed in conversations overheard in renting office
   C. Appearance and deportment of employees contacted during inspection
   D. System of employee control to ensure proper impression
IV. Interior
   A. Plan: room size, wall space, closet facilities, convenience of layout, and circulation
   B. Equipment: lighting fixtures, refrigeration, stove, plumbing fixtures, and window treatment
   C. Appointments: wardrobe equipment, built-in bookcases, etc.
   D. Beautification: decorations and finishes, colors, design of fixtures and hardware, floor treatment
   E. Exposure: light, view, prevailing winds, exterior noise

---

any individual differences. This adjusted, abstracted from the market, figure becomes the *market rent* for a specific unit within the building. The base unit varies among neighborhoods and, obviously, among property types. The rental schedule for an apartment is based on the unit, while the schedule for commercial space is based on square feet.

The factors of comparison between the subject space and the base unit are shown in figure 4.4. Although the factors listed relate specifically to residential space, they can be adapted for commercial real estate.

Since the base-unit-rate method establishes rental schedules by value comparison, changes in style, design, and unit composition affect the standard base unit. For instance, refrigerators in apartments once were luxury items that justified extra rent; now they are standard features. It is obvious that the employment of this comparative method of establishing rental values imposes the constant necessity of reviewing the base units for changes. Only by regular space shopping can the manager be certain of the validity of market conclusions.

When establishing a rental schedule based on comparison (for any property type), the manager must realize that each market and each neighborhood have definite economic limits beyond which prices cannot be raised, regardless of the desirability of the space. There is a point at which the installation of better equipment or improved accommodations are not economically feasible. The actual rental assigned to a space is ultimately determined by the property manager, whose decision, however, is based on the data accumulated in the property, regional, neighborhood, and market analyses and reflects the actual market. These procedures provide the manager with a thorough knowledge of the product, market, and competition. The final step in determining the rental schedule will reduce the percentage of error if the previous steps were performed accurately.

Any attempted shortcuts in the management plan process can result in an unbalanced view of market conditions and incorrect rents. Further, it should be recognized by the property manager that conclusions hold true only for a limited time period due to the ever-changing characteristics of income-producing real estate, which is sensitive to the nation's overall economic climate. For this reason, all rental schedules must be analyzed periodically. The property manager's awareness of trends and the ability to adapt to changes as they occur can make or break an investment. Management is responsible for constantly evaluating conditions that affect the viability of an investment and updating the management plan to reflect any changes.

Income and Expense Projection

A *budget* of income and expenses is essential to effective and intelligent real estate management. It predicts what will take place within a specific time period. The form is the same as that of the annual summary of operations, and its preparation need not be complicated, if performance records from previous periods are available. Without this information, a challenge confronts the manager: experience, analyses of comparable properties, and judgment must be the guide.

The income section of the budget should list the total value of all space at scheduled market rents less a provision for loss through vacancy and collection delinquency. The market analysis should have disclosed the amount of this deduction. If there is any seasonal trend in tenancy, it should be considered when the potential income is recorded. Some properties will have income from sources other than the renting of space (e.g., laundry room, parking, and vending machines). If so, the additional income should be computed and added to the effective rental income to determine the gross revenue.

In anticipating the yearly costs of operation, expenses should be thought of as belonging to one of two types—controllable and noncontrollable. *Noncontrollable*—or *fixed—expenses* include items such as real estate taxes, insurance, labor-union-established wages,

FIGURE 4.5
OPERATING BUDGET

Property						For Year							
	Jan.	Feb.	Mar.	Apr.	May	June	July	Aug.	Sept.	Oct.	Nov.	Dec.	Annual
Income													
Scheduled Rents (Including Employee Unit)													
Less:													
Vacancies													
Rent Loss													
Effective Rent													
Miscellaneous Income													
Total Income													
Expenses													
Administrative													
Management Costs													
Other Administrative Costs													
Operating													
Payroll													
Supplies													
Heating													
Electricity													
Water and Sewer													
Gas													

and manufacturer-set maintenance contracts. *Controllable*—or *operating*—expenses include those over which management has definite responsibility. While some expenses (e.g., utilities, water, and snow removal) are only partially controllable, budgets should reflect the degree to which they are. This distinction is especially important in periods of inflation, since it alerts management to factors beyond its control.

The manager preferably prepares a budget within two weeks after the end of a property's fiscal year. Some owners may request the budget in advance of this time. However, by waiting until immediately after the fiscal year's end, the actual cost of operating the property over the previous 12 months can be noted, and more accurate projections for the next 12 months made. If the owner insists on a budget prior to year's end, the projection should be based on actual expenses for the past ten or 11 months and estimated costs for the last month or two.

In addition to a monthly breakdown of budgeted items (as suggested by the format shown in figure 4.5), many property managers

FIGURE 4.5—*Continued*

	Jan.	Feb.	Mar.	Apr.	May	June	July	Aug.	Sept.	Oct.	Nov.	Dec.	Annual
Maintenance													
Grounds Maintenance													
Maintenance and Repairs													
Painting and Decorating, Interior													
Taxes and Insurance													
Real Estate Taxes													
Other Taxes, Fees, Etc.													
Insurance													
Contract Service													
Total Expenses													
Net Operating Income													
Less Reserves													
Net Income													
Less Debt Service													
Cash Flow													

Prepared by _____   Approved by _____

        Date_____   Date _____

also include the budget for the previous year and the actual expenses for the previous year. These are provided to facilitate comparisons.

The budget is not complete until a copy has been sent to the owner and approval given. Usually, there will be questions. The manager should plan to meet with the owner to discuss the budget and, if necessary, make changes.

The management plan, with its accompanying budget, is essential to successful management for two reasons: first, it is a guideline for the manager and the management organization; and second, it solidifies the relationship between the manager and the property owner and eliminates misunderstandings.

A budget should not be constructed as a background against which actual results appear favorable, nor should it set unrealistic goals. It serves as a warning when monthly comparisons of actual results deviate significantly from the budgetary predictions. As a long-term planning device, it prepares for major policy adjustments on rental rates and for major repair and improvement projects. As the manager analyzes previous years' results and determines a plan for the current year, a perspective develops that would not be acquired without detailed study.

Operations

When undertaking a new management account, the property manager not only must plan for the property's financial administration but also for its day-to-day operation. The complete property management plan, then, takes into account on-site staff requirements and the policies and procedures within which these employees will be expected to operate.

On-site personnel needs vary according to the type and size of the property. In a small apartment building, for example, a resident manager and a part-time janitor may be sufficient. In a large, high-rise office building, a leasing agent, building supervisor, and maintenance and security crews will be necessary.

But regardless of the property's type and size, the need to initiate a deliberate program of manpower planning remains constant. In developing a management plan, the property manager evaluates the work that is to be accomplished, determines the jobs to be performed, outlines the skills needed to perform them, estimates the number of people needed within each job category based on industry data and personal experience, and studies the property's current personnel and their skills. From this analysis, the property manager develops a personnel plan for the property. The task of filling vacant positions, according to the procedure detailed in chapter 9, then begins.

The relationship between the property manager and the on-site staff is made clear by a set of policies and procedures. Every professional property management firm has a manual containing the policies and procedures that govern its operations. When a new account is accepted, these policies and procedures are imposed on that property. In unique situations, adaptations can be made to accommodate special needs. However, changes to the management firm's policies and procedures should be avoided whenever possible.

Policies are guidelines within which decisions are to be made; *procedures* outline the steps for implementing a particular policy. An an example: assume a residential management firm has a policy that only rent-paying applicants with good housekeeping habits are to be accepted as tenants. The procedure designed to carry out this policy might detail the steps by which rental applications are to be completed and verified and assign the responsibility for this activity to the rental agent.

Together, policies and procedures let on-site personnel know the rules to be followed and enable them to work effectively in the absence of the property manager.

Investment Analysis

Real estate managers are becoming more sophisticated. A management plan once was considered complete when the projection of income and expenses was prepared, but now the plan must include an analysis of the property from an investment standpoint. In order to prepare a complete and accurate real estate investment analysis, the property manager must be familiar with financing sources and techniques, the valuation process, depreciation methods, income tax benefits, and cash flow calculations.

This financial analysis is essential for any property for which improvements are recommended. The analysis should indicate alternatives for financing the capital improvements and provide a recommendation of the most workable plan. Even if no improvements are recommended, the possibility of refinancing any existing loans on the property must be considered. The manager's goal is to determine the financing plan most compatible with the owner's objectives.

Basic to performing an analysis of the investment is computing the *cash flow* to the property. The formula for calculating cash flow is this:

	Gross Scheduled Rental
Minus	Vacancy and Rent Loss
Equals	Effective Gross Income
Plus	Other Income
Equals	Gross Operating Income
Minus	Operating Expenses
Equals	Net Operating Income
Minus	Debt Service (Interest and Principal)
Equals	Cash Flow

Furthermore, since the investor is most concerned with net returns, the property manager should compute the cash flow after federal income taxes. To do this, the manager must be familiar with depreciation methods and other tax benefits that accrue to the investor (i.e., real estate taxes, mortgage interest, and operating expenses as deductible items). If alterations or improvements have been suggested, the owner should be informed, on an after-tax basis, of the financial benefits of owning the property after the improvements have been made or the change effected.

The management plan should include a computation of the property's value, both before and after improvements have been made or alterations completed. The change in the value should prove that the improvements are justified economically. The value of an income property is estimated by applying an appropriate capitalization rate to the projected flow of annual net operating income. This process is referred to as *capitalization,* and the estimate of value that is obtained represents the benefits the owner anticipates receiving in future years.

Summary

A plan should be prepared for every property that is managed. A management plan documents the manner in which a property is to be run from physical, fiscal, and operational standpoints. Its aim is to achieve the objectives of the property owner.

In preparing a management plan, specific steps are taken. Each step requires the systematic gathering and subsequent study of data.

The first step is the regional analysis. This is the study of the economic and demographic conditions and physical aspects of the broad area surrounding the property. Next, the property manager focuses on the immediate neighborhood of which the property is a part and its population and population trends.

Also important to forming a management plan is becoming familiar with the property itself. The property manager should personally inspect the physical structure, analyze the property's operating budget, and study the policies and procedures under which it is being operated.

The fourth step in preparing the management plan is the market analysis. This involves: (1) identifying the submarket of which the property is a part, (2) measuring this submarket, (3) studying properties comparable to the subject property, and (4) comparing the subject property to its competition.

Having performed this series of analyses, the property manager then determines if the property is obtaining the highest possible net return for the owner and, if not, recommends an alternative course of action. In the fifth step, the analysis of alternatives, the manager considers what effect rehabilitating or modernizing the property or altering its use would have on its value. The alternative that would maximize the owner's objective is recommended in the management plan.

The details of operating the property, either on an as-is basis or in an alternative way, are focused on in the next part of the management plan. Here, the manager establishes a rental schedule based on market trends and conditions, prepares a projection of income and expenses, determines staffing requirements, establishes operational policies and procedures, and recommends financing, if necessary.

REVIEW QUESTIONS

1. What is a *management plan?* When is it prepared, and why is it necessary?
2. Define *region* and *neighborhood* from the point of view of the property manager.
3. How does the property manager perform a neighborhood analysis?
4. Outline the data a property manager should accumulate when performing a property analysis.

5. What is meant by *market analysis?* Why is this study difficult to perform?
6. Define *location* from the point of view of the property manager. What factors are involved in evaluating a property's location?
7. Define *rehabilitation, modernization,* and *alteration.* Give examples of each.
8. What basic premises should be used by a manager when proposing alterations?
9. When would it be advisable to convert a rental building into a condominium? Explain the steps a property manager would take prior to recommending a conversion.
10. What is the *base-unit-rate approach* to setting a rental schedule?
11. What is a *budget?* What is its value?
12. Define *policy* and *procedure.* Why are they needed? Give three examples of policies and suggest procedures to implement them.

Owner Relations and Record Keeping

ANYONE TECHNICALLY can manage property, but, in the real estate industry, *property management* refers specifically to having someone other than the owner supervise a property's operation according to the owner's objectives. There is a direct and explicit business relationship between the manager of real estate and its owner. The relationship is one of *agent* and *principal,* in which the property manager (the agent) enters into a legal, fiduciary, and confidential arrangement with the owner (the principal).

Although real property may be owned by a nonprofit entity (e.g., a condominium, the government, a nonprofit institution), this chapter will focus on real estate as an income-producing asset and those who own it for the benefits it offers as an investment.

Investors give different reasons for placing their money in real estate. Some turn to real estate because of the tax shelters it provides. Some want a steady flow of cash. Others want a hedge against inflation. Yet, in the final analysis, all want to maximize their income.

To be an effective manager of real estate investments, the manager must be keenly aware of the nature of the property's ownership and its reasons for investing in real estate and must understand the role of client relations.

Principal Forms of Income-Property Ownership

Real property in this nation's early years was owned almost exclusively by individuals, either alone or with partners, joint tenants, or tenants in common. So great was the fear that land ownership might follow the pattern of Europe, where large landholdings were common and restricted to the wealthy, that it was impossible for corporations to own property.

As the nation developed and an affluent society emerged, this fear gradually diminished. More importantly, as real estate was marketed in larger and larger projects, affordable only to very rich individuals and excluding investors of lesser means, it was necessary for alternative forms of ownership to be explored. Shared ownership was the only solution.

Although some real estate still is owned by individual investors, in the last several decades, new and revitalized forms of shared ownership have grown in popularity—such as corporations, limited partnerships, and real estate investment trusts.

Corporation

The depression of 1929 to 1933 created great changes in income-property ownership in the United States. In the prosperous 1920s, real estate bonds totaling millions of dollars were sold in denominations as low as $100 to small investors desiring the high yields these securities offered. Each holding represented a portion of the major mortgages placed on the larger developments of that period. All went well until these projects defaulted during the depression. The bondholders became unwilling owners of real estate. As a solution, they agreed to share in the ownership of the properties acquired through foreclosure. Liquidating *corporations* were created which held title to the real estate until satisfactory sales could be arranged. The bondholders were issued stock in the new owning corporations. For the first time, the corporation became a popular vehicle for real estate ownership.

The advantages of corporate ownership of real estate are numerous: a stockholder in a corporation has no individual liability (only the stockholder's capital contribution is at risk); the corporation is an entity in itself, entirely apart from its stockholders; stock in a corporation can be sold or otherwise disposed of at will; additional capital can be raised by issuing new securities or by borrowing.

While these characteristics made the corporation effective in reorganizing thousands of foreclosed properties during the depression, there are several disadvantages to corporate ownership of real estate. The tax issue is the most important.

Three kinds of taxes affect corporate-owned real estate. First, there is the tax levied against the property (ad valorem tax); second, there is the federal tax levied against the corporation's earnings (corporate tax); and third, there is the tax levied against the individual stockholder's share of corporate profits withdrawn in the form of dividends (individual income tax).

The effect of the last two types of taxation is that the corporation's earnings are subject to double taxation—at the corporate level and at the individual level. Because of the tax liability incurred in transferring a property's cash flow to investors, individuals usually consider it impractical to form a corporation as a vehicle for owning real estate. The exception would be if the investors are in extremely high tax brackets, in which case using a corporation might result in a lower cumulative tax liability.

The corporate form of ownership is used most commonly and successfully by institutional investors involved in long-term business activities. These corporate owners of investment real estate are of two major types. First, there are corporations that own and have responsibility for income properties but are not large enough to supervise the operations of these properties. These corporations usually engage the services of professional property managers. Second, there are the bulk users of space (principally commercial) who construct buildings primarily for their own business use. Whether for prestige or future expansion, these corporations often build structures too large for their own space requirements. As a result, regular administration is necessary, and periodic leasing, too. Some of these corporations hire managers on their own payrolls to administer the properties. Others —the majority—engage professional management firms for this work.

Limited Partnership

The limited partnership was designed to provide the benefits that corporate ownership did not offer. It too developed during the depression when thousands of properties defaulted to banks, insurance companies, trust companies, and other lenders. In most cases, these agencies came under pressure to liquidate the foreclosed real estate. As a result, the market was flooded at a time when funds were limited and investors were skeptical. With cash in short supply, many large properties were sold under terms requiring minimal down payments —often as low as ten percent and always much less than had been acceptable previously.

Yet despite the nation's depressed economy, many people considered income real estate an attractive investment, especially when the terms became more favorable to the buyer. These potential investors would not speculate all their capital in such investments, but they were willing to risk a small percentage in a combined ownership plan. Such a combination was called a *syndicate* and was, in effect, an early type of *limited partnership* formed to buy, own, and operate a specific piece of property.

Astute property managers recognized in this trend a unique opportunity. First, as a broker, a manager could earn a commission through the sale of property and the organization of the syndicate to become the buyer. Second, if the manager applied the commission to purchase a part of the syndicate, he would be a partner in the ownership of the property and then could control its management. Syndicates, therefore, presented a threefold income opportunity to the manager: a brokerage commission, a management fee, and a potential cash flow from the investment.

Although the special investment opportunities of the early recovery period gradually disappeared because of higher prices and greater market activity, other factors brought new buyers into the field. Rising prices that stimulated the purchase of real estate as an inflationary hedge and the earlier successes of syndicate members attracted prospective investors. More importantly, by using limited partnership interests to divide the equity in a property, the double taxation that applied to corporate ownership of real estate was avoided. Real estate ownership through limited partnerships became a significant factor in the property manager's potential operations.

In forming a limited partnership, several investors pool their capital, enabling them to acquire larger, more expensive properties. In this way, the limited partnership represents an opportunity to invest in real estate that otherwise would be out of the reach of the individual investors. The limited partnership can buy real estate to hold for a brief period before selling it; or, it may invest in income property and hold it for the ongoing income and tax shelter it will produce.

Under a limited partnership arrangement, one or more *general partners* manage the partnership and its investments and have unlimited liability for all claims against it. The property manager involved in a limited partnership usually acts as the general manager, providing the management of the syndicated real estate.

The *limited partners* supply the capital but are prevented by law from management activity. In return, their liability is restricted to their investment, and they are given the tax advantages of the partnership form of organization. For tax purposes, the limited partnership acts as a conduit and passes through to the limited partners the tax deductions and losses generated by the property. For this reason, the limited partnership usually outshines the corporation as a form of real estate ownership.

There are two types of limited partnerships: the traditional *private limited partnership* and the *public limited partnership*. The public limited partnership has a large number of limited partners— as many as 20,000 to 25,000—and must be registered under federal and state securities laws, a costly and time-consuming process. The private partnership is designed for modest-sized projects that do not attract major capital sources, even though the real estate may be quite desirable. The private limited partnership has less than 35 investors and ordinarily does not require registration under federal or state securities laws.

Real Estate Investment Trust

Another ownership form that broadens participation in income real estate is the *real estate investment trust (REIT)*, a type of trust established by the Real Estate Investment Trust Act of 1960. Qualified REITs obtain special tax treatment: if a REIT distributes at least 95 percent of its ordinary taxable income to investors as dividends, corporate-level taxation is avoided. A REIT, then, is a single-tax entity that enables small investors to take part in large real estate investments.

If conservative procedures had been followed, the REITs would have been a desirable investment, but the promoters and underwriters of many of these trusts overestimated their capacity to produce returns for their investors. After several years of phenomenal growth following the passage of the 1960 act, REITs accounted for a major percentage of all construction loans in the United States. But the situation changed as credit tightened, and many trusts sold their assets or filed for bankruptcy.

Several factors caused the REITs to fail, but the main reasons were that they had too much money to invest too quickly, and they made unsound investments. The fact that the REITs borrowed heavily on a short-term basis so they could obtain more funds added to their vulnerability. When shorter-term rates rose to 13 percent in 1974, the REITs were obligated to instruments that could not generate returns sufficient to meet commitments.

There is nothing essentially wrong with the REIT concept, except the judgment of certain promoters who often had little or no real estate experience. The REITs are regaining favor among smaller investors, although their outcome remains uncertain.

Individual Investor

Although individual ownership of investment real estate is usually limited to small-scale enterprises, the property manager should be familiar with it as well. Since individual owners often have their own businesses and consider income properties strictly as investments, they cannot assume the responsibilities of management nor do they wish to collect rents, handle rental inquiries and service complaints, and supervise maintenance. Also, there are many absentee landlords who neither work nor live near the properties they own and almost always require the services of local property managers.

The advantage to individual property ownership is that income and profits are taxed only once. A property's financial operations are listed on the owner's individual tax return. If the property sustains a taxable loss, this loss can be a tax shelter and reduce other taxable income.

Management Agreement

Regardless of the form of real estate ownership or the type of property, the duties and responsibilities assumed by the property manager for the owner and the owner's obligations to the manager are sufficiently important to require a written contract. A *management agreement,* agreed to and signed by both parties, is the first phase in creating a satisfied client, which is the primary objective of the property manager.

In a management agreement, the property owner contracts the management of the building to an individual property manager or management firm. The document should be an in-depth and complete statement of the terms and conditions of the understanding, including the fees involved and the duties, responsibilities, and limitations of the signatories. To ensure its validity, the agreement should be prepared, or at least approved, by legal counsel.

A sample agreement, formed by the Institute of Real Estate

Management, is included in the appendix. It is not necessary that this particular form be used, but it is essential that all management relationships be covered by a written contract that includes:

1. An adequate description of the property to be managed.
2. The exact names of the owner and the manager.
3. The fee to be paid for the management service.
4. A clear statement of the responsibility and authority of the property manager and any limitations placed on the operation of the property.
5. Provisions for adequate protection to both parties from any risks incurred.
6. The term of the agreement and termination provisions.

Within this framework, the management agreement must stipulate those activities that the property manager can assume freely versus those that must be referred to the owner for approval. For instance: When is the property manager free to execute leases with tenants? What about major repairs? Who pays for advertising? What about insurance and bank arrangements?

While it is essential that a written management agreement be contracted by and between the owner of the property and the manager, it need not be for a long-term period. There are advantages and disadvantages in a long-term management contract for both the owner and the manager. If special services are to be performed and adequate compensation will not be received in a short period, the manager may be justified in seeking a long-term agreement. For example, in assuming the management of a new office building, the manager may be involved in preleasing activity and operational planning several months before the building is ready for occupancy and management fees are earned. The management agreement should be of sufficient duration to guarantee the manager adequate reimbursement for time spent without compensation.

In all cases, the manager should realize that a satisfied client is far more important to long-term business than contractual ties alone. Even when long-term arrangements exist, the wise manager treats all clients as though the contracts had to be renewed monthly.

Maintaining Client Goodwill

Even though it is a specific property manager who negotiates a management agreement with an owner, the manager is not the one who

FIGURE 5.1
Summary of Operations

| Property _____ | Period _____ |
| Owner _____ | Prepared by _____ |

			Comments
Scheduled Rents (Including Employee Unit)			
Less			
Vacancies			
Rent Loss			
Effective Rent			
Miscellaneous Income			
Total Income			
Less Expenses			
Administrative			
Management Costs			
Other Administrative Costs			
Operating			
Payroll			
Supplies			
Heating			
Electricity			
Water and Sewer			
Gas			

will be on the site on a daily basis. Rather, employees of the property will be handling tenant requests, performing maintenance tasks, and assuming other ongoing operational responsibilities.

In forming a sound relationship with clients, this situation must be explained immediately to the owner. Only by such a frank disclosure can a manager satisfy the client. If the manager does not inform the owner that others will provide the necessary services, the business arrangement may be jeopardized.

Sound owner-manager relations also depend on the client understanding that the manager cannot control the economy. Management can only produce the highest possible net return under current economic conditions. In favorable times, poor management can return excellent earnings; in unfavorable times, it is often impossible for the best management to produce more than bare returns.

One of the basic reasons for analyzing current market conditions is to demonstrate to owners that properties are operated efficiently. There can be no sound relationship with a client if a manager's employment is based on fixed earnings or yields.

FIGURE 5.1—*Continued*

Property		Period	
Owner		Prepared by	
Maintenance			Comments
Grounds Maintenance			
Maintenance and Repairs			
Painting and Decorating, Interior			
Taxes and Insurance			
Real Estate Taxes			
Other Taxes, Fees, Etc.			
Insurance			
Contract Service			
Total Expenses			
Net Operating Income			
Less Reserves			
Net Income			
Less Debt Service			
Cash Flow			

Attitudes of property owners are formed in two ways. First is the owner's personal experience, based on the operating record of the manager and how it is presented to the owner. In preparing the budget as part of the management plan, the manager's focus is on maximizing the owner's objectives while being realistic in estimating income and expenses. The manager's ability is judged against this budget. If good management has prevailed, the property manager will be able to show the owner how closely actual income and expenses came to the projections.

A property manager's operating record also is founded on the owner's personal contact with the manager, or with members of the management team, and by communications sent to the owner from the management office.

The owner's attitude toward management also is influenced by secondary experience, or from contacts with and the opinions of others regarding the character, integrity, and ability of the manager—in short, reputation. Most of the responsibility for forming a positive owner-manager relationship lies with the manager—in a carefully

FIGURE 5.2
RENT ROLL

Unit Number	Occupant	Previous Balance	Current Rent	Date Received	Other Collections		Total Received	Balance Due
					Amount	Description		

Property _____ Period _____

Owner _____ Prepared by _____

worded operating experience record and in productive personal
contacts.

Statement of Operations

There is a fine point of distinction between too much and too little
written contact with clients. However, there is one document that
cannot be omitted; the most important written contact between the
manager and the owner is the periodic (usually monthly) *statement
of operations*. This report is the primary record produced by a management firm's accounting department. All other records are secondary: either necessary to the operation of the property, or used to
interpret the data in the monthly report.

The monthly report is an accounting to the owner of money
received and money paid out. The report should cover the principal
factors of operation, including collections (gross scheduled income,
occupancy, uncollected balances, evictions), disbursements (maintenance, payroll, purchasing), and the overall condition of the property.

Summary of Operations. One of the key statements in the report to the owner is the *summary of operations,* a brief description of income and expenses relative to the property for a specific period, usually one month. It is an at-a-glance reflection of the flow of cash from the property to the owner. (See figure 5.1.)

For most properties, especially larger ones, the summary should be supplemented by schedules that provide in-depth information about the operation. The summary enables both the owner and manager to evaluate the monthly results. If detailed information is needed, it can be found in the accompanying schedules.

Records of Income. Since rent is the major source of income, the chief report of collections is the *rent roll,* which is a record of tenants' names and their units or suite numbers. To account for all rentable space (and as a record of all rental income payable and paid by tenants of the building), vacant space as well as occupied space is listed on the transcript. (A sample appears as figure 5.2.) The rent roll is a balance sheet for the account of each rental area; the footings at the bottom, then, must balance. The record proves that the sum of rental income earned, plus the beginning balances owing, less collections made, produce a result equal to the unpaid balance at the end of the month. The total of rental income earned, plus the rental value of vacant space, should equal the rental value of total space in the building.

Subsidiary income records from which the rent roll is prepared may vary greatly, depending on the type of property and office procedures. In all cases, the manager must maintain some type of *rental ledger* for each tenant or rental area, such as sampled in figure 5.3. The typical ledger is a card in a record tray or a loose-leaf sheet in a post binder. It provides space to note the tenant's name, phone number, unit, regular rent and other recurring charges, security deposit information, move-in date, lease terms, and other pertinent facts about the leasing arrangement. Columns are provided for entries of charges, credits, and balances.

Some ledger cards must be updated manually, but offices with large volumes of rent collection usually have machine bookkeeping or electronic data processing systems. The property manager should adopt standard procedures for keeping rent records. Usually, as an invoice to the tenant is prepared, one copy is kept as a ledger, or receivable record, until paid. Other copies are prepared as needed, i.e., for branch offices.

FIGURE 5.3
RENTAL LEDGER

Unit Number _____ Property _____

Monthly Rent	Unit	$ _____
		_____
		_____
	Total	$ _____

Date	Occupant	Rent Period Mo./Yr.		Payment Credited To				Total Amount Received	Remarks
		From	To	Rent	Security Deposit	Miscellaneous Amount	Description		

Another record essential to the handling and control of income is the *rent receipt*. A receipt should be issued for every item of cash received and a carbon of the receipt be retained. The copies may be used as a ledger posting source and for determining the daily total receipts from bank deposits. Rental receipt copies also may be audited

FIGURE 5.4

STATEMENT OF MISCELLANEOUS RECEIPTS

| Property _____ | Period _____ |
| Owner _____ | Prepared by _____ |

Date	Received From	Description	Amount
		Total	

to confirm that the collector recorded the correct rental and noted the period covered by the payment.

Should the property acquire income from sources other than tenant rentals, such as parking or laundry facilities, this income should be reported on a subsidiary record to the owner as well. A form similar to the *statement of miscellaneous receipts* (figure 5.4) would be appropriate.

Records of Disbursements. Along with the summary of operations is a *statement of disbursements,* which lists all expenses incurred by a property during a specific operating period. (See figure 5.5.)

The source of information regarding expenses varies from one management company to another. Many small management offices order services, supplies, and repairs orally and keep no written records. This is not a sound practice, since it places complete reliance on the memory of the individual. Regardless of the size of the opera-

FIGURE 5.5

STATEMENT OF DISBURSEMENTS

Check Number	Date	Description	Amount Operating	Amount Nonoperating
Property _____ Owner _____		Period _____ Prepared by _____		
		Totals		

tion, written orders should be issued for every purchase, so that invoices are not approved for payment unless first compared with the order and misunderstandings do not develop. In large properties that have receiving rooms, an extra copy of the purchase order typically is sent to the receiving clerk so that shipment is expected and the quantity and condition of supplies may be checked.

Different types of checks may be used for paying bills. Most managers use a plain check and note on the reverse the dates of invoices covered. Other managers send the bill along with the check and ask that it be receipted. Some use voucher checks that describe the items being paid in the voucher portion of the check.

If the owner lacks confidence in the manager to the extent that all bills must be receipted by the vendor, then the manager should not have been retained in the first place. Reporting bills paid that are not paid (permitting the manager temporary use of funds for personal gain) does occur. However, the code of ethics of the Institute of Real Estate Management expressly prohibits commingling of an owner's

FIGURE 5.6

CHART OF ACCOUNTS: SUBURBAN OFFICE BUILDINGS

Income
  Offices
  Retail
  Parking
  Escalation
  Retail Percentage Income
  Miscellaneous Income
  Vacancy and Delinquent Rents (minus)

Expenses
  Utilities
    Electricity
    Water
    Sewer
    Heating Fuel
      Gas
      Fuel Oil
      Electricity
      Steam
      Other
    Combination Electric
  Janitorial
    Payroll/Contract
    Cleaning Supplies
    Miscellaneous
  Maintenance and Repair
    Payroll
    Supplies
    HVAC Repairs
    Plumbing Repairs
    Elevator Repair and Maintenance
    Exterior Repairs
    Roof Repairs
    Parking Lot Repairs
    Decorating—Tenant
    Decorating—Public
    Miscellaneous Repairs
  Administrative
    Payroll—Administrative
    Advertising
    Management Fee
    Other Administrative
  Other Payroll Costs
    Payroll Taxes
    Employee Benefits
  Insurance
  Services
    Landscape
    Trash Removal
    Security—Payroll
    Security—Contract
    Window Washing
    Snow Removal
    Miscellaneous
  Real Estate Taxes
  Other Taxes/Fees/Permits

funds with those of the manager, and if this standard is adopted, there is no need to have bills receipted.

Because of the many types of properties that may be managed, there is no one accepted format for classifying disbursements and reporting them to the owner. Still, there is a strong need for simple, straightforward methods of classifying and presenting disbursement data. Much has been accomplished in standardizing account classifications. The Institute of Real Estate Management has adopted charts of accounts for the purpose of analyzing income and expenses relating to suburban office buildings and apartments. These charts of accounts are presented in figures 5.6 and 5.7, respectively.

FIGURE 5.7
CHART OF ACCOUNTS: APARTMENTS

Income	Expenses
Rent—Apartments	Administrative
Rent—Garage/Parking	Management Costs
Rent—Stores/Offices	Other Administrative
Gross Possible Rents	Operating
Vacancies/Rent Loss (minus)	Supplies
Total Rents Collected	Heating Fuel
Other Income	Electricity
	Water/Sewer
	Gas
	Building Services
	Other Operating
	Maintenance
	Security
	Grounds Maintenance
	Maintenance and Repairs
	Painting/Decorating
	Taxes/Insurance
	Real Estate Taxes
	Other Taxes/Fees/Permits
	Insurance
	Service
	Recreational/Amenities
	Other Payroll

Owners of institutional property frequently provide their own classification styles. Federal housing agencies have designed extensive systems of account classification which include the following categories: renting, administrative, operating, maintenance, depreciation, financial expenses, and taxes and insurance. Any logical, comprehensive, and consistently maintained style of grouping expenses, however, would be valuable.

Narrative Report of Operations.   The owner of a building should be familiar with its operating potential and approximate monthly income, subject to seasonal variation. If the owner's statement indicates a net operating return equal to expectations and there are no unusual items in either the expense or income categories, then it is not essential to include a detailed letter with the statement. However, experience proves that a client should not receive a report without evidence of personal interest, which can be expressed by an accompanying letter. Even if the letter states no more than that operations were normal for the month, it should be sent with the statement.

In every building there are months in which income is either lower or expenses are higher than normal, or vice versa. The owner's primary interest in the monthly report is to learn the level of cash flow. Any deviation from normal income is a subject of immediate concern, and a decrease in anticipated income is of special concern.

Because less-than-normal income may cause the owner to doubt management's competence, the manager should explain the loss. A reasonable client will understand why income is less than expected if the explanation is clear and convincing. If, however, the letter is inadequate and does not cover the facts, the owner may be disappointed and lose confidence in the management firm.

Each monthly statement should be reviewed carefully by management and an explanatory letter prepared to support any factors that were responsible for a decline in net revenue.

If at all possible, the manager should inform the owner when an unusual expense or a decline in income is anticipated. Advising the owner of these circumstances before the monthly statement is sent eliminates much of the explaining that otherwise would be necessary.

Personal Communication

In addition to the monthly operating report, there are many occasions when managers believe it is necessary to contact their clients. Most managers agree that letters should be sent only when the owner is away from the area. Personal contact, either face to face or by telephone, is much more effective than a written communication. Only when in personal contact with the client can the manager obtain an immediate reaction to a question or a proposal and be assured of a satisfactory outcome. If possible, there should be an interview when the monthly statement deviates significantly from the norm and explanation by written communication is difficult. There is no substitute for personal contact; letters should be written only when an interview is impractical.

Although personal contact is preferred, there is frequently a need for written confirmation of understandings reached with the client. Whenever decisions made in a telephone conversation or personal interview require verification, the manager should send the client a memorandum.

When it is impossible to contact a client by interview or a telephone call, a letter should be prepared carefully. If the letter is written by someone other than the person directly responsible for the client relationship, at least it should be examined by the executive who is most familiar with the client.

Property managers must be aware of the special problems involved in retaining business during unfavorable periods. When real estate conditions reflect lower rentals, higher vacancies, and increased operating expenses, the property manager cannot present his clients with an operating record that they will consider satisfactory. To most owners or stockholders the greatest earnings produced become the owner's regular expectation.

Property owners (whether individual, corporation, partnership, or the government) will be dissatisfied, of course, with reports of steadily declining net income, and managers must assure owners that every effort is being made to obtain maximum earnings. During adverse times, the property manager must inform owners of general economic factors, and also must emphasize that results are better than average for conditions, even though net income is declining.

There are certain basic principles which the manager should observe with clients. The number of contacts is best decided by the situation. Some property owners retain managers to assume the operating details and reduce their own contacts with the building, or to be free from the responsibilities of tenant contact and personal administration. But, they still want the manager to keep them informed.

To the property manager whose clients are few enough to permit frequent personal contact, the frequency of contact is a matter of individual need: the corporate owner who wishes to be completely free from responsibilities should not be bothered, while the individual owner who is deeply interested in the property's operation should be contacted regularly.

In larger organizations where the chief executive cannot handle all client contacts, one *account executive* should be responsible for client relations in each operation. When a new property is acquired for management, it should be assigned to an account executive. In the initial interviews between the account executive and the client, the person responsible for acquiring the operation should be present to acquaint the two parties. The account executive, once familiar with the client and the account, can assume complete responsibility for the operative and financial services to be provided.

Sometimes the client's personal relations with the management firm extend beyond the individual manager or, in a larger organization, the account executive. Clients may visit the manager's office just to see how things are going or perform some specific errand in connection with their property. As clients, they believe they are important and judge the management firm by the manner in which they are received on these occasions. All employees in the management firm, therefore, should meet as many clients as possible, so that when they do visit the office, they are recognized and treated courteously.

Summary

Real estate management refers to having someone other than the owner of a property supervise its operations according to the owner's objectives. The property manager is the agent and the owner is the principal. To be an effective agent, the manager first determines the owner's reasons for investing in the property and then creates a management plan so that these objectives are met. To ensure a continuing agent/principal relationship, the manager also sets forth a client relations policy and establishes procedures to see that this policy is implemented.

Real estate ownership may take one of several forms. The principal ownership forms are: (1) corporation, (2) limited partnership, (3) real estate investment trust, and (4) individual investor. Each is characterized by a unique set of traits pertaining to income tax consequences, liability, and management requirements.

The relationship between the ownership and the property manager is documented in a written management agreement. This contract sets forth the terms and conditions of the business relationship, including the fees involved and the duties and responsibilities of and limitations on the parties.

Maintaining a sound ongoing relationship with the client requires two kinds of action: formal, written communication, and informal, personal contact.

The property manager reports on a property through a statement of operations. The statement of operations is made up of several parts: (1) the summary of operations, which briefly describes the income and expenses attributable to the property; (2) records of income, which include a rent roll and statement of miscellaneous receipts; (3) a statement of disbursements, which is tied to the chart of accounts; and (4) a narrative report of operations, which verbally explains what transpired at the property during the past period and why.

Complementing the formal statement of operations, which usually is prepared monthly and at least quarterly, is personal contact with the property owner. This communication comes from the property manager who is charged with the management account and is designed to display interest in the property being managed and sincere concern for the owner and the owner's investment.

REVIEW QUESTIONS

1. What took place in property ownership during the depression years that is significant to real estate managers?
2. Name the characteristics of a *corporation*. Is the corporation a viable form of owning real estate? Why or why not?
3. What is a *limited partnership?* Is it a viable form of investing in real estate? Why or why not?
4. What advantage does the *real estate investment trust* offer to investors?
5. When a property manager takes over a property, what agreement should be made with the owner? Should this agreement be in writing? Why?
6. How are opinions held by property owners of property managers formed?
7. Should a property manager tell the owner of a building that is being taken over that other persons actually will perform the various functions to which the manager has agreed? Justify the answer.
8. What should a manager's monthly report to the owner include?
9. What is a *rent roll?* Prepare a sample.
10. What is a *rental ledger?* How is it used?
11. When are tenant invoices for rent needed? When are they not?
12. Outline the steps in handling property expenses.
13. What is the purpose of the narrative report of operations?
14. What is an *account executive?* Outline the duties associated with this position.

15. A client expected a $1,000 cash flow from his building in June, but the monthly statement showed $685. What would the property manager do about this in the interest of retaining the client?

Chapter
Six

Marketing and Leasing

THE MARKETING PROGRAMS for all property types generally observe the same principles. Finding prospective tenants and closing arrangements for occupancy is called *renting* or *leasing,* and the process of keeping a tenant who is already in the space for an additional period is called *renewal.* Both processes are termed selling and merchandising, but the author believes the latter term is more appropriate.

To examine the distinction: A *sale* is defined as "the transfer from one person to another for a consideration of the possession and right of use of some particular article of value to both parties." Such a transfer can be accomplished only if the buyer: first, has an opportunity to buy; second, has the desire to buy; and third, has the ability to pay for the article. Both selling and merchandising can result in this kind of transfer, but there is a distinct difference in technique.

Selling involves the transfer of an article to someone who either had not wanted the article, admitted a need for it, or had an opportunity to purchase it. *Merchandising,* however, creates a desire for a particular article that people use almost universally by pointing out features in the specific item that will appeal to the buyer. Buyers in this category give themselves the opportunity to purchase. Whether or not they buy depends on the merchandiser's ability to offer a product that meets the buyer's needs—real or otherwise—and present it so that those values will move buyers to acquire the product.

Applying this distinction to the renting of residential and commercial space, it may be concluded that renting is merchandising rather than selling. People must live and work somewhere. The property manager's object is first, finding known prospects to see and desire a particular property, and, second, finding the type of prospects who can pay the rent being asked.

Factors Affecting Marketing Strategy

Successful merchandisers realize that the greater the number of people who view their merchandise, the greater will be their volume of sales. A large number of potential customers creates consumer pressure, which is a desirable condition for all who deal in merchandise the public needs or wants. The same principle of merchandising applies to renting space: the property manager's job is to attract as many prospective tenants as possible. The most effective and economical way of accomplishing this depends on several factors, chiefly, the property's age, size, and location.

It is much easier to attract prospects to a new building than to an old one. Natural curiosity about a new building plus its attractiveness to the renting public stimulate rental activity. This interest in new space varies with the number of similar structures under consideration, but it is safe to say that a new building has much greater appeal than an older one. And this extra appeal is necessary, since a new building must rent 100 percent of its space at one time, while the average standing structure needs to rent only a small percent of its space in a given period.

To profit from the interest created by a new building, developers sometimes construct a display model so that prospective tenants can see the kind of space available. This is especially important with office buildings and other properties that are preleased before the occupancy date. If it is not possible to construct such a model before the building's completion, it should be done at the earliest opportunity. In any case, signs should be displayed prominently to acquaint the public with the new building's features, its size, how it may be inspected, and whom to contact for rental information.

The size of the building is important, because the number of units or square feet determines the promotional program. With a proper rental schedule and with proper promotion, there should be a definite correlation between the space available for rent and the number of acceptable prospects.

The location of the property must be given most careful consideration when a marketing program is implemented. Since location makes some sites more valuable than others, a property in a premium location advertises itself through its physical presence.

If the building is located in a densely populated area with high occupancy levels, if its suites are of the size most in demand in the area, and if the rental schedule matches the consumer purchasing power within the area, marketing should not be costly. But, if the building is located in a sparsely populated area, if the size of the units does not match demand, or if rent prices greatly exceed the average purchasing power of consumers, then a carefully thought-out promotional program is absolutely necessary. Inflation, which causes construction and interest rates to rise continually, will probably increase rent for new space to previously unheard-of levels. This is another reason for the aggressive marketing of new space.

Types of Advertising

In analyzing the neighborhood and market as part of the management plan, the manager has discovered sources from which tenants could be selected. Although the problem of knowing where tenants may be found has been solved, the problem of reaching them at the lowest possible cost remains. Since there is extensive literature on the subject of advertising and business promotion, little space in this text is devoted to the subject. However, several types of advertising that may be used by property managers are analyzed.

Signs

Every property, whether it has vacancies or not, should display a small and tasteful sign, informing interested passers-by of the name of the managing agent and how rental information may be obtained. Although some managers (indeed, some occupants and landlords) believe that a sign is degrading, such an attitude should not prevail. A discreetly placed sign will stimulate prospects—and prospects are the foundation of the management business.

The use of signs as *institutional advertising* (i.e., advertising designed to raise the prestige of the property management firm or building) is a productive practice, too. The use of billboards and wall displays to promote certain types of buildings, especially those under construction, can be quite effective. The problem here is that circulation is relatively small, and these signs are successful only for large apartment complexes, office buildings, and shopping centers.

Newspaper Advertising

No other type of advertising can reach more people with such comprehensive coverage than a newspaper. In cities where there are two

FIGURE 6.1

CLASSIFIED ADVERTISEMENTS

WALK TO SCHOOLS, SHOPPING, PARK from Sutton Surrey. Studios, 1 & 2 bedroom apts. Available for immediate occupancy. Outstanding kitchen with self-cleaning oven, dishwasher. Central air and carpeting throughout. Pool and tennis courts. From $250.

Open daily 9 'til 6

2000 Ridge Avenue
440-8683

Olympia Fields

1 & 2 bedroom apts.

Spacious & bright apartments in wooded setting. Only 20 minutes to downtown.

• Wall-to-wall carpeting
• Central air conditioning
• Self-cleaning oven
• Dishwasher
• Patio or balcony
• Swimming pool
• Security

From $300

Open daily 9 am to 7 pm

Take I-57 to Central St. exit—
Go east 3 blocks.

2100 Central St.
492-9761

or more newspapers, one usually is dominant in real estate advertising and should be preferred when a marketing plan is formed.

Classified advertising, which is relatively inexpensive and appears in a special section of the newspaper, is a basic medium for announcing space for rent. Classified advertising is especially effective in promoting residential rental units. Since most prospective tenants search for apartments on weekends, promoting rental space in the weekend editions of a newspaper often yields fast results and saves advertising costs. (Sample classified ads appear in figure 6.1.)

A *display advertisement* is larger and more expensive but will attract more attention than a classified ad. This is the usual way of marketing a new property and is especially effective in promoting commercial and industrial space. Since a display advertisement can appear in any section of the newspaper, proper placement will ensure that the advertising message is aimed at the appropriate audience. (A sample display ad appears in figure 6.2.)

In metropolitan areas, major newspapers periodically publish special real estate sections with information for property owners, real estate salesmen, managers, tenants—in fact—the general public.

FIGURE 6.2
DISPLAY ADVERTISEMENT

BROADWAY SHORES
CAN'T PROMISE EVERYTHING.

We can't promise you expressway commuting and long hours in traffic. We're too close to things for that, only 10 minutes from downtown.

What we can promise is a self-contained community of modern apartments with vista views of the lake. We can promise free parking. We can promise a shopping center, with restaurant, supermarket, drugstore, and more. We can promise recreational facilities for tennis, shuffleboard, basketball, softball, volleyball, and an imaginative children's play area.

We can promise rentals ranging from $100 for studio apartments to $320 for three bedrooms.

Applications now being accepted for future availabilities.

ABC Management, Inc.
Model Apartments
Daily 9 'til 9
2500 Broadway Avenue/Kansas City
492-1000

This medium should not be overlooked when the marketing plan is designed.

Broadcast Advertising

Television advertising can be effective in describing new properties that are for rent or lease. Because it is so costly, television advertising should not promote individual rental units, but large properties.

Television advertising usually is less expensive in smaller communities. This means that, in large communities, TV advertising will be productive only for large properties that appeal to selected viewers.

Radio advertising also requires careful analysis of its cost-to-prospect ratio, primarily because there are so few potential renters in the listening audience. Most managers believe that radio advertising is economical only in smaller communities to promote large properties. In any case, the property manager must find ways to use the media for specific advertising objectives.

Direct Mail

Although every person is a prospect for an apartment and every business is a prospect for office space, this does not mean that all are prospects for a particular apartment or office building. However, if there are bona fide prospects for a specific property, then direct-mail advertising aimed at these individuals can be effective.

Preparing copy for direct-mail advertising and the expense of its format are secondary to compiling a list of prospects to whom the finished piece is mailed. Most purchased lists are ineffective and should be used carefully. The best method of direct-mail advertising for the average building is to prepare a personal list from local and private information.

If direct-mail advertising is chosen, the copy and format should be aimed at the intelligence and income level of the proper audience. Costly advertisements, unselectively composed, create the wrong impression and lose their effectiveness.

While brochures are ideal for direct-mail advertising, they also are useful in other situations. For example, a colorful, appealing brochure that fully describes a new office and includes sample floor plans should be available to give prospects who visit the property. (A sample brochure, which could be used for direct distribution to prospective tenants or as part of a direct-mail campaign, appears in figure 6.3.)

Economics of Advertising

Few buildings are large enough to require institutional advertising. Therefore, the only reason for advertising a building is to discover enough prospects to fill existing vacancies or those known about in advance. The answer to the question, "When is advertising neces-

FIGURE 6.3
DIRECT-MAIL BROCHURE

sary?" then, is definitely related to the occupancy level. If there are no vacancies and no prospect of vacancies, no advertising is needed. In larger buildings in which continuous turnover is normal, continuous advertising may be needed.

No set rule can determine the amount of advertising necessary for any individual property. Some buildings are so located and designed that there are always enough prospects to maintain occupancy levels without advertising. Other properties are so isolated from the renting public that the only practical method of obtaining prospects is through aggressive advertising.

The manager can decide on an advertising program by asking the following question: "If I advertised, could I increase consumer pressure enough to increase rents or occupancy? If so, would the amount needed to increase the volume of prospects be a profitable investment?" This question can be answered by experimenting with advertising in various media. If the space in a highly desirable building is properly priced, the experiment should prove that advertising for this purpose will not pay. However, a manager of a large property should make frequent experiments of this kind as a check against the rental price and the market.

For the smaller, isolated property that cannot attract prospects through any simple means, the need for advertising is obvious. The amount that should be spent can be determined only by a cost-per-prospect basis. For example, in a period of shortage, a small classified ad that informs the renting public that there is a five-room apartment at a given address for a rental of $400 per month may bring ten prospects to the building, two of whom would have rented the apartment. Suppose this ad costs $50. The cost per prospect would have been $5, and there would be no question as to the effectiveness of advertising.

On the other hand, suppose that there were many vacancies in the community. Suppose, too, that the manager placed an ad at a cost of $50, and only one prospect viewed the $400 apartment. If it is known that an average of five prospects are needed to contract a lease, this ad would have to be repeated for five days in order to complete a rental. Certainly, the expenditure of $250 (5 days × $50 per day) for a lease on a $400 apartment would be considered productive, so the manager would continue advertising for the five-day period.

Assume, however, that it was necessary to advertise in a weekly publication (or that Sunday was the paper's only effective advertising day) and that the manager would probably have to wait five weeks to

FIGURE 6.4
TRAFFIC REPORT

Property _____

Week of _____

Prepared by _____

	Monday	Tuesday	Wednesday	Thursday	Friday	Saturday	Sunday	Total
Nature of Inquiry								
Telephone call								
Visitor								
Time of Inquiry								
Morning (before noon)								
Afternoon (noon to 5 p.m.)								
Evening (after 5 p.m.)								
Referred by								
Large display ad in newspaper								
Classified ad								
Billboard								
Drive-by								
Telephone directory								
Word-of-mouth								
Direct mail								
Apartment locator service								
Television								
Radio								
Unit Desired								
One-bedroom								
Two-bedroom								
Three-bedroom								
Efficiency								
Furnished								
Unfurnished								
Weather Conditions								
Comments								

obtain a lease. Then, of course, the cost of the waiting period would have to be computed as an extra expense in leasing space. Five weeks' time in itself would be worth slightly more than $400, and, with the cost of the advertising, acquiring a new tenant would cost more than $650. Of course, it could be that the first prospect would be the one out of five who would rent the unit. However, a manager cannot deliberately gamble with the owner's money.

One solution to the property manager's dilemma centers on whether or not the rent should be lowered in an effort to lease the space more quickly. The answer to this depends on two factors: (1) the current trend of the market, and (2) the number of apartments of the same type in the building.

If there is a downward market trend (because of high vacancy and a poor economy), then the manager should consider a rent reduction in order to obtain a new tenant. If the market trend is upward, then the manager might consider a second factor, namely, "How will a reduction in the price of this unit affect tenants in other apartments?" If the reduction would have an adverse effect, then the manager should wait as long as necessary to find a customer.

Before lowering the rent on a single unit, both the property manager and owner must agree to having something other than a "one-price house"; i.e., they must be willing to negotiate the rent rate on every lease. Market conditions may require frequent changes in pricing, but often the manager creates a market by negotiating each lease.

The question of when and how much to advertise depends on common sense and simple cost calculations. Total cost is determined by the net cost to the building after combining the cost of vacancy with that of advertising. Many property managers consider only the expense of the purchased advertising and overlook the often greater cost of vacancy. An analysis, such as this, is useful in merchandising any type of rental space.

Determining the effectiveness of advertising is a matter of accurately checking on the number of prospects produced by various media and then analyzing the prospect-producing cost of each. A *traffic report,* such as the sample in figure 6.4, makes this record keeping easy by providing for space to note what led prospects to visit or make inquiries at the property. After evaluating the reports, the property manager can determine the effectiveness of the different marketing methods and respond to the rental activity accordingly.

FIGURE 6.5
RENTAL INQUIRY CARD

Name	
Address _____	Phone _____
Place Employed _____	Phone _____
Unit Desired	
Rent Desired $ _____ Date Desired _____	
How Many Occupants and Relationship _____	
Unit Shown _____ Rent Quoted $ _____	
Follow-up Remarks _____	
Date Inquiry Received _____ Inquiry Taken by _____	

The most effective approach is the one that produces the most prospects at the lowest, time, and volume.

Another management form used to increase advertising effectiveness is a *rental inquiry card* (figure 6.5). By keeping a record of all prospects who call or visit a property and reviewing that record when other units are available, more advertising may be unnecessary.

Renting Techniques

Renting is a process of interesting prospects in space once they have been given the opportunity to rent it. The desire to rent results from the property manager's maximizing the value of the space and then convincing prospects of this value.

Negotiating a lease requires the manager to stress how a given space satisfies the prospective tenant's needs. The prospect should receive all the information that could produce a favorable decision in a courteous, considerate, and sympathetic manner. This is accomplished when the property manager personally guides the prospect through the space to be leased, noting its features. At this time, the manager also should cite any amenities and services provided. The manager of an office building, for example, should mention special security arrangements or utility reduction systems. The property manager of an apartment complex would point out swimming pools and laundry facilities. In either case, the social and retail facilities found where the building is located can be stressed to create value. If it is an industrial property, the manager would mention the proximity of transportation facilities. (Specific techniques for marketing space in residential property, office buildings, and retail property are detailed in chapters 10, 12, and 13, respectively.)

Qualification of the prospective tenant (i.e., judging the prospect's acceptability) is an important, but sometimes neglected, aspect of renting. The rental agent has an obligation to both the owner and the prospect to qualify the potential tenant when pointing out the values in the space to be leased by determining if the space meets the prospect's needs and if the prospect meets the property's criteria. This can be accomplished by asking some unobtrusive questions and not only listening to the answers but also judging from what is not said.

Lease Document

The culmination of marketing activity is a written agreement between tenant and owner. By definition, a *lease* is a contract given by one person (the landlord or *lessor*) to another (the tenant or *lessee*) for use or possession of real property, for a specified time, and in exchange for fixed payments. The contract is usually written and binding in the legal sense with respect to the commitments given by the signatories.

Any agreement, even an oral one, is legal and enforceable within the bounds of the law, to the extent that the law applies and to the degree that the intent is clear. However, good management requires a written lease to establish a record of a contract made between an owner and a tenant.

Both parties should demand a written lease for one reason: protection. A landlord desires a lease to assure occupancy and income for the period which it covers. At least theoretically, there should be no loss due to a sudden vacancy.

The tenant desires a lease, too, because it provides security of possession for the length of its term. Without a lease, tenants theoretically can be evicted at the whim of the landlord and, therefore, cannot feel secure in the possession of the leased premises. In certain areas, residential tenants may be protected by laws regulating rental and eviction, but, without such laws, the tenant has no guarantee of possession other than the lease.

Since leases are designed primarily to eliminate misunderstandings between owner and tenant, the lease provisions must be understood by both. It is always a good policy for the manager to ask a new tenant if the lease has been read and to explain provisions not understood.

There are lease forms that are definitely unfair to tenants and contain provisions that will be eliminated by the informed or those whose lawyers review the lease before signature. Other clauses, while not unfair to tenants in view of the landlord's rights, are frequently eliminated by tenants after legal advice. The lease must always conform to local or state legal requirements.

The professional manager should not adopt a lease form simply because it is popular but should use a form that is reasonable, standardized, and suitable for all tenants. The professional manager interested in establishing goodwill does not use a lease from which informed people will remove basic clauses and which uninformed people will sign as a matter of faith. A proper lease form is suitable to both the informed and uninformed and its contents upheld. When properly prepared and presented as a means of protecting the tenant, the lease has excellent marketing value.

Types of Leases

The type of lease used depends on the kind of property being managed. A prepared property manager should be informed about three basic types of leases.

The first of these is the *occupancy agreement,* a euphemism for "residential lease" used to soften any hostility that sometimes is felt by tenants for landords. An occupancy agreement is often a form of *gross lease;* that is, the tenant pays a fixed rental and the owner pays all the expenses associated with the operation of the property, including taxes, insurance, and other expenses. Responsibility for utility costs and extraordinary repairs may be negotiated between the parties.

The second type of lease is the *net lease,* under which the tenant not only pays the rent but also assumes responsibility for certain expenses connected with the leased premises. The landlord, then, receives a net figure as rent. Actually, there are three types of net leases. Under the *single-net lease,* the tenant pays for maintenance and operating expenses associated with the space being leased. Under the *net-net lease,* the tenant pays all maintenance and operating expenses plus property taxes. Under the *net-net-net* (or *triple-net*) *lease,* the tenant pays all maintenance and operating expenses, property taxes, and insurance. The net lease and its variations most commonly are long-term leases designed for large office buildings and other commercial properties.

The third type of lease is the *percentage lease,* which is used for retail properties. Under a percentage lease, the rental usually is based on a percentage of gross sales or net income made on the premises or a minimum fixed rent, whichever is greater. With this type of lease, the landlord shares in the financial benefits of the leased premises. In contrast to the percentage lease, major retail tenants often negotiate a lease with a fixed charge per square foot.

Lease Provisions

Despite the differences in the three basic types of leases, all leases must have certain characteristics to be considered valid.

Standard lease forms have been accepted throughout the country by local and state real estate boards, building owner groups, trade associations, and property managers. These forms contain provisions that apply to the specific types of buildings leased as well as local laws.

Essentially, a lease is a written agreement that describes the *demised premises* (i.e., the property covered by the lease agreement), sets forth the term of tenure, and states the amount and method of rent payment. A simple contract of this type, dated and signed by both parties, is a valid lease. Because of the complexities of the legal system, however, it is necessary to add conditions and agreements to cover possible areas of misunderstanding and dispute.

Specifically, a lease must contain:

- The complete and legal names of both lessor and lessee. Next, the lease must be signed by the tenant (or authorized agent of the tenant) and the property owner. If empowered to execute leases for the owner, the managing agent may sign the lease.
- Description of the leased premises. For an occupancy agreement, the apartment number and address of the building are usually sufficient. For commercial space, legal descriptions and even floor plans may be added.
- Term of the lease. The lease should cite the dates on which the lease is to begin and terminate as well as note the total period

to be covered. Provisions relating to renewal or cancellation also should be stated.

- Rental. A lease must indicate the type of consideration given by the tenant to the landlord in exchange for the right to occupy the leased premises. In any type of lease, the amount and date of rent payment must be stated.
- Use of premises. All leases stipulate that tenants will use the premises for a set purpose. Prohibition against illegal use, with termination penalties, usually is included under this condition.
- Rights and obligations of the parties. This section of the lease, which usually is quite lengthy and detailed, states who is to do what and eliminates the possibility of misunderstandings between landlord and tenant.

Certain clauses that outline the rights and obligations of the parties to a lease require special attention. One of these is the fire clause. Since it is possible for a building or specific premises to become untenantable by fire or other disaster, a clause is universally contained which provides for the disposition of the lease after such an event. This clause either allows the landlord to terminate the lease after destruction to the premises or to repair the premises within a certain length of time.

Also among the specific provisions in every lease are those that provide the landlord with legal means for terminating the lease, recovering possession of the premises, and collecting rents and damages. These agreements are usually contained in a series of clauses that apply to re-entry and recovery of possession by the landlord, legal dispossession proceedings, actions to recover rent, provision for attachment to enforce the collecion of rent, statutory liens, judgment liens, and other collection procedures. Provisions pertaining to subletting the leased premises, renewing the lease, and performing ongoing and extraordinary repairs also are contained in most agreements.

Many leases also contain clauses that permit rents to be raised under certain economic conditions during the lease term. With the value of the dollar fluctuating so rapidly and the cost of utilities, services, and supplies contantly increasing, a rent adjustment clause is universal in all leases for longer than one year. Even under a net-lease arrangement with the tenant paying many or all expenses, an escalation clause is necessary. The owner should expect dollars received five years from the date of the lease to purchase the same as on the date the rent was negotiated. If this is to be achieved, all

FIGURE 6.6

SECURITY DEPOSIT CLOSING STATEMENT

Property _____ Unit _____

Type of Unit _____ Occupant _____ Move-In Date _____

Term of Rental Agreement _____ to _____ Move-Out Date _____

1. Date "Notice to Vacate" Received _____

2. Cleaning and Maintenance

    a. Estimated cleaning time _____ hours

    b. It was necessary to paint _____

    c. It was necessary to shampoo carpet _____

    d. It was necessary to clean drapes _____

    e. Damage beyond ordinary wear and tear from check-out column _____

    Occupant _____ On-Site Manager _____

Forwarding Address:

Name _____

Address _____

City _____ State _____ Zip _____

- -

For Office Use Only

Total security deposit on record $ _____

Less:

    Deposit held for unpaid rent

      $ _____ per day for _____ days $ _____

    Cleaning (actual time)

      $ _____ per hour for _____ hours   _____

    Damage (above ordinary wear and tear)   _____

    Improper notice   _____

    Other (specify)   _____

    Total security deposit held   _____

Total security deposit refund $ _____

                Managing Agent _____

long-term leases must contain some type of rent adjustment provision. Escalation clauses are common in commercial leases and are becoming more common in residential leases as well. There are many types of escalation clauses, and the manager should choose the provision that best serves the property owner and is acceptable to the tenant.

While much that is contained in lease clauses originates in common law, landlords' rights can vary from state to state. Action taken under these clauses throughout the nation, however, is strictly the concern of lawyers and not real estate managers.

Because the purpose of the written lease is to cover all possible areas of misunderstanding and disagreement, any situation that is not covered by a specific provision in the lease form should be expressed in a special *rider* or *exhibit,* signed by both the lessor and the lessee and incorporated into the lease.

Security Deposits

At the time a tenant signs a lease, most property managers require that tenant—especially a residential tenant—to pay a *security deposit.* This deposit is supposed to guarantee that the tenant fulfills lease conditions. It protects the building owner from tenants who might damage the rental units or otherwise fail in their obligations. If all conditions are met by the tenant, the landlord must return the security deposit. The security deposit, therefore, does not belong to the owner and usually is kept in an escrow account.

Incorporated into the statutes of several states is the Uniform Residential Landlord and Tenant Act (URLTA). The URLTA stipulates that the owner of residential rental property may not demand a security deposit of more than one month's rent. It also states that when a tenancy is terminated, the deposit must be returned to the tenant within 14 days. If a portion of the security deposit is kept to repair damages, an itemized notice of these maintenance costs should be prepared. A closing statement similar to the sample in figure 6.6 will standardize this procedure.

Some states also require the owner to pay interest to residents on their security deposits. With heightened interest in consumerism, more and more states probably will enact similar pro-tenant legislation in the near future.

The property manager should make sure that no security deposit is considered as a tenant's final month's rent. If it is, the deposit will be taxable income. Tax liability is avoided if the deposit is kept in an escrow account, one way of recognizing that the deposit does not belong to the owner and restricting the owner's use of it.

Renewal Techniques

Renewing an existing lease is more important than making a new one. First, renewal eliminates vacancy loss, which occurs in a normal market when one tenant moves out and a replacement must be found. Second, it is less expensive to satisfy an existing tenant than to improve space for a new tenant. Finally, a building has greater stability with long-term tenants.

Renewing a lease means that customers have been satisfied. The property manager who succeeds in this remembers that every contact with a tenant is a sales contact and that all tenant leases are subject to renewal.

There are legitimate reasons for failing to renew a lease, which are beyond the control of the manager. But under normal circumstances, when the tenant whose lease is expiring is under no pressure to move, renewal is a matter of negotiation. There are very few periods in the economy when leases expire in a stable market. Rents are either going up or going down; vacancy is either increasing or decreasing. Lease expiration, then, is a time for bargaining between the tenant and the building owner. These bargaining points are:

1. Whether or not the tenant will renew at all.
2. The amount of rent to be paid, usually an increase.
3. The length of the lease.
4. The extent of repairs and rehabilitation to be performed under the renewal terms.

All four factors must be considered by the property manager and the tenant. In any type of property, the manager must realize that the good tenant is a valuable asset, that an existing tenant's requirements usually are less than those of a new tenant, and that renewing a lease is the best form of maintaining a high occupancy level and stable earnings.

The renewal process also requires that administrative action be taken. There are three basic steps. First, a list of all tenants whose leases are expiring should be made regularly. This list can note the progress of renewal activity. Second, tenants on the list should be notified by mail that their leases are due to expire. For residential tenants, lease renewal notices usually are mailed 60 days before lease expiration. This should allow management sufficient time to find new tenants without losing rent. Third, the property manager should follow up on the notices. This should be done in person or by phone shortly after the notices are mailed, allowing tenants little time to look elsewhere or otherwise decide not to renew.

Different administrative action may be called for if a property's leases contain *automatic renewal clauses* (as opposed to leases that expire unless the tenant gives notice to the contrary). With an automatic renewal clause, the old lease is automatically renewed unless either the tenant or the landlord notifies the other party of a desire to terminate the agreement. If neither party gives such notice, the lease is automatically renewed under the same terms and conditions.

Summary

Property managers consider marketing a significant management activity. Merchandising techniques vary among property types; however, marketing strategy always depends on the given building's size, location, and age.

Property managers often turn to advertising to introduce rental space to the market. Appropriate forms of advertising are: (1) signs, including billboards (to announce large new projects) and small institutional signs on buildings (to note who is managing them); (2) newspaper advertising, including both classified and display ads; (3) in some instances, radio and television advertising; and (4) direct-mail advertising, which is expensive but can be effective if the manager has a list of viable prospects.

The best type of advertising is that which produces the most prospective tenants at the least cost and in the least time. This requires analysis of the cost of advertising plus the cost of vacancy. Also worthwhile in judging advertising effectiveness is to maintain a traffic report, used to record the number of prospects who visit a property and what brought them there.

Attracting prospects is only part of marketing. In all types of space, prospects must be qualified according to their needs and then shown units that satisfy those needs. Only when a tenant's needs are met will a lease be negotiated.

A lease is the contract that creates the landlord-tenant relationship. There are three principal types of leases: (1) gross lease, under which the tenant pays a fixed rent and the owner pays the property's operating expenses; (2) net lease, under which the tenant pays rent plus assumes responsibility for specific expenses connected with the leased premises; and (3) percentage lease, under which the rent is based on a percentage of gross sales or net income made on the premises.

All leases should include: (1) legal names of lessor and lessee; (2) description of the demised (i.e., leased) premises; (3) lease term; (4) rent rate; (5) use of the premises; and (6) rights and obligations of both parties.

Usually when a lease is signed, the tenant is asked to pay a security deposit. This deposit protects the landlord from a tenant who might damage the leased premises or fail to meet other obligations.

As important to renting space is renewing leases. When a lease is renewed, it means that the tenant has been satisfied. The property manager should adopt a policy of handling tenant requests so that tenants will be satisfied and consequently will renew their leases. Also needed are administrative procedures for handling lease renewals.

REVIEW QUESTIONS

1. What impact does a building's age have on marketing strategy? Its size? Its location?
2. Define *renting, merchandising, selling,* and *renewal.*
3. Name the principal types of advertising used in announcing rental space. List them in order of importance from experience in the real estate field.
4. How does a manager determine the effectiveness of advertising?
5. What is a *traffic report?* Why is it used?
6. Define *lessee* and *lessor.* What is a *lease* and for what purpose is it written?
7. List the advantages (1) to tenants, and (2) to the landlord, when a lease is written for longer than one month.
8. What is the point of written leases if oral agreements are binding by the law? Is it possible to have a written lease that has all of its provisions stated in a completely unambiguous way?
9. Define *gross lease, net lease,* and *percentage lease.* Why has the term *occupancy agreement* been adopted?
10. Why do property managers require security deposits? What impact does the law have on security deposits?
11. Why is it more important to renew a tenant's lease than to lease to a new tenant?
12. What is *automatic renewal?*
13. What are the basic points of bargaining between tenant and property manager?

Chapter
Seven

Tenant Administration

Tenants are the foundation of property management activity and, in fact, are ownership's greatest asset. To develop this potential, a series of tenant-oriented property management programs should be adopted. First, a tenant selection policy is needed to ensure that leases are signed only with acceptable applicants. Second, an ongoing tenant relations program is required to satisfy existing tenants and encourage them to renew their leases. And third, a rental collection program is necessary to ensure prompt payment of rents by tenants.

Tenant Selection

A property manager is a mediator between tenants who want an acceptable place to live or work at the lowest possible price and property owners who want to maximize their profits. The position is often difficult. If the owner is not satisfied with the manager's operation, the latter may be discharged. But if tenants do not perform according to the lease, even for reasons beyond management's control, the owner still will be dissatisfied. It is a game of double jeopardy. The property manager works within a framework in which owner interests must be balanced with tenant interests. This requires a workable compromise between the seller wishing to maximize profits and the buyer wishing to minimize cost.

The property manager makes a living by maintaining a harmonious relationship with all parties. First, the property manager chooses which properties to manage and consequently which owners

139

to represent; then, after selecting a particular property, the property manager chooses the tenants. Tenant selection should guarantee that the respective interests of the parties concerned are satisfied as fully as possible. The tenant expects maximum services for the rent, and the owner expects maximum profit on the investment.

To many uninformed owners and managers, the sole criterion of tenant desirability is rent-pay ability. Certainly, the credit rating of a tenant is extremely important in tenant selection. However, based on long-term experience, more than 90 percent of all tenants voluntarily pay their rent near the due date. But, 90 percent of all managerial problems can be attributed to the other ten percent of a building's tenants. This emphasizes the need to apply criteria other than rent-paying ability when selecting tenants. For residential tenants, criteria might include employment stability and housekeeping ability, while selection might be based on business reputation, expansion plans, and service requirements for commercial tenants. (Selection criteria for tenants of the three major income-property types are discussed in detail in chapters 10, 12, and 13.)

While the specific nature of the selection criteria varies from residential to commercial and retail tenants, every effort must be made so that only those tenants are selected who are responsible and suited to the particular property. Also, since long-term tenants are more profitable than short-term tenants, consideration should be given to the permanence factor.

Data are needed to make appropriate tenant selections, and each prospective tenant should be asked to complete a rental application. The kind of information requested will depend on the type of property involved. A residential rental application, for example, would ask for data concerning the applicant's personal identity, income, all the persons who would occupy the unit, and rental history. A commercial rental application would request the company's history plus banking and business references. Once this information is verified, the property manager can make careful tenant selections.

Tenant Relations

While selecting the proper tenants is important to the successful operation of a property, this process cannot take precedence over keeping them once they are chosen. The role of tenant relations is to listen to complaints against the owner and manager and correct any erroneous ideas about their intentions. In the real estate management business, dissatisfied tenants present serious problems.

Nothing is more disturbing to the property manager than a landlord-tenant conflict over mutually exclusive interests. While there is a point of bargaining at the beginning of the landlord-tenant relationship, the conflict of interest between the two has been exaggerated. Most landlords want a fair return from property in line with current market conditions; tenants are mostly concerned with obtaining the best value for rent money and receiving all the services for which they bargained. Much of the conflict between the two parties is avoidable when sound management practices are employed.

The conscientious property manager educates both landlord and tenant to a realistic understanding of their mutual concerns and objectives. A mutual understanding can be achieved, if the manager works at it.

It is important to understand the owner-manager-tenant relationship. Although the manager must see that the tenant is given fair treatment, the tenant's goodwill cannot be bought at the building owner's expense. On the other hand, the manager cannot refuse a tenant's reasonable request or withhold services for the sole purpose of increasing the building owner's advantage.

In most cases, a poor relationship between a building owner and a tenant stems from misunderstanding. The first step in correcting this problem must be taken during the original negotiations with the tenant. As often as possible, the results of these negotiations should be in written form (the lease) and the contents reviewed with the tenant at the time the discussions are completed.

Besides a written agreement covering the fundamental points of the tenancy arrangement, the manager should explain rent collection policies, review carefully the operating regulations that control the property and discuss the methods of enforcing them, and be certain that the tenant understands building maintenance policies and how responsibilities are divided between building owner and tenant. Ideally, a tenant brochure is given to each new tenant that outlines all of these policies and procedures. (Pages from a sample tenant handbook appear in figure 7.1.)

There is no substitute for frankness and honesty in human relations. The manager who seeks a successful tenant relations program must thoroughly understand that procrastination is deadly. Most problems center on service requests. When such a request is made, the tenant should be told immediately whether or not it will be granted. The most serious mistake made by many managers is accepting service requests they know will not be granted. If the manager explains the reason for the refusal, much of the sting will

FIGURE 7.1

Tenant Handbook

VACATING AND CLEANING PROCEDURES

Thirty days prior to vacating the apartment and at the termination of the rental agreement:

Step I:

1. Notify Resident Manager in writing intention to vacate apartment. Obtain form from the Manager.
2. Inspect the apartment with the Manager. Review these procedures with the Manager at the time the 30 days written notice is obtained. Electricity turned off after apartment is vacated.

Step II:

1. General.
   1. Dust throughout.
   2. Clean window sills, wash windows
   3. Clean air-conditioning and heating Obtain new filters from the Manager
   4. Clean all light fixture lenses, inside
   5. Mop and wax resilient floors.
   6. Clean kitchen exhaust fan hood and
   7. Carpets and drapes must be vacuum rods cleaned. If carpets and drapes soiled beyond what is normal wear be commercially cleaned at the resid prorated and participated in by the same basis as painting charges.

AGREEMENTS

APPLICATION DEPOSIT
Deposit will be credited towards apartment rent if resident's credit check is acceptable to management.

Deposit will be refunded if credit check is not acceptable to management. Deposit will be retained if credit check is acceptable but individual does not desire to rent.

MOVE-IN CHECK LIST
Prior to moving into apartment the resident in company of management shall inspect apartment. Any condition not acceptable to the resident must be so noted by the resident. Upon acceptance of apartment condition and prior to moving in resident and manager shall sign check-list.

MEMOS TO MANAGEMENT
Notify management on memos provided for any work required in apartment. Notify management immediately of any emergencies.

RENTAL PAYMENTS
Rent is due on the 1st of each month and is delinquent on the 2nd. Payment shall be by check and made out to the name of the apartment complex and shall be delivered to the resident manager.

Residents shall be charged for writing insufficient funds checks.

MOVING
Schedule moving between the hours of 8:00 a.m. and 5:00 p.m. on weekdays. No moving is permitted on Sundays or legal holidays. Notify management in writing on forms provided 30 days prior to moving.

INSURANCE
Resident is responsible for insurance on own personal property.

PEST CONTROL
Tenant is responsible for control inside of apartment.

be removed, and the tenant's respect will be won. If the manager accepts a request and procrastinates, the tenant will lose confidence and never forget. This is the worst public relations and has no place in well-organized property management.

While everyone who deals with the public knows that some tenants demand unreasonable service, most tenant requests are warranted, and the property manager should not automatically classify tenant requests as complaints. Management should consider requests as a measure of the maintenance program and/or the condition of the property. Actually, the tenant who calls about a leaking faucet is doing the property manager and owner a favor. The problem can be corrected rather than be permitted to worsen.

A sound tenant relations program requires more than a sympathetic attitude on the part of the manager. Since tenants are frequently in contact with on-site managers, leasing agents, maintenance people, building supervisors, janitors, telephone operators, or clerks of the maintenance office, these people must be acquainted with the manager's tenant relations policies as well. While property managers cannot claim "the customer is always right," the basis for training on-site personnel should be that the tenant is always entitled to considerate treatment.

Efficient management realizes that good tenants are a tangible asset. Good tenants remain in residence and eliminate expensive turnover. Good tenants protect the manager's property and minimize the cost of maintenance. Good tenants advertise the reputation of the building and the manager, which reduces vacancy losses and promotional expenses.

Keeping in mind the values of a solid, well-satisfied tenancy, managers of large buildings try to increase tenant goodwill by making life in the project as pleasant as possible. In an apartment complex, arrangements can be made for children to have supervised play and for preschool care; recreational events are staged and tenant organization groups are recognized and accommodated. All of these activities promote sound tenant relations and solidify the earning power of the property.

The property manager must realize, however, that becoming closely associated with any tenant on a social basis would be dangerous. These associations lead only to embarrassing situations and convince other tenants that the manager is playing favorites—a belief that will increase tenant demands at the time of lease renewal and weaken management's negotiating position.

Credit and Collections

In a typical building operation, a property manager's compensation is a percentage of the gross rents actually collected; this percentage is negotiated between the property manager and the owner. Consequently, there is a strong incentive to collect rents because the manager's income depends on these collections. Even for institutional and public housing properties, rent collection is an important part of the manager's activities.

Operating costs, taxes, and general overhead expenses mount steadily, each day a building stands. These expenses are best paid from cash income, since they will never be paid by promises. The chief source of income is tenant rentals, and it is, therefore, essential that tenants' credit be screened carefully and current and future rent collected promptly.

The nearly universal practice of collecting rents once a month (generally on the first day) requires the property manager to be completely informed about all aspects of tenant credit and the associated duties of collection. Careful screening of applicants for rental space contributes to the eventual success of the collection program. Nevertheless, it is vital for management to establish firm and definite collection policies. Exceptions should be allowed only for special cases. For example, it would be reasonable to accommodate a tenant who is paid a few days after the day that rent is due.

While laxities and grace periods may be justified in some business arrangements, late-payment clauses (regardless of the amount of the penalty) are counterproductive in rental-lease agreements. The main protection that property managers have for their percentage-based income is to insist on regular rental payments. There should be no idle threats but rather a set of enforceable (and enforced) rules regulating collections.

For example, as standard operating procedure, the management firm could have the established policy that rents are due on the first of each month, late on the second, with first notices of delinquency being sent out then, and eviction notices issued for all accounts that are past due for longer than a week. Door knocking by management should begin on the third day. Exceptions would be made only with cause and as little publicity as possible (lest other renters claim similar rights for deferred payments).

Any favoritism in rent collection must be avoided. The tenant who has missed one rental payment is in a tight position, not only for the overdue payment but also for making the next payment. To carry someone on credit is asking for trouble; it is against the tenant's long-range interests and those of the property manager and the property owner. By screening the tenant before asking for a lease to be signed (for example, through a credit check), most collection problems can be avoided.

While credit is important in the selection of tenants for all types of properties, questions about credit for commercial and industrial tenants are unique in themselves. They are less complicated than those questions concerning the credit of residential tenants. Because of the complexity of residential tenant credit, its effect on tenant selection is discussed in detail in chapter 10, which deals exclusively with the management of residential property.

Rental Collection Policy

It is an accepted policy that rentals—whether for office, store, loft, or residence—be paid in advance. Monthly rentals are usually due on the first day of each month. It is the practice for some property owners and managers to have rents due on the anniversary of the date on which the tenant moved into the property. This is a poor practice and hinders efficient rent collection. There is a definite advantage in having all rentals due on the first day of each month: most bills for operating expenses are paid on the tenth of the month. Time is important, therefore, in all phases of property management.

Despite this emphasis on rental delinquencies, it must be pointed out that most tenants pay their rents promptly. In a well-run real estate management office, more than 75 percent of all rentals due on the first day of each month will be paid on that date, and more than 95 percent of all rentals due on the first day of the month will be paid before the fifth of the month. Any deviation from these norms is probably due to the management firm's inefficiency rather than to the quality of the tenants. Students of property management must realize that tenants will pay their rents as promptly as the efficiency, effectiveness, and reasonableness of the property manager's collection policy permits.

Having tenants fulfill their financial obligations requires prompt action when rent is not paid on the due date. If the property manager does not act immediately, the tenant loses a sense of responsibility and becomes slack in rental payments. Tenants may be inclined to delay any monetary payments: there are so many demands on their income—either business or family—that they will put off those that are least pressing, or not in line with their priorities. Therefore, the property manager's continuous supervision is essential to a successful operation. The only sound policy is to collect promptly or initiate legal action.

Management firms often fear that aggressive collection action will result in vacancy. This is especially feared in a declining market period, when general vacancy may be high. In these periods many managers tolerate substantial rent delinquencies rather than take action that will result either in the payment of rent or eviction. The manager must realize that it is better to have a vacant apartment than a unit on which the tenant is not paying rent. After all, when a space is vacant, a small saving can be made in heat and wear and tear. Also, there is a chance to find a tenant who will pay the rent.

There are several methods that will produce prompt payment by tenants. The first, and most important, is a clear-cut original understanding between the property manager and tenants. When a tenant applies to lease an apartment, office, or store, the person who takes the application should explain to the prospective tenant that it is management's policy to take immediate action against tenants when rentals are not paid promptly. This warning can be made in a firm but friendly manner. The property manager should repeat the warning when the prospective tenant's credit has been approved and final arrangements are made for transferring possession of the space. In this way, the manager will emphasize the point and hopefully avoid the embarrassment caused by unexpected and rigid collection methods.

When a tenant is delinquent, money is actually being taken from the landlord. The property owner is furnishing the tenant with the facilities and services that were promised only in return for rental payments. Just because the tenant does not pay the rental when it is due does not release the owner from the responsibility of the space and paying its pro rata financing charges as well as the taxes attributable to it. The property owner, therefore, is actually advancing money to the delinquent tenant. When this situation is explained to tenants, they can see their negligence in a different light.

Delinquency Procedure
The effectiveness of any system depends on how closely it is observed by the people in control. Property management is a service profession, operated by individuals with various responsibilities. A collection system will be effective only if it is supported consistently by the property management firm.

A series of forms is the foundation of a good collection system. These forms may vary in type and design but basically consist of the following:

- *Rent Bill.* Whether or not to send each tenant a bill on the first day of the month is a matter of policy set by the property manager. Some computerized and machine-operated systems print a tenant rent bill and receipt form at the same time. Many property managers, who operate general real estate offices, prefer to mail rent bills so that they can enclose advertising. Many managers claim, however, that it is not necessary to send out rent bills in order to collect; when tenants are accustomed to paying their rents promptly, they will do so without receiving bills. Every tenant must be made to realize that the rental must be paid on the first day of the month. Tenants should not rely on the management firm to remind them when obligations are due. There are exceptions: in buildings in which there are special charges of varying amounts (electricity, maid service, laundry, and escalation clauses), rent bills are, of course, necessary.
- *Reminder Notice.* A reminder notice, such as the one shown in figure 7.2, should be sent to a tenant on the first day that rent

FIGURE 7.2
RENT REMINDER NOTICE

Date_____

Resident_____ Unit Number_____

Total Rent Due $_____ From_____ To_____

Please bring the above amount and appropriate late charges to the office within the next 24 hours.

Thank you.

_____
Resident Manager

is delinquent. The first notice is a friendly reminder that the rent is due and should not be so harsh as to antagonize the tenant. If payment still is not made, a more strongly worded notice may be sent.
- *Eviction Notice.* Even though there are differences in eviction notices from state to state, the form is a notice to the violator

to pay the rent immediately or leave the leased premises within a specified time. (See figure 7.3.)

FIGURE 7.3
EVICTION NOTICE

To: _____
_____
_____

and all tenants in possession.

Please take notice that rent has not been paid for the premises hereinafter described and now held and occupied

by you and that the sum of _____

_____ Dollars ($_____) is now due and unpaid.

being the rent due from the _____ day of _____, 19_____, to the_____

_____ day of _____ 19_____.

You are hereby required to pay said rent to the undersigned within three (3) days after service of this notice

upon you or to remove yourself and personal belongings from and deliver the possession of said premises to

the undersigned within said three (3) days, or the undersigned will institute legal proceedings against you to

receive possession of said premises, to declare a forfeiture of the agreement under which you occupy the same,

and to recover treble damages.

The premises herein referred to are described as _____

_____

Manager_____ Date _____

By adopting these forms and appropriate procedures, the manager restates the collection policy: all rentals are to be paid in advance and monthly rentals are late on the morning of the second day of each month. This policy makes it clear that the property manager will take legal action against delinquent tenants if necessary.

Action against delinquents in which these forms are used can be divided into two general categories. The first is organizational action, taken to stimulate rental payment; the second is legal action, designed to guarantee payment of rental or the eviction of the tenant. It is necessary to analyze both types of action and the timing of each.

If a tenant is delinquent on the morning of the second day of the month, the account requires organizational activity, usually in the form of a reminder letter. While the property manager's collection procedure has already been explained to the tenant (who can expect prompt action), it is still good policy for the property manager to allow a reasonable time between the date the rent is due and legal action for its payment. In most cases, this period should be no longer than five days, during which time the tenant should be reminded of the delinquency and warned that further action will be taken if the rental is not paid promptly.

Most firms use a reminder form, while others prefer an individually addressed letter that serves the same purpose. The form should be mailed or personally delivered at the close of business on the second or third day of each month, so the tenant realizes that the delinquency is noted immediately.

The distribution of these reminder notices should become routine. For commercial and industrial properties, this duty should be assumed by the accounting department or the property manager's bookkeeper, since the basic records of rental collections are the responsibility of these employees. In the case of residential properties, the property manager may ask the accounting department to prepare a list of unpaid rentals and direct it to the resident manager responsible for the building in which the delinquent tenants reside. These tenants then could be contacted personally or by telephone, usually by the on-site manager.

Whichever reminder method is used, the important fact is that the tenant is notified of the delinquency immediately and warned that, unless the rental is paid on or before the date noted, action will be taken on behalf of the building owner. This action should be promised rather than threatened. The reminder can be handled in a courteous and pleasant manner, without losing impact or firmness. It is the property manager's responsibility to see that collection is made with the least possible loss of goodwill. The desire to please, however, should not be carried to the point of failing to collect the rent. In the long run, it does not benefit the building owner or the property manager to establish goodwill by permitting delinquency. It is possible to establish and carry through a firm collection policy without losing the respect of tenants. People agree, in principle, that bills should be paid promptly, and the sensible tenant is seldom offended by a well-conducted, firm collection policy.

Eviction Procedure

If a tenant refuses to make a delinquent rental payment, it will be necessary for the property manager to implement eviction proceedings.

Eviction refers to the ejection of a tenant from the leased premises by the landlord. Although the laws governing eviction vary widely from state to state, most provide for the serving of eviction notices by property owners or their agents. These notices are usually returnable in court after a certain number of days have elapsed, ranging, according to the state, from three days to seven days or more.

The eviction notice usually proceeds as follows. The property manager fills out an eviction form, usually in triplicate: one copy is served to the tenant as stipulated by local or state law, one is filed in court by the attorney representing the property manager or the building owner, and one is filed at the management office. (In some small claims courts, the property manager can personally represent the owner in an unlawful detainer action.) It is most important that the form be filled out in strict accordance with the legal procedures specified in it. Eviction notices frequently are thrown out of court on technicalities because they were improperly drawn.

When the form has been properly completed, it is given to the manager responsible for the building in which the delinquent tenant resides. This form is then served on the tenant. In some states, the form must be served on a person who is above a specified legal age and is actually on the premises in which the delinquency has occurred. In other states, it is possible, if no one answers the door, to serve the form by posting it on the main entrance of the premises involved. The form usually provides for an affidavit of service (a sworn statement that the notice has been properly served), which is filled out by the person who serves the notice. This affidavit then is presented to the court.

In the usual procedure, if the tenant has not paid the rent to the property manager within the specified number of days, the eviction notice is filed in the court by the attorney representing the property manager or building owner. Once the notice is filed, the court will set a date for the hearing on the eviction suit and notify the tenant to appear in court.

When in court, the tenant may be given an opportunity to pay the rent. Legally, the landlord does not necessarily have to accept this rent, yet court procedure is such that, if a tenant offers to pay, the judge may direct the landlord to accept payment. If the tenant is unable to pay, the judge usually will set a date by which the tenant must vacate. If the tenant has not vacated by that date, then the attorney for the landlord, or the property manager, obtains a writ of possession. If the tenant ignores the writ of possession ordered by the court and does not vacate voluntarily, then the owner or agent returns to the court to obtain a writ of eviction, which orders a court officer to physically eject and dispossess the tenant. This eviction process can involve a considerable sum of money and, even under the most favorable circumstances, can require 30 to 45 days.

The laws regarding suits for possession by landlords have been changed in many states to broaden the rights of tenants. Even in cases where nonpayment of rent is admittedly involved, courts are more and more reluctant to evict families, especially those in the lower income brackets. This is a greater reason why action must be prompt when delinquency occurs.

In several states, there are other possibilities for legal action against delinquent tenants. Most of these involve complicated legal maneuvers that should only be directed by an attorney.

Summary

Tenants are the foundation of property management activity, and, if carefully chosen and satisfied, they will be recognized by management as its most valuable asset.

Tenants should not be selected haphazardly. The professional property manager establishes criteria a rental applicant must meet before a lease is offered. All tenants—for both commercial and residential property—must have the capacity to pay the rent being asked. A credit check is useful in making this determination. Acceptable tenants also display the ability to properly maintain the leased premises and a compatibility with the property itself and with the other tenants.

In addition to setting tenant selection criteria, the property manager also must adopt measures to see that tenants are satisfied throughout the terms of their leases. The manager is a buffer between the property owner and the tenant, striving to see that both parties to each lease agreement are treated fairly.

The key factor in assuring tenant satisfaction is responsive handling of tenant requests for maintenance. Reasonable requests should be performed as promptly as possible. If requests are impossible to fulfill or there will be delays, an explanation is in order. In all cases, on-site personnel who are in actual contact with tenants should be courteous and accommodating.

The cornerstone of the success of any management organization is promptness in collecting rents. Even if tenant selection criteria have been established and rigidly adhered to, there will be a few collection problems. For tenants who either cannot pay their rents on time or do not take the responsibility seriously, rent collection policies and procedures are needed.

A rent collection policy that indicates when, where, and how rents are to be paid should be established and communicated to all tenants. Procedures also are needed for taking action against tenants who fail to meet their rental obligations. This usually entails sending reminder notices to delinquents and, if they get no response, initiating legal action with the intent of eviction if the rent is not paid.

REVIEW QUESTIONS

1. What measurements should be made by the property manager in selecting tenants? List in order of importance.
2. What is the purpose of a rental application?
3. What is the objective of a property manager's tenant relations program?
4. Basically, what does a landlord expect from the property? What does the tenant expect in turn for rent money?
5. How should the property manager handle a tenant who wants a storm door installed if the manager knows it cannot be done?
6. What is the primary reason for tenant misunderstandings? How can they be prevented?
7. What is the basis of a good rent collection policy?
8. When should rents on all properties be due and payable? Why?
9. What two types of action should be taken when a tenant is delinquent? Explain each.
10. Define *eviction*. When should legal action against a tenant be taken? Explain.

Chapter
Eight

Maintenance

ONE OF THE RESPONSIBILITIES of property management is to supervise the physical operation of properties under its control. This requires experience in maintaining the physical plant and selecting and training the on-site staff to perform the necessary activities. *Maintenance* is a process that provides the repairs and services necessary to satisfy tenants and preserve the physical condition of the building and still hold down operating expenses and maximize earnings for the owner. Management is in a delicate position. Only by an accurate evaluation of a property's maintenance needs, including manpower requirements, can the property manager balance the two forces.

Maintenance Process

Within the professions, there has been a trend toward intellectual rather than vocational courses. Instruction in "how to" subjects has trained those assisting professionals (i.e., nurses' and teachers' aides, paramedics and paralegals) rather than the professionals themselves.

In the initial stages of property management, education focused on vocational trades, such as plumbing, heating and ventilating, and painting and decorating. But as the profession of property management matured, education's focus shifted. Managers no longer must have the practical skills involved in maintaining physical structures. It is necessary, however, for students and practitioners to understand the manager's role in the physical operation of real property.

There are four types of services that must be incorporated into a maintenance program:

1. Maintenance activities that protect the physical integrity of structures under management.
2. Maintenance activities that assure the continuous performance of a property's mechanical, electrical, plumbing, and other equipment.
3. Routine chores that maintain cleanliness and order.
4. Maintenance activities that create or sustain physical attractiveness for merchandising purposes.

Within this framework, the property manager will encounter three categories of maintenance activities. The first is *preventive maintenence*. This is a program of regular inspection and care that allows potential problems to be prevented or at least detected and solved before major repairs are required.

The second kind is *corrective maintenance*. This involves the actual repairs that must be made to the building and its equipment because of failure to perform proper preventive maintenance or natural wear and tear.

The third type is *custodial maintenance,* which refers to policing and housekeeping duties.

Programs can and should be prepared for these three types of maintenance, but cannot always be prepared for a fourth type of maintenance—*emergency maintenance*. Even far-sighted preventive, corrective, and custodial maintenance programs cannot predict emergencies, but, the property manager can establish procedures for dealing with emergency situations.

Maintenance for Physical Integrity

All structures have two lives—a physical life and an economic life. The *economic life* of a building is the period of time it can be used in the production of assets or services. The time period depends on a variety of factors: some can be controlled by the property manager and others depend on the economy. In virtually all instances, the *physical life* of a building depends on the quality of its maintenance. As proof, there are structures in all parts of the world that are as sound physically as they were when they were built, even though they may be hundreds of years old.

The property manager is responsible for making certain that each element of the physical structure functions as it should. When conditions lessen the structure's earning power, there is a temptation among private owners to avoid those expenditures necessary to maintain physical integrity, in order to hold down operating costs. In public buildings, politicians sometimes postpone maintenance expenditures to hold taxes at falsely computed levels. *Deferred maintenance* compounds a building's physical problems and greatly increases the long-range operating costs. Often, the property manager will have to balance the owner's wishes with a personal knowledge of what should be done to protect the property. Management must make clear to the owner who resists maintenance the consequences of neglect. When an owner constantly overrules needed expenditures and earns the ill will of tenants, the manager should terminate the business relationship, or risk identification with poor management.

The following is a checklist of those structural elements that require a manager's attention.

Walks, Driveways, and Parking Areas. Most walks and driveways are made of concrete, asphalt, brick, or stone which, though durable, deteriorate from erosion, wear, and weather. Sometimes preventive maintenance is possible, but usually repairs restore neither visual nor functional utility, and replacement rather than maintenance is preferred.

Foundations. Building foundations unsupported by caissons resting on bedrock are subject to deterioration, movement, leakage, and other faults. Unless defects are severe, correction is possible. Even large buildings can be shored up to compensate for settling and movement. Waterproofing materials stop leakage, and foundation materials can be replaced or repaired systematically to preserve their integrity.

Exterior Walls. Most exterior building walls can be maintained. Wooden walls can be preserved almost indefinitely so long as there is an effective coating—usually paint—to protect the surfaces from weather. Brick and stone walls resist erosion insofar as the basic materials are concerned. However, the brick or stone walls are cemented together by some type of mortar which, in cold climates especially, deteriorates from moisture. The repair of these surfaces by restoring the mortar joints is called *tuck-pointing*. Mortar joints must be inspected regularly—at least once every five years—to determine the need for repair.

Exterior Porches, Stairways, and Fire Escapes.   Exterior stairways, porches, and fire escapes (constructed of wood, steel, concrete, and iron) require constant surface restoration to avoid deterioration from oxidation, moisture, and wear. Depending on the climate, these surfaces need renewal every three to five years. The number of coats of paint or other surface covering required depends on the individual location.

Roofs.   Roofs take much abuse from climatic conditions of extreme heat, cold, or moisture. A roof either must be replaced or repaired many times during the life of the average structure. Under especially severe conditions, roofs often weaken in critical areas ahead of schedule and repairs may be required before complete replacement is necessary.

Fenestration.   Window glass, while subject to breakage, is virtually impervious to wear. The framing material and the operating parts, however, require regular attention. In the past, window frames were constructed from wood, regardless of the structure's basic material. Recently, however, metal frames have become popular, and their manufacturers claim that some of these metals are impervious to weather and are maintenance-free. This claim has yet to be proved, even though it is certain that many of the new materials will require less maintenance than either wood or the metals that previously were employed. All types of windows, however, are subject to functional defects that must be repaired.

Gutters and Downspouts.   Roofs are drained by gutters and downspouts, which protect exterior walls from moisture and prevent accumulations of water. Gutters and downspouts often are made from galvanized iron. The outside surface of this material is protected by paint, but its interior is subject to rust and wear. Replacement time is approximately the same as for the roof.

Interior Wall Surfaces.   Shielded from exterior climatic abuse, most interior walls, when properly treated, require far less maintenance than other structural elements. But, they are subject to wear and misuse. Perhaps the greatest problem is the accumulation of too many wall coverings or the improper application of them. Too many coats of wallpaper on a plaster wall will cause the plaster finish coat to break away. This also applies to too many coats of paint. A shift in the building's foundation and what is known as settlement frequently cause surface walls and ceilings to crack. Tenants sometimes disturb or disfigure walls by hanging pictures, drapery brackets, and other decorations. Also, of course, there is outright abuse by children or careless adults.

Interior walls in service areas present the most difficult maintenance problems. Movers, delivery men, and the public in general often damage walls. Experienced managers order materials for service area walls specifically designed to minimize problems. Tile, for instance, not only provides a tough surface but also eliminates painting. Steel shields installed where damage is most likely to occur are sound preventive maintenance aids.

Maintenance for Functional Performance

In the modern world, structures must do more than merely exist; they must work.

Perhaps the most recurring maintenance problems are represented by equipment that does not operate. One of the major responsibilities of a building manager is to assure the functional operation of the structure's mechanical equipment. The number of mechanical devices is increasing constantly through technological development. Usually demanding maintenance attention is the following equipment:

Heating, Ventilating, and Air-Conditioning System. With increasing affluence, society expects a higher degree of physical comfort. People are not satisfied with a building that merely keeps them warm and dry in inclement weather. Tenants want a constant year-round temperature, a guaranteed range of humidity, and an adequate supply of clean, fresh air (despite the current energy crisis). The equipment controlling these conditions is complex, expensive to maintain, and requires maintenance.

Heating, ventilating, and air-conditioning (HVAC) systems all regulate one element—heat. The heating plant stores heat and releases it evenly throughout the structure, while the air-conditioning system absorbs heat from various parts of the structure and removes it from the building. The ventilating system removes stale, foul air from a building and replaces it with fresh air. A technical discussion of heating, air-conditioning, and ventilating systems is beyond the scope of this text. However, the student manager should become familiar with the types of equipment most frequently used.

Plumbing System.   The plumbing system distributes and controls water and disposes of waste. Maintaining this system includes the care of fixtures and equipment, the conservation of water, the anticipation and prevention of stoppages in waste lines, the selection of new equipment for replacement, and secondary activities that support the essential functions of the system.

Adding garbage disposal units to the plumbing system (especially where drainage pipes cannot handle the bulk loads they develop) creates many problems. In some areas, these units cannot be installed. Where they are found, tenants should be properly instructed in their use, and building personnel should be trained in maintenance procedures.

Electrical System.   The use of electricity in the United States is increasing steadily. When buildings were originally wired for electrical current, use was limited to illumination of tenant spaces and power for elevators and centrally located pumps. The wiring system was relatively simple, since it led only to light fixtures and the actual power installations that were part of the building's mechanical equipment.

The wiring system in today's building (whether residential, commercial, or industrial) is much more complicated. Electric energy is required everywhere in the modern structure—not just for lighting, but to provide portable heat, operate housekeeping and business machinery, and service electrical appliances.

From the property manager's point of view, capacity is the chief problem of the electrical distribution system. As the volume of electrical energy distributed to tenants increases, the transmission lines also must be enlarged, just as large pipes are needed to increase water flow.

If the capacity of the wiring and the number of electrical outlets in tenant spaces are adequate, there is no need for further concern. If tenants install electricity-draining equipment (e.g., large-capacity room coolers, heaters, or business machines), arrangements should be made when occupancy terms are negotiated as to who is to pay for the special wiring. Also, if electricity is furnished to the tenant as part of the rent, the manager must arrange for the tenant to pay for excess charges.

One of the manager's primary concerns is maintaining electric motors in proper operating condition, for these affect the entire structure. Motors are used to power pumps, fans, hoisting devices, and for many other purposes. Also important to the manager are the communications system, if one has been installed, and maintenance of radio and television antennae and their connection to individual receiving sets in units occupied by tenants.

Elevators.   Two factors have led to increased use of vertical transportation devices in modern buildings. One was the development of steel and reinforced concrete building techniques that made multistory structures possible, and, second, has been the unwillingness of tenants to climb stairs. Today, even an outlying office building of two stories (especially if it contains physicians' offices) must be elevator-equipped.

An elevator consists of a cab, a set of rails or tracks, cables, a hoisting machine, and a set of controls that directs its operation. Vertical transportation devices also include lifts (usually for freight), dumbwaiters, and escalators.

Maintaining any form of vertical transportation is so technical that most managers arrange for contract maintenance, either with the manufacturer or other specialist in this field.

Fenestration.   Although windows were discussed previously, there is more to be said about the maintenance of their moving parts. The window frame itself must be in working order, which may mean the installation of window ropes, counterweights, weather stripping, and locks and fasteners. It also may involve the purchase and maintenance of window shades, venetian blinds, draperies, drapery hanging devices, and awnings.

Window cleaning is handled differently in various types of properties. In most residential buildings, the tenant is responsible for cleaning windows. Window cleaning contractors usually offer their services to tenants on a per-window charge. The tenant's responsibility to clean windows extends to store tenants, who usually have the work done by one of their maintenance crew. In office buildings, window cleaning is the responsibility of the owner. It is handled in one of two ways—either by a window washer who is an employee of the maintenance staff or by outside contract. The time between window washings is set by the management, usually on an arranged schedule. The frequency of window washing varies with location and season.

Laundries.   Most residential buildings provide laundry facilities for tenants. In large multifamily structures, laundry rooms are located on each floor or in the basement. Standard equipment in these areas includes laundry tubs and automatic washers and dryers. Although the tubs are provided free for tenant use, laundry appliances are usually coin-operated machines. They may be installed in the building on consignment by a vendor, who collects the fees and assumes responsibility for maintaining the machines, or they are owned by the landlord, who either contracts for their maintenance or assigns it to the building staff. The cleaning and interior maintenance of the laundry rooms themselves are the responsibility of the landlord and are delegated to building employees.

Storage Areas.   Many buildings provide storage space for residential tenants' excess belongings. Sometimes, storage is limited to trunks and travel gear in a large room used in common by tenants.

In many larger buildings with higher rentals, an individual storeroom is provided for each apartment. Tenants are given keys for their storerooms, and they assume full responsibility for the contents.

In well-run properties, management assumes the responsibility for guarding storage areas and upholding rules and regulations pertaining to their use.

Swimming Pools and Other Recreational Amenities.   Residential property management is a competitive field, and more apartment buildings are providing recreational facilities to lure tenants. If there is a swimming pool, its maintenance is the responsibility of the building management and can be assigned to staff or contracted to firms specializing in such maintenance. However the pools are maintained physically, they still present a serious responsibility to the management in consideration of safety and order. Since many apartment buildings are not large enough to staff their pools with lifeguards, rigid rules must be enforced, especially to avoid accidents to children. Often, pools are fenced (sometimes by law) with locked gates, and keys are furnished only to tenants.

Aside from safety factors, strict pool supervision is needed to prevent disturbing the peace and quiet of tenants who may not use this facility. A schedule of hours of use by adults and children and regulations for the entertainment of guests, use of radio and television, and picnicking and drinking should definitely be adopted and enforced.

Many properties provide recreation rooms for parties that cannot be accommodated in individual tenants' quarters. These recreation areas often contain small kitchens with stoves, refrigerators, and bars, available either for a rental charge or gratis after advance reservations are made with the management. Obviously, rules and regulations for the use of such spaces are required. This is also true of workshops, sewing rooms, and other areas provided in many modern buildings.

Playgrounds and common parking areas represent definite responsibilities to management with conditions of use, care of equipment, and maintenance.

Recreational rooms and other facilities were especially popular among developers in the early 1970s. However, there is some question about whether the investment is justified. These social facilities seldom were sufficiently attractive to apartment tenants to warrant their cost, especially in the inflationary years after the early 1970s.

Housekeeping and Cleanliness

No matter how well a building's physical equipment is maintained, it is poorly operated if it does not have high standards of cleanliness. Similarly, the readiness and capability of the maintenance staff in responding to tenant requests for service affect a building's reputation.

Cleanliness is achieved through education and habits. Managers must realize that neatness and order are fundamental to profitable real estate operation and communicate this concept to employees, tenants, and the public through supervision and training.

Cleanliness and order begin with the design of a building. Obviously, it is impossible to keep a dirt floor clean, and it is also apparent that a marble floor is much easier to maintain than a porous wood floor. When a property manager has an opportunity to review specifications for a new structure, suggestions can be made that will make maintenance easier and more economical.

Good housekeeping also requires adequate equipment. Tenants' waste materials are less of a problem if they are deposited in the proper container or incinerator. Building lobbies will not be so soiled if door mats and all-weather runner mats are installed. And, maintenance personnel can perform much more efficiently when they have proper tools and appliances to assist them in their duties.

Some managers wrongly lay the entire responsibility for cleanliness and good housekeeping on the building's janitorial and maintenance crew. Yet, no building will be desirable and attractive unless the tenants and the public cooperate. In an office building, for example, one cannot expect to keep the floors free from cigaret stubs, gum wrappers, and other litter unless ash and rubbish containers are provided. Management also has a definite responsibility to enforce cleanliness as one of the conditions of using the property. This includes taking action against tenants, or requesting their removal from the premises, if they fail to cooperate with the program.

Maintenance for Merchandising

This text has emphasized management techniques that enhance the saleability and profits of income property. Since an investment property's success depends on marketing its space, it follows that certain maintenance operations are performed solely for merchandising reasons.

For example, exterior surfaces must be protectively coated to prevent deterioration, but this is not true for the interior walls of apartments, offices, or public spaces. These surfaces are not subject to the influences of weather and wear: the chief reason to paint them is to beautify, increasing their attractiveness to present and prospective tenants. The use of color inside buildings achieves the same objective as the use of color in a full-page magazine advertisement. A tenant is more likely to rent if a space is attractive and probably will pay a higher rent if it is noticeably more attractive.

There are many other maintenance activities more related to merchandising than to maintenance. When spending the client's money in the operation of any property, the property manager must recognize the desirability of creating the maximum beautification and functional utility per dollar spent. Landscaping does not add to the actual utility of interior rental spaces, but the planting of shrubs and flowers can measurably increase the value of every apartment or office suite in the property. Similarly, carpets in the lobby often present greater maintenance costs than other floor coverings but, under certain circumstances, are justified because of the value and marketability they add to interior rentable space.

In the case of a residential property, much of the maintenance performed to get a vacant unit ready to show to prospects is done with merchandising in mind. To ensure that vacant units are as marketable as possible, a *unit make-ready report,* such as the one in figure 8.1, should be adopted by the property manager. As the inspection of a newly vacated unit is made, any observed defects can be noted on this checklist, which is then given to the maintenance department so that the necessary correction steps can be taken. When

FIGURE 8.1

UNIT MAKE-READY REPORT

| Property |
| Unit _____ Type _____ |
| Date Vacated _____ Date To Be Occupied _____ |
| Initial Inspection by _____ Date _____ |

Checklist Before Move-In	Instructions
☐ Check all plumbing. (Toilets, faucets, all plumbing in unit.) Make sure no leaks.	
☐ Check all appliances. (Run dishwasher once on each cycle, check for proper operation of refrigerator, disposal, and range.)	
☐ Check hardware in unit. (All door knobs, closet hooks, closet rods, door pulls, night locks, door stops, magnetic catches, etc.)	
☐ Check windows and screens. (No breaks in either. All sliding glass windows and screens working correctly.) Clean out tracks on all sliding glass windows and doors. Ensure that all screws are installed where needed.	
☐ Check venetian blinds for proper operation.	
☐ Check all walls for holes, seams, cuts, nail pops.	
☐ Check paint. (All walls, ceilings, woodwork, trim which need to be cleaned or painted. No spots, streaks, or scratches.)	
☐ Check flooring. (All floors cleaned and waxed, parquet block floors or wood strip and asphalt tile included. Carpet vacuumed.)	
☐ Bathroom(s) cleaned. (Tubs, toilets, tile walls, tile floor, vanities, mirrors, medicine cabinets, and sinks clean.)	
☐ All towel bars, toilet paper holders, soap dishes installed and cleaned.	
☐ Check tile in bathroom(s) for cracks or flaws.	

each deficiency is corrected and all items are checked off, the apartment is ready for showing. A similar form can be adopted for commercial properties.

How much maintenance is warranted solely for merchandising purposes is a matter of managerial judgment. Only through experi-

FIGURE 8.1—*Continued*

Checklist Before Move-In	Instructions
☐ All baseboard, shelves in closet, electrical outlet plates installed properly.	
☐ All threshholds and metal strips installed where needed.	
☐ Check that all doors close properly, with no rubbing or warping.	
☐ Check that all vents and registers are installed.	
☐ Check heating and air conditioning (when appropriate) to be sure working properly.	
☐ Check that filters are installed in all air handling units or air conditioning units (when appropriate).	
☐ All kitchen cabinets cleaned inside and outside.	
☐ Windows cleaned.	
☐ Check all lighting. (New bulbs in all fixtures, and all fixtures hung and working.)	
☐ Check for chips or cracks in plumbing fixtures and kitchen appliances.	
☐	
☐	
☐	

Final Inspection by _____ Date _____

Approved by _____ Date _____

ence and careful analysis can the property manager determine if these expenditures will be productive financially.

The student of property management must have an understanding of building maintenance that extends beyond the simple protection and functional utility of the property. Maintenance also includes relating monetary expenditures to the overall profitability of the property and increasing returns.

Performance of Maintenance Activities

Knowing what must be done to maintain property is pointless if no one is assigned to perform the necessary duties and no schedule of maintenance inspections is prepared.

Staff vs. Contract Maintenance

The professional management organization can handle its maintenance problems in a variety of ways. The most common is through contractors or service agencies engaged in building maintenance, either across-the-board or for individual jobs, such as plumbing, heating, and elevator maintenance. The work is performed on order from the property management firm, and bills are rendered by the service agency or contractor. After examination and approval of the work and its cost, expenses are charged to the owner's account. The management firm assures that the work is done promptly, efficiently, and economically.

Another method of handling the maintenance is through a maintenance department formed by the property management firm. Skilled mechanics and laborers are hired who can perform the many maintenance tasks that are presented by the various properties. In this case, the management firm itself is a contractor or service agency.

While this policy is followed in many areas of the country by individual management firms, it does present problems. First, there is a conflict of interest when the manager certifies and approves payment of invoices for work performed for building owners. The management firm is actually judging its own efficiency and economy of operation. This custom should only be practiced with full disclosure to the client.

Second, in the operation of a maintenance division by a management firm, disputes may arise which threaten the management arrangement. The very nature of building maintenance will present unexpected and sometimes heavy expenditures which are an aggravation to the property owner. When the bill for these expenditures is rendered directly by the management firm, the building owner may believe that some of the expense can be charged to the manager. The owner may suspect that the manager has profited unduly from the expenditure. It is, therefore, preferable to handle the maintenance in another way.

In larger individual buildings, money can be saved by the direct employment—on the building payroll—of maintenance people. Again, there is considerable variation in local practice, depending on location and labor union organization. The main employee of a building with a one-man staff is a janitor. During the winter, the janitor's responsibility is the care of the heating plant and the removal of tenant garbage and snow; in the summer, it is the maintenance of grounds, walks, and public spaces. In efficiently operated properties, the janitor also makes minor repairs to most of the building's equipment. If the building cannot be maintained by only one person, others are employed as assistants.

In buildings with high-pressure steam plants supplying heat and power, the basic job is performed by an engineer. When assistants are necessary, they are called assistant engineers, and they work at the direction of the chief engineer.

In large residential complexes, office buildings, hotels, and other major structures, the building payroll may employ full-time painters and decorators, electricians, plumbers, carpenters, and other specialized tradesmen.

Schedules and Inspections

Even though a property manager may not be able to correct faulty plumbing or repair an air conditioning unit, the manager must be able to establish a program for performing these and other maintenance activities. A maintenance schedule should include daily housekeeping and routine policing duties. However, primary emphasis should be on regular inspections of the property's equipment and its physical structure. Through these inspections, potential problems can be detected early and often prevented altogether. The benefit of a strong preventive maintenance program is lower operating costs and, consequently, increased profits to the owner.

A conscientious real estate manager realizes that every managed property deserves regular inspection. This inspection will be successful only if conducted on a routine schedule and if it is a check against certain end results. The real estate manager should have a checklist of items to be inspected; this checklist need not be identical for each visit. If a new roof has just been put on a building, there is no need for the manager to inspect the roof's surface or its flashing; it may be looked at superficially, but a detailed examination is unnecessary.

FIGURE 8.2
WORK ORDER

Work Order Number _____

Property _____ Date _____

Location _____

Maintenance Required

_____
_____
_____
_____

Maintenance Performed

_____
_____
_____

Materials Used

_____
_____
_____

Time Required _____

Cost of Labor	$
Cost of Materials	
Total	**$**

Maintenance Performed by _____

Unable to Complete Because of _____

_____
_____

The same is true if the outside sash and trim of the building have just been painted. On the other hand, there are certain items that should be checked on each visit: lawns, landscaping and walks, rear halls and stairways, entrance halls, and other public areas. Boiler rooms, shops, tenant storage spaces, and laundry rooms should also be inspected regularly.

All of these items should be listed on a master schedule of inspection for each property maintained by the manager. With such a

FIGURE 8.3

PROPERTY MAINTENANCE RECORD

Property _____

Date	Action	Location	by Whom	Time	Cost

system, it is not necessary to inspect each item on each visit to a building; but, the manager can avoid neglecting any item by using an inspection report. For example, examining the building's screens when they are removed in the fall aids in estimating the time required for repair. In the spring, these screens can be inspected as they are painted and reinstalled. Scheduling these factors not only will conserve the manager's time but will ensure proper attention to details.

(Inspection forms for apartment buildings and for both the interior and exterior of office buildings appear in the appendix of this text.)

The maintenance function requires a certain amount of administrative record keeping. For example, if an inspection reveals a deficiency, the property manager must take action to see that the problem is corrected. A *work order,* such as the one in figure 8.2, is useful in implementing corrective maintenance. Not only does the work order advise maintenance personnel of the job that is to be done, but it also becomes a record of the work that was performed, the date it was completed, the person who handled the assignment, and the cost of repairs and replacements. Work orders also can be used to follow up on tenant requests for maintenance.

Many professional property managers also keep master lists of all repairs that are performed at a property and other maintenance activities that are undertaken. A *property maintenance record,* such as the sample in figure 8.3, can be useful. When accurately maintained, this record can alert the property manager to any troublesome patterns so that recurring problems can be corrected with long-term solutions.

Summary

The objective of a maintenance program is to preserve a property owner's investment while satisfying and providing for the well-being of tenants. Conscientious concern for the physical aspects of a real estate investment may mean the difference between its success and failure. While not necessarily proficient in performing maintenance tasks, the manager must be able to identify the various types of maintenance activities and plan for their performance.

A complete maintenance program incorporates four types of maintenance activities: (1) maintenance to protect a property's physical integrity; (2) maintenance to assure continuous performance of a property's functioning parts; (3) housekeeping; and (4) maintenance to make the property's rental space more marketable.

In addition to understanding the types of maintenance, the property manager also must assign someone to perform the specific needs associated with each type. This may be done in one of three ways: (1) the manager may contract with a service agency or individual maintenance engineers; (2) the management agency may form a maintenance department, which then contracts with the property; or (3) on-site personnel may be hired to service the property.

To judge the quality of maintenance being performed and uncover small problems before they become big ones, the property
manager must establish a schedule of regular inspections. This
schedule should cover all interior and exterior public areas and
rental areas, with particular emphasis on the building's structure
and equipment.

REVIEW QUESTIONS

1. What are the principal types of maintenance that must be per-
    formed?
2. What is *corrective maintenance?* Relate this to the tenant rela-
    tions program adopted by the property manager. What impact
    does this have on renewals?
3. Define *physical life* and *economic life.* What is the impact of
    maintenance on each?
4. Name five items that require functional maintenance. Elaborate
    on each.
5. What impact does a building's design have on its housekeeping?
    Give three examples.
6. What effect does maintenance have on a building's market-
    ability? How can the property manager justify maintenance
    performed for marketing reasons?
7. What arguments are used to support the formation of a main-
    tenance department within a management company? What
    arguments are used against such formation?
8. What is *preventive maintenance?* Explain the relationship be-
    tween preventive maintenance and inspections.

Chapter
Nine

Staffing and
Employee Relations

PROPERTY MANAGEMENT is a business that depends on people. The real estate manager cannot work alone.

In organizing a management operation, the property manager has to determine what staff responsibilities must be met to ensure the effective management of properties under the firm's supervision and then select and train the appropriate individuals to fill these requirements. Even the largest property management firm begins as a one-person operation. As operational needs develop, new employees are hired. The property manager ideally evaluates not only current staffing requirements but also long-term ones, planning for the future so that employees are ready and trained to handle new business as it is obtained. Staff should be added according to a specific plan rather than haphazardly.

Job Descriptions

Because of differences in both type of work assignments and size of operations, there is no single organizational pattern that will apply in all cases. Nevertheless, certain job functions and responsibilities exist in every management office—large or small.

Each organization will have its own arrangements, reflecting both the nature of the company's business and the style of the proprietor. In a large management company, one or more persons most likely will perform each of the job descriptions listed. For practical purposes, especially in smaller management organizations, one person probably will perform several job functions.

The size of the management staff depends on four basic factors: the number of tenants to be served, the number of clients served, the average size of the properties handled, and the number of fiscal accounts involved. For example, the property supervisor is the principal employee of the management company. This person is in the field during most working hours; so, an administrative assistant often is needed to handle detail work, take messages, and receive the public at the office. Together, they form a team. In a small firm, this team is the entire staff, with a secretary performing both clerical duties and also those related to the accounting operation.

In larger organizations, the supervisor, with adequate assistance, is assigned a specific number of units or square feet. For residential income properties, experience suggests that the maximum number of single-family residences that can be handled efficiently by one supervisor is approximately 150. The supervisor, then, would be managing 150 buildings with 150 tenant families. But, if the average building contains ten units, it might be possible for the manager to supervise as many as 300 tenant families, or 30 buildings. If the average size of the buildings is 20 units, the manager might be able to supervise the 500 units contained in 25 buildings.

In organizations managing several thousand units of property, it is a working rule to have an executive-level property manager for every five management supervisors. These suggested workloads are not by any means fixed, but they do allow the student some idea of the personnel requirements of the property management organization. Similar relationships between properties being managed and personnel requirements can be established for office buildings and shopping centers.

Executive Property Manager

The executive property manager (or the vice president of property management in a large, full-service real estate firm) has two major responsibilities: to obtain new management business and to arbitrate management policies and procedures. This person also must respond to the needs of all employees of the organization.

Executive Property Manager

I. Responsible for Policies
   A. Rates to be charged for services

  B. Commission to be charged for services
   1. Amount
   2. Cooperating with other real estate professionals
 II. Developing New Business
  A. Direction of new account solicitation
  B. Determining desirability of new accounts
  C. Institutional contacts
   1. Through clubs, social affiliations, and identification with professional activities
   2. Through publicity in trade journals and newspapers
 III. Direction of Business
  A. Supervising operational costs
  B. Supervising departmental activities
   1. Reports from department heads
   2. Occasional inspection of properties
  C. Reviewing all legal charges and insurance claims against the firm
 IV. Employee Relations
  A. Organizing department and general staff meetings
  B. Hiring and firing staff
  C. Handling union matters, if applicable
  D. Ensuring fair employment practices

Director of Property Management

The director of property management is chiefly responsible for directing the activities of the organization's property supervisors. In-depth management experience is needed, and the skills to operate real property effectively must be mastered.

Director of Property Management

 I. Directing and Supervising Activities and Personnel
  A. Reports from managers
   1. Inspections
   2. Tenant contacts
   3. Building personnel: number of employee changes and reason, and total payroll under the management supervisor's control
  B. Reports from cashier
   1. Record of all delinquencies
   2. Number of units vacant, including those under maintenance, availability dates, and turnover rates
   3. Monthly rent roll
   4. Gain or loss of business

          a. In units
          b. In rent roll
       5. Monthly operating statement
   C. Reports from service request clerks: number of requests handled, number referred to building staff, and number of orders written to contractors and supply houses
   D. Reports from purchasing agent on labor and commodity costs
  II. Personal Examination of Statements to Owners
   A. Meetings and interviews with staff
   B. Directing collections and collection policy
 III. Owner Contacts
   A. Personal interviews with management team
   B. Letters with owners' statements
   C. Frequent communications about matters interesting and beneficial to owners
   D. Semi-social calls to strengthen personal relationships

Director of Leasing

The director of leasing joins with the director of property management to form a sales team. Each analyzes the property and prepares a proposal that may be used for intelligent discussion and planning. Although the executive property manager promotes the solicitation of new business, the managers of the leasing and management departments do the actual selling.

Director of Leasing

   I. General Supervision of Rental Agents
   A. Through daily reports
   B. By sales meetings
   C. Through personal interviews and discussion of the individual broker's work and problems
  II. Knowledge of Market Conditions and Trends
   A. Personal investigation of districts and buildings
   B. Reports from the management department
   C. Information supplied by brokers
 III. Supervising Activities in the Rental Department
   A. Examining prospect cards
   B. Daily check with listing clerks
   C. Examining and personally approving earned commission or credit slips
   D. Inspecting units available to rent
  IV. Soliciting New Business
   V. Training and Motivating Leasing Staff

Property Supervisor

The property supervisor has direct responsibility for specific properties. In this position, the respective on-site managers account to the property supervisor.

While the job description for the property supervisor outlined below applies to residential property management, it easily could be adapted to commercial and other property management operations.

Property Supervisor

I. General Responsibility for Assigned Buildings
   A. Collections
   B. Cost of operation
   C. Occupancy and turnover rates
   D. Condition of building: cleanliness and need for repair
   E. Manners and efficiency of personnel
II. General Administration of Properties Under Supervision
   A. Collections
      1. Based on cashier's reports
      2. Telephone calls
      3. Personal contact
      4. Letters
      5. Five-day notices
      6. Direction of legal action through attorney
   B. Cost of operation
      1. Personal approval of orders for labor and materials
      2. Knowledge of conditions incidental to ordering labor or materials
      3. Knowledge of assistance required to maintain building in first-class condition, basing payrolls on the building's actual requirements
   C. Assuring occupancy
      1. Maintaining units in attractive condition: turnover upkeep, decorating, cleanliness, improvements needed to meet competition, keeping price in line with market
      2. Making sure certain buildings are shown
   D. Building maintenance: regular inspections, checking personnel
III. Contact with Tenants
   A. Personal calls and recording reactions
   B. Personal attention to tenant correspondence
IV. Contact with Owner
   A. Frequent personal interviews
   B. Advising owner of conditions in building

    V. Supervising Building Personnel
       A. Hiring janitors or chief janitors
       B. Approving assistants hired by chief janitors
       C. Control of efficiency and manners
   VI. Lease Renewal
 VII. Cooperation in Soliciting New Business
       A. Observation
       B. Submitting ideas for improving the management of
          competing buildings
       C. Assisting the director of leasing in analyzing
          prospective business

Resident Manager

The resident, or on-site, manager is responsible for all phases of a particular property operation. Special emphasis is placed on general administration and maintenance of the property and supervising its personnel and resources.

    The job description listed below applies to the apartment manager but could be adapted to similar positions at other types of properties.

Resident Manager

    I. Regulating Maintenance and Purchase Orders
       A. Inspecting interior and exterior of building, including
          landscaping and grounds
       B. Issuing maintenance work orders and establishing
          schedules and controls
       C. Adhering to purchase order, stock control, and petty
          cash systems
       D. Supervising outside contractors who work on the
          property
       E. Preparing required operating statements
   II. Performing Marketing Duties
       A. Overseeing details of move-ins and move-outs, with
          special attention to apartment inspections
       B. Preparing and processing leases and related forms
       C. Working with tenants and tenant organizations
 III. Maintaining Records of Financial Transactions
       A. Collecting rents and handling delinquent accounts
       B. Adhering to all directives related to account numbers,
          expense and income requirements, and rent roll
       C. Preparing daily bank deposits
       D. Preparing required reports

    IV. Supervising On-Site Staff
        A. Hiring and terminating according to company policies
        B. Performing written evaluations of employees
        C. Maintaining accurate payroll records

Leasing Agent

The leasing agent's responsibilities parallel those of the property supervisor but emphasize leasing the space in assigned properties rather than their ongoing operation.

The job description for the leasing agent also is designed for residential properties but is adaptable to other management operations.

Leasing Agent

    I. Leasing Apartment Units and Houses
        A. Knowledge of rental units
        B. Diligent follow-up of leads
            1. Telephone inquiries
            2. Recording calls and interviews on prospect cards
            3. Noting prospect needs for future vacancies
        C. Cultivating prospects
            1. Recording individual requirements
            2. Visiting prospect's home when possible, and noting type of furniture and living standards
            3. Carefully selecting units for display that match prospect's needs and preferences
            4. Discovering what the prospect likes when viewing available units, and concentrating the sales effort accordingly
            5. Appealing to prospect's interests: price, love of family, or desire for modern conveniences
    II. Cooperating in Soliciting New Business
        A. Observing competitive buildings and performing comparisons
            1. Condition of the building
            2. Condition of available space
            3. Accessibility of available space
            4. Price compared to other units
        B. Personal contact
            1. Owners when renting units in their buildings
            2. Janitors and employees in buildings
    III. Promoting Goodwill

  A. Businesslike, well-mannered, courteous, and generous
     in dealing with the public, building owners, tenants,
     and competitors
  B. Reflects satisfaction with the company and contributes
     personally to its activities

Listing Clerk

The listing clerk must be impartial in distributing leads to rental
agents. Favoritism weakens the respect of those who believe they have
been ill-treated and, therefore, prevents the kind of cooperation that
produces maximum rentals.

Listing Clerk

   I. Preparing and Maintaining the Listing Book
      A. Securing information from the management
         department
      B. Securing information from other real estate firms
  II. Maintaining a Prospect File
      A. Recording names and expiration dates
      B. Systematic filing (for later follow-up) of prospect cards
      C. Recording leads and assigning rental spaces

Purchasing Agent

Properties under management often have a purchasing agent to
supervise the purchase of goods and services. Control of such purchases is essential to protecting a property's assets.

Purchasing Agent

    I. Supervising All Purchases by or Through the Organization
       A. Preparing and maintaining purchase outline used by
          service request clerks
       B. Maintaining data on labor and supply costs
       C. Analyzing products purchased to determine their
          worth, with advice from building engineers serving as
          technical advisors
   II. Examining New Appliances, Equipment, and Materials
  III. Directing Activities of Service Request Clerks
   IV. Approving All Bills Paid for Labor and Materials
    V. Preparing Cost Estimates for Operating Buildings Being
       Considered for Management
   VI. Responsible for Inventory Control

Cashier

The property management organization has a distinct fiduciary relationship with each of its clients. To satisfy this responsibility, all property income must be recorded accurately. A staff member is needed to implement this policy.

Cashier

I. Record and Bank All Money Received by Office (Daily if Possible)
   A. Enter rents on tenants' collection cards
   B. Complete journal entries, cash disbursements, and check orders
II. File Reports to Management Supervisors
III. Bill Special Accounts on Duo-Account Buildings
   A. Electric light current and lamps
   B. Special service
   C. Telephone
   D. Maid service
   E. Garage rent
   F. Garage special service
IV. Check Rent Bills and Their Balances
V. Bill Tenants for Vandalism Recorded on Vouchers
VI. Draw Building Payrolls and Janitors' Expense Slips

Service Request Clerk

The foundation of a solid tenant relations program depends on speedy attention to maintenance requests. Service request clerks, therefore, have key positions within the management organization.

Service Request Clerk

I. Handle All Telephone Calls for Management Supervisors and All Requests for Service from Tenants
   (Note: These persons should be patient, courteous, and service-minded. They have more contacts with customers than other members of the organization. Their performance should be checked frequently. They should be familiar with all the properties managed by the organization.)
II. Disposition of All Service Requests
   A. Calling janitor at the building
   B. Calling management supervisor
   C. Written order to contractor

1. Using purchasing outline
2. Advertising disposition to tenant
III. Disposition of Janitor's Supply and Labor Requisitions
   A. Obtaining management supervisor's approval
   B. Written order

Hiring Qualified Personnel

Property managers spend their working lives among people in a very close sort of business association. They must study people and be able to judge an introvert from an extrovert, an efficient worker from an inefficient one.

Sound personnel relations involve a dual responsibility. An employee is responsible to himself and his employer. An employer is responsible to the organization and the employee. This dual responsibility, based on mutual benefit, is the foundation of good employer-employee relations. Without it there can be no true organizational spirit.

Establishing such an interdependent relationship should be considered maturely by both the employer and the worker. Yet, many employer-employee relationships are formed with little care or thought.

The employer interested in building a successful organization must have a more efficient means of selecting personnel than simply needing a particular ability or just the presence of an attractive applicant. There are time-tested principles to be followed in selecting personnel.

First, when a new employee is hired for a property management organization, the employer should regard that employment as long-term. Personnel changes are expensive and contribute to organizational inefficiency. Effectively training an employee requires much time and money. A wise employer, therefore, does not hire anyone without considering long-term possibilities.

Second, an employer's hiring policy must be based on more than simply needing an employee. Scientific selection is made only when an applicant matches prescribed qualifications, not just when one applicant is the best of three or four interviewed.

Job specifications should be prepared for every position in the real estate management office, and an applicant hired only when these specifications have been met. Perhaps such a hiring policy involves more work for the employer, or maybe it will take longer to find the right person, or perhaps temporary help will have to be engaged while the permanent employee is sought. Nevertheless, this procedure will help establish a successful organization. Haphazard employment methods create dispirited, inefficient, and ineffective associations.

Recruitment

There are several methods of finding people to fill positions. The most common of these are promotion from within, employment agencies, help-wanted advertisements, reference by friends or associates, and outright recruiting.

Strangely enough, many employers overlook the benefits of maintaining valuable employees within their organizations. Upward movement within a firm is necessary in developing the esprit de corps so important in long-term personnel satisfaction. Frequently, employers hesitate to promote from within because it means that two people must be trained instead of one: the new employee must first learn the work of the person promoted, and the promoted worker must learn the new job. Creating a hard-hitting, enthusiastic group of coworkers is not easy, but it is worth achieving.

If no employees are available for promotion, then other methods must be used. Classified advertising can yield good results if prepared carefully. Many candidates, however, who are either under or over qualified will apply for the position. Classified advertising will be productive in filling a job vacancy, with the minimum expense of time, if applicants are screened from their letters of introduction and résumés.

Employment agencies also can assist. Again, the property manager first must prepare a detailed job description with qualifications for the agency to use in its search. Also, the manager should choose an agency that carefully screens candidates before recommending them.

Job candidates who are referred by friends or other employees, or, even better, people who are recruited for employment because they are performing well elsewhere, are preferred. This approach increases the employer's chances of finding the qualified person.

Selection

After recruiting prospective employees, it is necessary to judge their eligibility.

FIGURE 9.1

EMPLOYMENT APPLICATION

We are an equal opportunity employment company, dedicated to a policy of nondiscrimination in employment on any basis including race, creed, color, age, sex, religion, or national origin.

Please print all information.

Date _____

Personal Information

Name _____

Address _____

City _____ State _____ Zip _____

Phone _____ Social Security Number _____

Referred by _____

Employment Desired

Position _____ Date you can start _____ Salary desired $ _____

Are you currently employed? _____ If so, may we contact your employer? _____

Have you ever applied to this company before? _____ Where _____ When _____

Education

	Name and Location of School	Years Attended	Date Graduated	Subjects Studied
Grammar School				
High School				
College				
Other (Specify)				

Subjects of special study or research work _____

_____

_____

Activities (civic, athletic, fraternal, etc.; exclude organizations whose name or character indicates the
the race, creed, color, or national origin of its members)

_____

_____

_____

_____

Professional services are available to employers to assist in both selecting and training new employees. These services offer psychological tests that determine a prospective employee's suitability for the type of work under consideration. They also evaluate an individual's background and report on employment stability, character, and so forth. Special services of this kind frequently are employed by large firms in all lines of business.

FIGURE 9.1—*Continued*

Former Employers (List former employers, starting with the most recent)

Month and Year	Employer: Name, Address, Phone, and Supervisor	Salary	Position	Reason for Leaving
From				
To				
From				
To				
From				
To				
From				
To				

References (Give names of two persons not related to you whom you have known at least one year)

1. Name _____ Years Acquainted _____

Address _____

Business _____ Phone _____

2. Name _____ Years Acquainted _____

Address _____

Business _____ Phone _____

Nearest relative _____

Relative's address _____ Phone _____

Person to contact in the event of an emergency:

Name _____

Address _____ Phone _____

I authorize investigation of all statements contained in this application. I understand that misrepresentation or omission of facts called for is cause for denial of employment.

Signature _____ Date _____

Do Not Write Below This Line

Interviewed by _____ Date _____

Remarks _____

_____

_____

Neatness _____ Character _____

Personality _____ Ability _____

Hired _____ Department _____ Position _____ To report _____ Salary $ _____

Inefficient hiring practices found in many offices are paralleled by indifference in evaluating employees before they are hired. This continues to be true after employees are members of the organization. For example, many firms do not maintain adequate records of their employees' raises and absences from work. These employers cannot even consider promotion from within, since they lack basic information about their employees to do so.

Most reference letters are meaningless, because few previous employers write unfavorable comments about former employees. If the employee was at all acceptable, the employer is likely to "give him a break." If the employee was discharged, the employer probably would not answer the letter.

An *employment application* is most important to the hiring process. (See figure 9.1.) When properly and accurately completed, this form should contain a complete record of the applicant's employment since school and become the basis for screening applicants.

Arrangements should be made, then, for a personal interview or telephone call with at least the two most recent employers. This interview is necessary to confirm the information provided on the application form as well as determine the applicant's capabilities. Most firms have developed interviewing procedures and can arrange for this check without much difficulty.

Also important to the hiring process is an interview with the applicant by the person who would supervise the individual in the position. Certainly, the interviewer should ask about previous employment and other specific questions of fact. However, the interview is also important as a means of judging the applicant's knowledge about the job and appraising the applicant's attitudes, abilities, experiences, and personality.

Training Personnel

Observation of the training procedures in many offices has revealed much negligence. Some executives do not evaluate the performance of a new associate as thoroughly as the performance of a new car. When an automobile is purchased, it is driven carefully for the first several thousand miles and given devoted attention. But, when a new employee reports for work, the instructions too often are: "Here is your desk. Start right in. If you have any problems, everyone will be glad to help you." Nobody takes the new employee aside and carefully explains the firm's policies, ideals, and objectives. The new employee is left to learn the job alone and pick up piecemeal whatever knowledge can be obtained about how and why the organization functions. Too often the employee is thrown into work. There is no introduction, no graduation to the ultimately high speeds of full production, and no 500-mile checkup. It is amazing that employees perform as well as they do. Certainly, it is not because of adequate or sympathetic training.

The chief executive of a busy organization cannot always personally instruct a new employee in every phase of a new job, but there is no excuse for failing to arrange for instruction by someone else. Shortcuts often achieve the same result without requiring a lot of time. For example, many organizations prepare an employee policy manual which is given to each new employee. This manual, listing every job from chief executive to elevator operator, should contain the following information:

1. The general rules of employment, such as hours of work, pay schedules, holidays, sick leave, and vacations.
2. The policies of the organization affecting public relations, employee attitudes, and an employee's future.
3. A description of the particular job—how it is performed, its meaning and importance.
4. A brief history of the company and a statement of its objectives.

Retaining Valuable Employees

People are the principal resource of the property manager, and it is as important to satisfy trained workers as it is to satisfy clients. Without efficient employees, the management service will deteriorate, and clients will be lost.

Compensating Employees

One of the most important requirements of employees is adequate compensation. No amount of talk and backslapping substitutes for a full pay envelope. Too many property managers fail in this respect. They hire more people to increase business, yet they wish to hire them for a fraction of what they reserve for themselves. Employees are aware of this situation, and if they believe they are treated unfairly, they will be disgruntled and their attitude will be reflected in their work.

Every employer should ask this question about each employee: "Am I paying Jones just a little more than anyone else would who knows his value as well as I do?" An employee should be worth more to the current employer than to a new one. In most cases, personnel relations have failed when an employee leaves a firm in order to get more money. Either it is a lack of adequate pay by the employer or a failure to convince the individual that the firm has as bright a future as that of its competitor. In either case, it is not the employee's fault.

Salary is only one factor affecting job satisfaction. Often of equal importance are so-called fringe benefits that are offered as inducements to employment and a means of ensuring long-term employment. As taxes on wages increase with earnings, more employees seriously weigh these benefits. Commonly included among these are provisions for retirement, hospitalization, medical care, group insurance, paid holidays, vacations, stock options, and the use of a company car.

While salary remains the basic concern, the manager should also consider satisfying employees' other needs to retain their employment. A wise employer forms a program to increase job attractiveness. It is just as important to point out additional benefits to an employee as it is to a prospective client.

Promoting Morale

To encourage staff congeniality, many successful organizations publish house newsletters, which keep employees informed and recognize significant service. The newsletter need not be expensive. It could just as well be mimeographed, if it is carefully and interestingly written.

Another way to promote the general morale is through regularly scheduled recreation. Bowling leagues, dinner meetings, and golf outings all create traditional good feelings when they are well planned and held regularly.

It also is to the employer's benefit to display interest in employees on a personal level. The employer who has a genuine interest in the welfare of employees, can remember details about their families, and renders kind services at significant times builds a strong and loyal corps.

All people need kindness to make them happy or ease their problems. A small present, the offer of a loan, or expressing sympathy at the right moment are essential to human relations. However common it may seem to visit the sick or cheer those with problems, these are gestures of goodwill, which are indispensable in building enduring friendships and professional loyalty.

Inspiring Confidence

There is an old saying that "nothing succeeds like success." This applies to employees as well. They want to be associated with a firm, or an individual, that is going places, even if they are not ambitious themselves. They need to believe that their employer will succeed in any kind of business, because one of their basic desires is job security. They wish to work for and with a person who faces the future with confidence, who is anxious to succeed, and who is obviously ambitious.

One test of confidence is the treatment an employee receives when time off is needed. If he believes he will not be paid when ill or if he believes his employer will not allow a reasonable time off for personal business, then he probably will lie about the absence. Very few people abuse privileges. If they do, they are not acceptable employees. If they do not, the employer loses nothing by granting their requests. Also, when granting an employee's request for time off, it should be done graciously, not in a manner that might cause the employee to feel guilty. Generosity stimulates gratitude. A grateful employee is a great asset to the employer.

Encouraging Development

There are employers who fear that employees will become well known, well respected, and then siphon off their business. They uphold the "divine right" of proprietorship. Modern professional executives who operate property management firms realize, however, that they can remain at the top only so long as they are capable. Moreover, they recognize that people form management, and their organization will be larger and more successful if they have a team of well-known, well-respected individuals.

Every person desires recognition. The employer who realizes that the first duty of employees is to themselves need not feel threatened. By gratifying their desire for significance, employees actually improve the organization. Employers, therefore, should encourage staff participation in trade and community affairs and allow sufficient time for these activities. Membership in professional societies also should be encouraged, as should writing for trade papers and public speaking.

Summary

A foremost challenge to the property manager is recruiting, selecting, and training qualified personnel to carry out the manager's policies and actually provide the management service.

In planning personnel needs, the property manager should establish job descriptions for the key positions within the firm. Each description should be a statement of overall responsibilities and specific duties pertaining to the job. The number of job descriptions needed and the extensiveness of each is determined by the size and complexity of the management organization.

In addition to job descriptions, more detailed job specifications also should be prepared. If they outline the personal characteristics and qualifications of each job, these specifications can be invaluable in selecting, placing, and training employees.

Having determined the types of employees needed, the next step is to recruit applicants. There are several sources for employees: (1) promotion from within the organization; (2) classified advertising; (3) employment agencies; and (4) referrals from friends, business associates, and existing employees.

Mistakes in hiring can be reduced if a systematic selection procedure is adopted. The property manager should: (1) have each applicant complete an employment application form; (2) conduct a personal interview with the applicant; and (3) investigate the applicant's employment history and check personal references. In some cases, the applicant also may be asked to take employment tests to determine compatibility with the job.

The personnel function does not stop with hiring. New employees should not be left to themselves but should be given a formal orientation. An employee policy manual is helpful in introducing a new worker to the job and to the work environment.

The property manager also must focus attention on satisfying existing employees so that long-term business relationships will be formed. To this end, the manager should see that employees receive both monetary rewards (i.e., salaries and fringe benefits) and psychological rewards (i.e., personal encouragement and interest and recognition of accomplishments).

REVIEW QUESTIONS

1. What factors influence the size of the management staff? Explain in detail.
2. How would a property manager look for a new bookkeeper if the present bookkeeper resigned?
3. Suggest a method of indoctrinating a new resident manager in his job.
4. What is the difference between a *job description* and a *job specification?* How is each used?

5. What are the principal sources of property management personnel?
6. What factors influence an employee's satisfaction with his job?
7. What can an employer do to see that employees are retained? What is the value of low employee turnover?
8. What is an *employee policy manual?* How can it be used?

Scope of
Real Estate
Management

Chapter Ten

Rental Housing

THE TECHNIQUES THAT a property manager must master in order to become proficient were described in the previous six chapters. They include creating a management plan, maintaining records and sound owner relations, marketing rental space, establishing a tenant relations program, physically caring for the property, and providing the staff for the property's operation. In this and the next three chapters, the effect that the specific property has on the performance of these management activities is discussed.

Residential property is the largest single area in the real estate industry that has required professional management. Throughout the twentieth century, social trends have greatly affected American lifestyles. Literacy and educational opportunities are increasing. Racial barriers are disintegrating. People are more mobile and less subject to traditional constraints. While family life is changing throughout most of the world, it is important to consider how the trend affects American housing needs. Three contributing factors are these:

1. The prolonging of life through improved health care and nutrition, the conquering of disease, and advances in preventive medicine.
2. Youth orientation, resulting from the large percentage of young people in the total population and also from educational opportunities available to them.
3. Advances in birth control, resulting in smaller families; automobiles and airplanes, making Americans more mobile and less

rooted to fixed residential and employment locations; and urbanization, creating a need for high-rise buildings. Consequently, new mores have developed, and the concept of a family unit has widened to include lifestyles that formerly would have been considered unconventional.

To accommodate these new, mobile lifestyles throughout the country, many types of multifamily communities have evolved.

Opportunities in
Residential Property Management

Rental housing possibilities range from fully furnished efficiency units in multistory high-rises to unfurnished, three-bedroom units in sprawling suburban apartment communities to mobile homes in park-like settings. The type of property and the services and facilities provided have a direct effect on the management function.

Multifamily Rental Housing

There have been tremendous changes in the location, size, design, equipment, amenities, and overall number of private, multifamily apartment buildings in the last four decades. Whether garden apartments or high-rises, multifamily living structures are a major—perhaps the largest—factor in the increased demand for real estate management professionals.

Garden apartments designed for multifamily living are low-rise buildings, often located in suburban areas where land is relatively inexpensive. These suburban garden apartment complexes became popular in the 1960s and remain so. Their typical characteristics include extensive landscaping, low building structure, recreational amenities, and ample parking.

High-rise apartments are especially popular in major metropolitan areas where space is at a premium and a high concentration of dwelling units is necessary. While the typical building contains approximately 25 stories and 300 units, some high-rise apartments rival the tallest office buildings and house thousands of occupants.

Found in both cities and suburbs are *mid-rise apartment buildings* that range from six to nine stories. Similar to the high-rise, a mid-rise is equipped with elevators, a common lobby and mail room, and perhaps such amenities as exercise rooms, swimming pools, and parking.

Other types of multifamily rental housing are available as well. The more traditional three-story walkups, duplexes, and six-flats still can be found.

The architectural design of a multifamily dwelling has a direct effect on the complexity of its management. For instance, high-rises require sophisticated equipment, such as elevators and HVAC systems, and special upkeep like window washing. Technical knowledge is needed to supervise these buildings. The suburban apartment complex, however, with its sophisticated HVAC system plus recreational facilities and spacious lawns, has its own unique management problems. The tenant in a three-story walkup probably receives the least extra services and facilities, and, therefore, the building has fewer management requirements.

Government-Assisted Housing

Although increasing government involvement—federal, state, and local—is discussed in chapter 3, it must be noted here that this trend has created opportunities for the professional real estate management team.

A large public and subsidized housing inventory presents a challenge to the creative capabilities of all citizens and the real estate manager in particular. Originally designed to provide "decent, safe, and sanitary" housing for low- and moderate-income citizens, the nation's housing program has disappointed many of its supporters. While some local housing authorities have served their communities ably, the deterioration of much of the government-assisted housing stock has resulted in dissatisfaction with both the original concept and the attending programs. However, new programs are being enacted which hold the promise that many of the problems yet may be solved, especially if professional management is provided.

The sheer volume of subsidized and public housing programs creates a strong demand for property managers who are skilled in balancing the interests of the various parties (owners, government sponsors, tenants, and citizen action groups) and in easing situations that may stir social unrest. Government housing can have various locations and involve many groups (suburban versus inner-city, garden versus high-rise versus townhouse, elderly versus large-family), and it is evident that each possible management problem will not be met in every situation.

For the most part, the management of government-assisted housing is similar to the management of conventional rental housing.

However, there are unique demands. Sometimes managers must act on the rights of tenants, regardless of their income level. Often, they must handle the problems of single-parent families, joblessness, or teen-age dominance. Communication lines must be formed across ethnic, racial, economic, and religious barriers. Many times, there will be an enormous amount of paperwork because of bureaucratic regulations. Tenant turnover, vacancy rates, rent loss, and collection costs are likely to be higher in government-assisted housing than in conventional rental housing.

As a result of these factors, government-assisted housing, with its complicated administrative problems having social, political, physical, and fiscal dimensions, virtually has created a new field of property management.

Single-Family Housing

The single-family house is the basic American dwelling structure. Although the majority of these are detached, the rising price of urban land has caused home builders to construct attached and semi-detached row houses, frequently called *townhouses*. In these dwellings, renters enjoy the features of the conventional single-family house (e.g., private entrance, multistory separation of living and work spaces, and backyard patio), yet the higher-density land use means a lesser land investment cost, an important offsetting factor to investors and renters. Single-family houses usually are built at a density of from three to eight houses per acre, while row houses require less than half that area.

Formerly, single-family houses were purchased for personal use (seldom as investments), and consequently professional management was not needed. In large cities and suburban areas, however, there now are property managers who specialize in managing single-family rental houses. This is because investors have purchased them either for a tax allowance or appreciation of the property or because owners' employment causes them to temporarily relocate from their homes.

Mobile Home Parks

The term *mobile home* has become a misnomer and hopefully will be eliminated. Most are located on fixed lots and are permanently connected to local utilities. The mobility of the mobile home definitely has been reduced.

Mobile homes and single-family dwellings differ in that the mobile home is factory-manufactured and delivered as an assembled product, while the single-family house, even the prefabricated variety, is site-assembled and finished. Another difference is that mobile homes and the sites on which they are located often have different owners, while houses with fixed locations rarely do (with the exception of Hawaii, where leasehold interests on land under homes is commonplace). In any case, many new mobile home units appear each year as they become an acceptable housing alternative for those who cannot afford a conventional home. Still, the future of this trend is not clear. The government has considered eliminating the tax advantage that mobile home owners now enjoy by considering the home personalty instead of realty. If this occurs, there likely will be a slowing of the industry.

Although the manufacture and distribution of mobile homes is a well-established and growing industry, the business of providing locations and service for owners of these units has not equalled it. What is really needed is specialized mobile-home park management.

Institutional Housing

The student of residential property management also must examine those private institutions that own housing without concern for maximizing dollar income.

Examples of these institutions are colleges and universities that construct housing to accommodate both students and faculty, military service installations that provide housing for recruiting and retaining personnel, and corporations operating in remote locations that must provide homes for employees. There are many other times when the need for accommodations warrants their creation, without the promise of any direct monetary profit. When these projects are completed and ready for occupancy, it is obviously necessary to manage them efficiently in order to minimize operating expenses and, thus, the subsidy involved.

Another type of institutional housing is *ad hoc,* or socially sponsored, *housing.* The design that produces the best possible housing units at the lowest occupancy cost, either to benefit some specific group or satisfy the sponsors, is the main concern. Housing for the aged, nursing homes, extended-care facilities, and convalescent homes are examples. While these kinds of properties demand highly specialized real estate management skills, many general management principles can be adapted to their operations.

Market Analysis

Studying the market in which a property is located is necessary in evaluating it as an investment and establishing a realistic rental schedule. While the general market analysis outlined in chapter 4 applies here, the residential market has certain peculiarities, especially concerning family size and domestic status, that demand separate attention.

The unit of consumption in residential real estate is the family. If there is a community of 1,000 people in which the average family numbers five people, then there will be a need for 200 housing units. If, however, the average family numbers only four, then the same community will require 250 housing units. The market analyst, then, must know the current average family size in the given neighborhood.

For the past 50 years, the size of the average American family has decreased due to economic pressure, ability to plan family size, more divorces, and greater longevity. This trend is particularly evident in urban centers and has created *social obsolescence,* a significant factor in a neighborhood study. Many cities have neighborhoods whose locations are desirable but whose homes were designed to house families of five and six persons. Although these buildings may be structurally sound and reasonably modern in design, they are too large for families of two and three persons (excluding the very rich). To counteract social obsolescence, these buildings are converted into rooming houses, light housekeeping suites, and other uses designed to avoid the problem of blight. In some neighborhoods, older buildings are converted into more profitable properties by increasing their availability to more families without reducing their desirability.

Facts relating to neighborhood size, obtained from census studies or other sources, will be informative to the property manager. Large-size families indicate the presence of children. In middle- to upper-midde-income areas, this usually means residential stability, while in substandard areas it can prove the opposite. However, the converse is not always true. While large numbers of one- and two-person families once indicated a high degree of transiency, with the new lifestyles, this trend may reflect the presence of couples who either have raised their children or have none.

At this time, the manager also should study the domestic status of the population, including the numbers of divorced persons, single and married persons of adult age, and the other new (e.g., communal) relationships.

Another aspect of neighborhood market analysis is the manager's study of land use within an area. This analysis should provide information about: (1) the character, age, condition, and visual desirability of residential buildings in the area, and (2) the types of accommodations that are offered to the renting public. The size of units in the zone's buildings must be determined, sample units inspected, and prevailing rates for various sizes and types of units obtained. After establishing neighborhood boundaries, a property manager can obtain much information about the buildings in the area by driving through its streets and observing the structures.

During this phase of the study, the property manager correlates the supply (units in the area) with the demand (families in the area) and then can determine if the two factors match.

One of the chief reasons for an in-depth neighborhood market study is to evaluate the area's purchasing power. This is necessary for a realistic appraisal of a particular property's renting potential. Generally speaking, a neighborhood in which the average rental for residential units is $200 will not support even a single property with rentals of $800. The level of comparative neighborhood rentals moves downward (due to age, obsolescence, and deterioration) over a period of years, and even isolated low rentals in a neighborhood erode the high rentals.

A neighborhood's average residential rental level indicates the type of facilities (commercial and social) that the neighborhood can support; the amount it can contribute to maintaining its own desirability; and, from an objective point of view, the desirability of its population.

Marketing Apartment Space

Even when the rental schedule is established according to current market activity (as detailed in chapter 4), a promotional program to attract prospective tenants usually is necessary. The advertising program must be well planned and well executed; its extent will depend on market conditions and the level of vacancies.

While the importance of advertising should not be underrated, seldom will a lease be signed without a tour of the space by the prospective tenant. Consequently, personal salesmanship is a strong factor in leasing apartment units.

A prospect never rents an apartment he does not want. The prospect who even visits a building already has considered that: it meets most qualifications, the general location is suitable, the price is somewhere near the budget allowance for rent, the size of the units is appropriate, and the building's exterior is attractive.

When a prospective tenant makes an inquiry, the capable manager, who realizes that prospects mean advertising dollars and are vital to maintaining a high occupancy level, first discovers the prospect's requirements for location, price range, and unit size. If it is impossible to meet the prospect's needs, this should be mentioned—creating goodwill toward the firm; however, the prospect's name should be noted for possible future use. The smart manager realizes that the property cannot appeal to everyone, and sales efforts are reserved for the most likely prospects.

Since personally escorting a prospect to the apartment is best, the manager or rental agent should either accompany the potential tenant or arrange to have a qualified caretaker on the premises. On the way to the apartment, the best features of the property should be pointed out: the attractive exterior; character of tenancy; the maintenance methods employed; the neatness of entrances, halls, and corridors; the services and amenities (such as laundries or recreation rooms) available to tenants; management policies that ensure peace, quiet, and wholesome comfort; and security measures that protect the residents.

When they enter the apartment, the manager should state positively, "Here is an apartment I know you'll like." Then, the manager watches unobtrusively to see what features the prospect examines and points out the values of those items. For example, if the prospect looks out the window, the pleasant view should be noted. If there is no noteworthy view but plenty of light, this as well as an attractive window treatment might be emphasized. On the first tour, the manager should not force information on the prospect but simply point out attractive qualities of seemingly important items.

If the prospect is ready to take the apartment, he should be guided to the office to complete a rental application. If not sold to the point of closing immediately, then the agent should mention any overlooked features by saying, "Did you notice that the hardware throughout the apartment has been refinished, that the closet off this small hall is especially handy for linens, that the bedroom is away from the living room and is unusually quiet if your neighbors are entertaining?" The manager should never appear anxious over a deal but rather offer additional information casually, showing enthusiasm for the building without high-pressure salesmanship.

After touring the apartment, the prospect probably will have questions. These should be answered fully but without too much detail and, again, without any anxiety. When the prospect is ready to leave the apartment, the manager should not delay the departure but maintain the casual enthusiasm, mentioning again the conveniences and advantages of the location and the best qualities of the neighborhood.

The manager can rely on knowledge of the prospect when pointing out the neighborhood's features. For instance, if there are children, the prospect should be told about nearby school facilities, the distance to them, and the comparative safety of the route the children travel. If there are no children, the building's proximity to movies, shopping areas, and churches may be noted.

Most prospects do not rent on the first visit but, if they are impressed, return, accompanied by a spouse or roommate. For this reason, the manager should determine if the prospect has been favorably impressed. If so, arrangements for a return visit can be made. If the prospect appears hesitant, the manager can press subtly for an appointment, expressing concern on the prospect's account and still not indicating anything but genuine interest.

A prospect will not return unless the apartment had a positive impact. On the second (accompanied) visit, the prospect usually assumes the role of the salesman, emphasizing those points that will favorably influence the companion. There usually is no need for the manager to supplement these descriptions and arguments.

Anyone can merchandise rental space reasonably well if sincere interest and a pleasant personality are displayed. The prospect definitely wants an apartment; applying this desire to a specific building and unit is the property manager's challenge.

Tenant Selection

The objectives of a residential tenant selection system is to obtain good tenants from both the manager's and the owner's standpoint. To do this, the criteria of a desirable applicant must be identified. An acceptable residential tenant has four basic characteristics:

1. One who can and will pay the rental promptly.
2. One who will adequately care for the physical premises being leased.
3. One whose family or household occupants' conduct presents no problems for either neighbors or management.
4. One whose tenant history indicates long-term occupancy.

FIGURE 10.1

RENTAL APPLICATION

	Date _____
	Property _____
	Unit _____
	Monthly Rental $ _____

The undersigned hereby makes application to rent unit number _____ located at _____

_____

beginning on _____ , 19 _____ , at a monthly rental of $ _____ ,

and submits the following information:

Name of Applicant _____

Name of Co-Applicant _____

Number of Dependents _____ Ages _____

Other Occupants and Their Relationship _____

Pets (Number and Kind) _____

Current Address _____ Phone _____

How Long? _____ Reason for Leaving _____

Owner or Agent _____ Phone _____

Previous Address _____

How Long? _____ Reason for Leaving _____

Owner or Agent _____ Phone _____

Current Employer _____

How Long? _____ Employed as _____

Supervisor _____ Phone _____

Address _____

Social Security Number _____ Salary $ _____ per _____

Name of Bank _____ Checking Account Number _____

_____ Savings Account Number _____

Credit References:

Name   Account Number

_____   _____

_____   _____

_____   _____

Automobile License Number _____ State of Registry _____

Automobile Make, Model, Year _____

Driver's License Number _____

Have you ever: filed for bankruptcy? ( ) Yes   ( ) No

been evicted from tenancy? ( ) Yes   ( ) No

willfully or intentionally refused to pay rent when due? ( ) Yes   ( ) No

When fully and accurately completed, the tenant application form is the best source of data for judging the prospective tenant. Application forms are available and fairly well standardized (figure 10.1). When properly completed, an application form should provide information on the prospect's current employment or other source of income, the present residence and the name of its owner or manager, the number and relationship of the people who will be residing in

FIGURE 10.1—*Continued*

I hereby apply to lease the above described premises for the term and upon the conditions above set forth and agree that the rental is to be payable the _____ day of each month in advance. As an inducement to the owner of the property and to the agent to accept this application, I warrant that all statements above set forth are true; however, should any statement made above be a misrepresentation or not a true statement of facts, S _____ of the deposit will be retained to offset the agent's cost, time, and effort in processing my application.

I hereby deposit S _____ as earnest money to be refunded to me if this application is not accepted within _____ business banking days. Upon acceptance of this application, this deposit shall be retained as part of the security deposit. When so approved and accepted I agree to execute a lease for _____ months before possession is given and to pay the balance of the security deposit within _____ business banking days after being notified of acceptance, or the deposit will be forfeited as liquidated damages in payment for the agent's time and effort in processing my inquiry and application, including making necessary investigation of my credit, character, and reputation. If this application is not approved and accepted by the owner or agent, the deposit will be refunded, the applicant hereby waiving any claim for damages by reason of nonacceptance which the owner or his agent may reject without stating any reason for so doing.

I RECOGNIZE THAT AS A PART OF YOUR PROCEDURE FOR PROCESSING MY APPLICATION, AN INVESTIGATIVE CONSUMER REPORT MAY BE PREPARED WHEREBY INFORMATION IS OBTAINED THROUGH PERSONAL INTERVIEWS WITH MY NEIGHBORS, FRIENDS, AND OTHERS WITH WHOM I MAY BE ACQUAINTED. THIS INQUIRY INCLUDES INFORMATION AS TO MY CHARACTER, GENERAL REPUTATION, PERSONAL CHARACTERISTICS, AND MODE OF LIVING. I UNDERSTAND THAT I MAY HAVE THE RIGHT TO MAKE A WRITTEN REQUEST WITHIN A REASONABLE PERIOD OF TIME TO RECEIVE ADDITIONAL, DETAILED INFORMATION ABOUT THE NATURE AND SCOPE OF THIS INVESTIGATION.

The above information, to the best of my knowledge, is true and correct.

Signature of Applicant _____

_____

Application and Deposit of S _____   Date Received _____

Received by _____

Co-applicants must file separate applications.

the unit, others in the unit who are employed and their employers, and, if possible, the previous place of residence and length of that occupancy.

The manager's evaluation of each applicant ideally resembles one that a two-flat owner gives to a prospective tenant interested in sharing the premises. Important considerations, then, are long-term potential, housekeeping ability, child care, living habits, and tenant compatibility, as well as credit and rent-paying ability.

Permanence Potential

Just as some workers change jobs frequently, and indeed sometimes because of this, many tenants are moving continuously from one place to another. Frequent turnover is costly, both in terms of greater-than-normal maintenance expenses and also the revenue loss attributable to vacancies. Whenever possible, then, the occupancy history of a prospective tenant should be examined carefully.

Most well-adjusted and stable families dislike moving. If they have established roots in a community, and especially if they carefully selected their apartment home, they try to avoid moving.

Some relocations are justified and in no way discredit those involved. Some moves actually benefit the property manager (providing a chance to perform a major overhaul or increase the rent) and other tenants (getting rid of undesirable neighbors). Still, the property manager can act only after the facts are known, taking precautions against the prospect with a poor record.

Housekeeping Ability

A large problem in apartment building maintenance is its housekeeping. This applies equally to tenant quarters and public areas and grounds.

One of the main purposes of interior decoration is to motivate the tenant toward cleanliness. A tenant who is a good housekeeper is preferable—from the standpoint of both the building owner and neighboring tenants—to the slovenly and untidy tenant. The good housekeeper creates less maintenance expense of any kind. A good housekeeper takes pride in keeping the leased premises (and public areas too) as attractive as possible, which automatically protects the owner's investment. This tenant reports a leaking faucet before it discolors the wash basin, prevents children from marking on walls, disposes of garbage before it attracts insects, and maintains the standards of the building. It often is helpful for the manager to discuss the concept of "ordinary wear and tear" with the prospective tenant.

Child Care

Even the person most sympathetic toward children realizes that, unless controlled, they can create disturbances and be destructive. Some property owners and managers refuse to rent to families with children. This policy should be avoided, except when the building in question is not suitable for occupancy by children.

Families with children usually make stable tenants. The wise building manager and owner want these families as tenants, especially if they appear to lead well-ordered lives. It is impossible for a manager to determine from an application form whether parents discipline their children. Therefore, facilities must be provided to accommodate children's special needs. Game rooms, playgrounds, and swimming pools are examples of facilities that make modern residential properties more appropriate for children.

Living Habits

In single-family residences, there is usually enough distance between neighbors to prevent one from annoying the other. In multiunit apartment buildings, however, tenants live so closely together that any disruptive behavior can result in unpleasant living conditions. Many tenant families have one or more members who often use alcohol. Other families argue violently. Still others turn night into day, with parties that carry on into the hours when most tenants are trying to rest for the next day's work. While managers certainly uphold personal freedom, intervention is necessary when one pattern of living jeopardizes the rights of other individuals within a building.

Laws that protect the inviolability of the home make it very difficult to regain possession of an apartment that has been rented to an annoying tenant. Ironically, while tenants who fail to pay their rent are comparatively easy to evict, much time is spent checking prospective tenants' credit records. On the other hand, because there are no simple answers to behavior problems, greater emphasis should be placed on other criteria of tenant selection.

It is extremely difficult, for example, to evict a tenant for being consistently under the influence of alcohol. Yet, the habits of this one tenant in an apartment building may make the building undesirable for other tenants who are raising families. Again, a manager cannot discover from an application form or an interview if a prospect has a problem. Checking a prospective tenant's background at one or more places of previous residence might uncover difficulties with former neighbors and prevent the manager from renting to an objectionable neighbor. These investigations, however, are usually avoided, since living habits today are considered private matters.

Tenant Compatibility

The happiness of each tenant, to a degree, depends on the ability of the group to be congenial. When an apartment becomes vacant, the manager should judge the prospective tenants in light of their compatibility with those already living there. To use an exaggerated example, if 11 tenants in a 12-unit building were thieves, a manager would, of course, hesitate to rent the 12th apartment to a detective. An effective manager strives for overall tenant harmony in considering a prospective tenant for any property.

Rent-Paying Ability

While the social criteria of tenant selection are important, the property manager cannot overlook the tenant's financial ability to pay the rent.

For many years it was a rule of thumb that a family could afford 25 percent of its monthly income for housing. However, social and economic conditions in recent years have changed this guideline. For example:

- A family's rent-paying ability depends on its size and whether or not both spouses work. The larger the family (especially if the wife is not employed), the less of its income can be applied to housing.
- In all families, new "necessities," such as automobiles, hospitalization, insurance, beauty care, recreation, sports, and travel, compete for disposable dollars.
- A significantly higher percentage of housing units are occupied by households of young people, childless couples, divorcees, empty-nest older people—all of whom, as a group, have relatively high rent-paying ability.
- Under present conditions, one must consider supply and demand as indicated by the market itself in order to determine rent-paying capacity.

Most tenants in the United States pay their rent from current income. The typical tenant who loses a job soon will be unable to make rent payments, not having a sufficient cash reserve to meet living costs for an extended period of time. Therefore, a credit check should reveal the source of tenant income.

In most cases, the principal source of income is the tenant's current employment, since few people in the tenant consumer class live on investments. Jobs in the United States differ in both compensation rates and stability of employment. Therefore, the property manager must analyze the prospective tenant's current job from several points of view. The first is type of compensation—usually weekly or monthly. Generally speaking, most stable types of employees have a regular salary, payable semimonthly or monthly. It is easier for these employees to meet regular monthly rental payments than it is for those who are paid weekly, especially if wages are computed on an hourly basis. Weekly income is spent more freely, and it is often difficult for tenants to systematically withhold a portion of each week's pay for the monthly rental payment.

The property manager also is concerned with stability of employment. This is especially true of industrial wage earners, since the interdependence of manufacturing processes frequently results in layoffs beyond the control of either the tenant or (in some cases) the employer. The most stable type of employment usually is governmental or institutional. A person who works for a post office, police department, local telephone company, public utility, life insurance company, or bank is likely to have steady and permanent work. But, an individual who works in an automobile plant, the building trades, or the entertainment field often has major as well as minor employment interruptions.

Most property managers are sufficiently familiar with local employers to gauge the long-term stability of employment provided by the prospective tenant's employer. Length of employment is an excellent basis for judging overall credit stability. Highly unstable people change employment frequently; on the other hand, steady, reliable people have a low frequency of job turnover.

The attitude of the applicant's employer about employee obligations also must be weighed. Some employers are sympathetic to legitimate claims of their employees' creditors and may cooperate with a manager who has a claim on an employee for rent. This policy may benefit the property manager who must take legal action against a delinquent tenant.

After verifying the prospective tenant's employment, the applicant's history of meeting financial obligations must be checked. The best source for this information is the former landlord. A person who has paid rent promptly in the past is likely to pay it promptly in the future. Contacting the former landlord (preferably in person) is important, therefore, to confirm that the prospective tenant actually lives there and has a favorable rent-paying record and that the name of the landlord given by the potential tenant is correct.

Other facts to be weighed in a credit check are those relating to the prospective tenant's time-payment history. Any records of judgments on file (either satisfied or of record) against the prospective tenant should be obtained.

In most larger cities, credit investigation agencies prepare credit reports for property owners at a fixed fee per report. The property manager may arrange to have one of these agencies perform credit investigations. If this service is retained, however, the property manager must be assured that the investigating agency actually will contact the previous landlord of each tenant being checked. Although many property managers believe that the costs of these investigations are excessive, it is poor economy to fail to investigate thoroughly.

If a credit information agency is used, the Fair Credit Reporting Act requires the property manager to advise applicants that their credit is being checked. The rental application form usually states, "a credit report will be obtained on all applications" or has a statement similar to that on the sample application form in figure 10.1. The Act also requires the user of the credit report to make certain disclosures to the applicant whose credit is being checked, should the information lead to a credit denial.

Fair Housing

In making tenant selections, the property manager must be mindful of the government's commitment to assuring fair housing throughout the United States and take care not to violate the Fair Housing Act.

HUD administers the federal fair housing law, which prohibits discrimination in housing on the basis of race, color, religion, sex, or national origin. Complaints of housing discrimination are investigated by HUD, which attempts to resolve them through conciliation and/or refers them to state and local fair housing agencies. Any individual aggrieved by housing discrimination may file a complaint with any HUD office as well as file suit in a federal or local court. To avoid such suits and to be able to fulfill obligations under the Fair Housing Act, the property manager must be familiar with its terms.

Equal Opportunity

In developing a tenant-selection policy for public and subsidized housing, managers must be knowledgeable about the equal opportunity in HUD-assisted housing program. This program is designed to assure equal opportunity to participate in and benefit from HUD-funded activities without regard to race, color, or national origin.

Under this program, HUD ascertains the extent to which its programs comply with federal law forbidding discrimination in all federally funded activities. The Office of Fair Housing and Equal Opportunity investigates complaints and reviews HUD programs to eliminate discrimination. Changes that would make HUD activities more responsive to the problems of minorities and which would promote their participation in HUD activities are encouraged by this program.

Social Responsibility

As indicated, the property manager has a legal obligation not to refuse a prospective tenant on the basis of race, religion, sex, or nationality. It also can be argued that the selection of residential tenants involves still another obligation—a social responsibility to consider the question of need when a choice must be made between two prospective tenants.

Suppose a manager operates a property containing one- and two-bedroom apartments. Assume also that a tenant renting a one-bedroom apartment has had a child and has asked for the first two-bedroom apartment that is available. Assume further that a two-bedroom apartment becomes available and a friend of the manager, who has no children, applies for it. If the two tenants are equally desirable in terms of other criteria, the manager should rent the apartment to the tenant with the child. In this way, the family with the greater need is being accommodated, and community interests are being served.

Although these decisions may conflict with the manager's responsibility to obtain the highest possible income from a given property, there are times when social responsibilities must outweigh the profit factor.

Rental Collection

Many property managers mistakenly believe that concern for tenant credit ceases once a prospective tenant is admitted to the building. However, in a rapidly changing economy and a dynamic society, the economic status of both the group and the individual fluctuate widely, even in a period no longer than the average tenancy. The property manager's interest in tenant credit standing, therefore, should be continuous.

Information about each tenant's ability to pay rent on time should be maintained in a tenant credit file. This information can be reviewed at the time of lease renewal and renegotiation of lease terms. Data on rent-paying ability is especially valuable when the rent market is moving upward (and the property manager wishes to raise rents) or downward (and the tenant requests a rent reduction).

However, while collecting information on tenants' rent-paying

ability is a constructive management activity, even more important
is adopting a firm rent collection program. The property manager
should establish a collection policy that details when, where, and how
rent is to be paid and assumes that any deviation is unacceptable.
This policy should be noted to tenants before leases are signed and
emphasized when they move in.

In addition to outlining rent payment procedures, the rent
collection policy also should state all actions to be taken when rent
payments are delinquent. As mentioned in chapter 7, this includes
the mailing of late letters, personal contact with delinquent tenants
by the resident manager, and, if necessary, the filing of judgment and
eviction suits. To ensure that all delinquent accounts are handled
consistently, a schedule, to be followed rigidly by the resident manager, should be adopted.

All property management firms should insist on the full payment of one month's rent, or another fixed sum, before a new tenant
is permitted to take possession of a unit. This security deposit is protection against rent loss or damage to the premises during tenancy.
It rightfully is assumed that the tenant who cannot pay one month's
rent as a security deposit probably will have financial trouble
throughout the period of tenancy.

On moving out, the tenant may be entitled to receive a fair
rate of interest on the security deposit and a prompt return of all
or part of the total amount. Some states require an accounting of any
deductions and the return of the residual amount, often with interest
on the deposit, within a given number of days. The property manager
should be familiar with any such statute and reflect the appropriate
provisions in the property's operating policy. (See chapter 6, figure 6.6.)

Occupancy Agreement

What is referred to here as an *occupancy agreement* is commonly
termed a residential lease. Because of historical connotations, the
word "lease" relates to landlord and tenant and, whether properly
or not, is associated with wealth and poverty, respectively—at least in
the public's opinion. Implied is that the landlord is a first-class citizen
while the tenant is something less. Occupancy agreement, then, is a
euphemism for lease, used to reduce any hostility that may be felt
by tenants for landlords.

Acceptable euphemisms have not been found for the words

landlord and *tenant*. To say that one is the owner and the other the occupant or resident overlooks the fact that owners of certain properties (for example, private homes) also may be the occupants and residents. But with growing social awareness, managers must be sensitive to the feelings of others, especially the disadvantaged and deprived. Otherwise, misunderstandings may arise which will only complicate the property manager's work.

The property manager very often must arbitrate tenant-landlord disputes. The manager who favors one side against the other may win the approval of one but lose the respect of the other. Since an occupancy agreement is primarily between landlord and tenant—with the property manager serving as the direct representative of the owner—it is obviously important that the negotiator be impartial.

The property manager should develop contractual arrangements that emphasize the mutual interests—rather than the historical conflicts—of landlords and tenants. Leases at one time seemed to favor owners, but they now must be written in accord with local laws that explicitly protect and guarantee individual rights.

Chapter 6 outlines the provisions generally included in a lease. However, two provisions warrant special attention here. One concerns the term of the lease, and the other concerns the services provided by the owner for the tenant.

Term of Lease

There is no standard lease term within the residential property industry. In some cities, written leases for a term of six months or one year are common. In other locations, all tenancy (with or without written leases) is on a month-to-month basis. In almost every city, residential units commanding high rents are covered by written leases for terms of at least one year.

From both the landlord's and the tenant's standpoint, there are advantages and disadvantages to term leases rather than monthly agreements. A *term lease* is an instrument in which a landlord obtains more or less rent than may be justified by the market. In a rising market, the lease restricts the landlord's right to adjust the rental with upward market movements. In a declining market, the tenant is committed to a rental that may be above the going rate for comparable space.

Because of seasonal variations in the demand for residential housing in many sections of the country, there are advantages to both parties in having an annual lease. Without annual leases, owners might suffer heavy losses from vacancy at certain seasons of the year. For example, in Boston, everyone who can afford to live at the seashore during the summer months faces the expense of two residences. To avoid this double expense, large numbers of tenants, if not tied to annual leases, would give up their city homes during the summer months and return to them in the winter. On the other hand, tenants without term leases who live and work in Miami all year would be evicted during the winter to provide for transient, vacationing tenants who would be willing to pay a much higher rental. In the first case, it is an advantage to the landlord to have an annual lease; in the second case, it is an advantage to the tenant.

There are a number of disadvantages in a written term lease for both the lessor and the lessee. If the landlord desires to obtain possession of the property, it cannot be done until the termination of the lease. (However, a lease can be terminated by the tenant's nonpayment of rent or failure to meet other obligations.) Also, if the tenant is required to move from the city or if a change in family or income status develops, the lease remains effective.

Another disadvantage of residential lease terms beyond one month is the fact that lease expiration creates bargaining between lessor and lessee. This is a disadvantage to the lessor because the lessee can make demands for maintenance, decorations, or equipment. It also can initiate periodic rent review by both lessor and lessee, and one or the other may seek an adjustment.

In a declining market, for example, a tenant with steady employment and adequate income may be satisfied with the amount being paid for rent and not even consider a reduction. But, if the lease expires, the tenant may compare the rent to others and, in negotiating with the landlord, drive as hard a bargain as possible. Even though the tenant simply wants a rent in line with rentals being charged for comparable units, the bargaining might not have occurred if the lease had not expired.

A similar situation exists in a rising market. A landlord, obtaining a satisfactory return on a building, might not think about raising rents if all leases are monthly. However, when annual leases expire, the owner is encouraged to analyze price trends, occupancy conditions, and tenant income to ensure that the highest possible income is being realized.

The advantages and disadvantages of leases shift from the lessor to the lessee, depending on existing economic conditions. The ideal leasing arrangement may be a written document that extends for an indefinite period and provides for mutual termination, depending on tenant and landlord requirements for protection. These leases would provide both parties the advantages of a written agreement without the disadvantage of instigating negotiation.

Services

Under the terms of most leases, the lessor must provide services over and above the tenant's right to possess the described space for a stated term. To avoid misunderstandings, the lease should specify the extent and amount of such service. In single-family dwellings and townhouses, the lease should state if the tenant is responsible for care of the grounds, exterior and interior painting, maintaining equipment, and any or all repairs to the structure.

In apartment buildings, the lease should describe the janitorial service, if any, that is provided by the lessor. It also should specify if the landlord supplies the heat, and, if so—in the absence of applicable city ordinances—state when such heat is to be furnished.

The lease also should state if hot and cold water is provided by the landlord and, if so, for what purpose. Because more appliances are being installed today (air conditioning, for example), the lease should provide for the possible installation of such equipment by the tenant. If the building has elevators, the lease should stipulate the extent of the landlord's responsibility regarding their operation and should protect the lessor against possible liability connected with this equipment.

In larger properties where utilities other than heat and water are furnished by the landlord, the conditions under which they are furnished must be included in the lease, as well as provisions for their payment and the lessor's rights in the event of nonpayment.

Tenant Relations

Tenant relations is a prime consideration in managing any type of property, but especially residential properties. An organized, effective program designed to create a strong tenant-manager bond can make the difference between efficient, successful management and mediocre management.

Experience proves that some managers and their employees have problems with tenants and others do not. The difficulty is more likely to be with management than with the tenants. Managers whose employees are truthful, courteous, and patient, who immediately respond to tenant requests with prompt action and follow through on promises—these managers not only retain the goodwill of tenants but also serve the building owners well. As long as there is a written agreement covering the terms of occupancy, there should be no misunderstanding of responsibilities. The manager's duty is to uphold that agreement.

In some urban areas, tenants form unions to represent their interests in collective bargaining negotiations with landlords. So far, this organizing has been limited to residential properties in slum or near-slum areas. The first action by *tenant unions* is usually to call a strike in which tenants withhold their rental payments in order to force landlords or their agents to the bargaining table. Currently, there is no legal recognition of the rights of tenants of conventional housing either to withhold rents or bargain collectively over rents, maintenance policies, tenant services, or general grievances. Under traditional landlord-tenant law, it is presumed that a tenant will either pay the rental being asked and accept the premises in the negotiated condition or find accommodations elsewhere. The landlord has had the right to set terms and conditions arbitrarily, and the tenant has had the right to accept or reject them.

In recent years, however, there has been increased recognition of the landlord's obligation to meet certain minimum standards for occupancy. Housing codes specifying such standards have been adopted by municipalities and other local governments, and their enforcement has been more rigidly prosecuted. Yet tenants do not have the right to withhold rentals as a means of forcing their demands. Under the law, the proper governing agency alone assumes this enforcement.

This change in the legal foundation of the landlord-tenant relationship has already begun and undoubtedly will develop further in the years to come. In many states, laws have been enacted which obligate the landlord to set the premises in habitable condition.

It must be noted that tenant organizations are a legal requirement for many subsidized housing developments. These organizations work with management to resolve difficulties stemming from poor management, on one side, and from poor performance and objectionable tenant behavior, on the other.

Tenant organizations also are sometimes formed in luxury apartment buildings where a collective voice is needed to obtain landlord action.

Under somewhat vague laws, tenant organizations must define services that are thought to be lacking and also promote tenant education programs. Often, when the leaders of these organizations meet with management representatives, issues can be discussed and resolved without formal legal actions. It should be emphasized, however, that many of these difficulties result from poor management—or at least from misunderstood management. An effective public and tenant relations policy is essential, therefore, to avert these disputes.

Eventually, stricter laws will be enacted to guarantee a balance between the conflicting owner-manager and tenant interests. Whether the law someday will recognize the tenant's right to withhold rents under conditions of extreme provocation is another matter. But, welfare departments already have declared their right to withhold subsidy payments under certain conditions.

Staffing Requirements

While the property manager is the general overseer of an apartment building's operation, the *resident manager* is the direct representative of management and ownership on the site. As the member of the management team most accessible to tenants, the resident manager is instrumental in creating an image of the building. Whatever actions the resident manager takes, they will reflect on the building, the parent management firm, and the goals of the property owner. For this reason, the property manager must select a resident manager carefully.

The specific responsibilities of the resident manager vary according to the location, size, and type of residential property. As a rule, however, the resident manager's duties comprise three major categories: marketing and tenant relations, rent collection and record keeping, and maintenance supervision.

The property manager determines the general policies and procedures under which all properties managed by the agency will be operated. The resident manager's duty is to ensure that these policies and procedures are adhered to at the given property.

For example, the property manager prepares the marketing plan for a project and establishes a budget for promotional activities. The resident manager then implements this plan by identifying the building's selling points, showing the units, explaining the building's facilities and benefits, and, ultimately, closing rental transactions. Also, in meeting administrative responsibilities for rent collection and other procedures, the resident manager maintains records on the forms provided by and according to the system adopted by the management firm. This includes strict adherence to all rent collection schedules.

Quite obviously, the resident manager does not perform these duties alone. Usually, the resident manager hires and supervises a support staff: the number of employees depends on the size and type of property and the agency's operating policies. In larger projects, for example, a maintenance supervisor and staff, a rental agent, and a bookkeeper may be needed. Job specifications for these positions should be prepared by both the property manager and the resident manager, according to hiring practices outlined in chapter 9.

In the case of government-assisted housing, personnel regulations may apply. Equal Employment Opportunity programs are designed to ensure that neither federal and federally assisted contractors nor local government agencies funded by HUD discriminate in employment because of race, color, religion, sex, or national origin. There also may be requirements as to the on-site office versus the central management office as the administrative center of a government-assisted property.

In addition to performing specific operational tasks with on-site staff assistance, the resident manager also can provide higher-level management with valuable data. No one is better equipped to supply information about the property, the neighborhood, the competition, and other important facets of the operation than the resident manager who has daily, personal contact with and exposure to the marketplace. The property manager's analysis of this kind of information is necessary to the ongoing success of any residential development, regardless of the owner's objectives.

Summary

Most professional management opportunities are in the residential field. Property managers are needed to administer multifamily rental housing, public and subsidized housing, single-family rental housing, mobile home parks, and institutional housing.

In accepting a residential management account, a study must be performed of the region and the neighborhood in which the property is located. This market analysis focuses on the family, which is the unit of consumption of residential real estate; existing land use and land use trends in the neighborhood; and the supply and demand ratio. From this analysis, a rental schedule can be established that realistically reflects market activity.

Successful marketing of apartment space depends largely on personal salesmanship. Emphasis must be on showing prospective tenants how a property's units fit their individual needs.

However, not only must the tenant's needs be considered; the property also has needs, i.e., good tenants. Tenants should be judged on: (1) permanence potential; (2) housekeeping ability; (3) child care habits; (4) personal living habits; (5) compatibility with other tenants; and (6) rent-paying ability.

To complement the tenant selection policy, a rental collection policy is needed. Such a policy's goal should be to enable management to be firm with delinquencies without arousing hostility.

The relationship between the landlord and the tenant is expressed in a written lease (often called an occupancy agreement to dispel the antagonism often felt between the two parties). The term of the lease varies according to individual management practices and local customs; in some areas, month-to-month leases are most common, while elsewhere leases of one year or longer are the rule. The advantages and disadvantages to term leases shift from the landlord to the tenant, depending on economic conditions.

Part of the property manager's job is to maintain the goodwill of tenants toward the property owner. Good tenant relations depends on how management responds to tenant complaints, relates to tenant organizations, and, in short, communicates with residents.

The most visible representative of the management team is the resident manager. This on-site employee, the daily contact with the property and its tenants, administers the policies and procedures established by the management agency. The specific responsibilities of, and the support staff assigned to, the resident manager depend on the location, size, and type of property.

REVIEW QUESTIONS

1. List the forms of residential property management. Describe each briefly.
2. What impact do social trends in the United States have on the nation's housing needs? What consequent impact does this have on property management?

3. Why is the family the unit of consumption in residential real estate? What effect does this have in performing a market analysis?

4. How would a property manager handle a prospect who comes to the rental office to inquire about an apartment?

5. What criteria does a property manager use to judge a prospective residential tenant?

6. Explain *social responsibility* from the standpoint of the property manager dealing in residential rentals. Give an example.

7. How are a prospective tenant's housekeeping habits judged? Of what value is such information to the property manager?

8. What factors influence the percentage of income a family can apply toward housing?

9. What is the Fair Housing Act? What impact does it have on tenant selection criteria?

10. What effect does the Fair Credit Reporting Act have on the tenant selection process?

11. Where should the credit record of the tenant be located? Why?

12. What is considered the most important phase of investigating a residential tenant's credit rating?

13. List the advantages and disadvantages to tenants and to the landlord when a lease is written for longer than a one-month period.

14. Define *occupancy agreement*. What is the significance of this term?

15. How would a professional property manager respond if a tenant union was organized at an apartment building under management?

16. What is the significance of the *resident manager?* What are the responsibilities of this position?

Condominiums
and Cooperatives

INTRODUCED AFTER WORLD WAR II, condominium ownership is relatively new in the United States. Yet, already it has become a significant alternative to home ownership in many parts of the country. The popularity of condominium ownership rose sharply during the 1970s, when the desirability of owning real estate increased.

Long before condominiums in their present form came into being in the United States, cooperatives were common. However, condominium ownership to some extent has made the cooperative form less popular in recent years. Most future business opportunities for property managers will be reserved for those who specialize in condominium buildings.

On the surface, the management of condominiums and cooperatives may appear similar to the management of rental apartment buildings. They are, after all, ordinary buildings from the point of view of their management problems. The only difference between them and rental properties is in the form of their ownership and their tenancy. However, careful analysis of this difference reveals that condominium and cooperative managers encounter unique problems. For this reason, the subject of condominium and cooperative management is given special treatment in this text, with emphasis on the differences between it and rental apartment management.

Condominium Ownership

Condominium ownership represents the most radical development that has occurred in the United States real estate industry in the last two decades. It has spread with inflation, and now virtually every kind of multitenant property is owned in condominium. The concept has been applied to single-family home developments, office buildings, and resort properties but is employed more frequently with multifamily dwellings. The focus here is on management of residential condominiums.

Condominium refers to a form of ownership: the apartment-like unit in the real estate development that is occupied by the individual tenant is owned in fee simple absolute interest; that portion of the development that is used in common with others is owned jointly, or in condominium. (*Fee simple absolute* is the greatest and most absolute ownership of land, subject to the least number of limitations.)

The owner has title to the *condominium unit,* often legally defined as a three-dimensional space of air located within the walls, floor, and ceiling of the structure. The unit may be mortgaged separately, assessed for real estate taxes, insured, and sold in the same manner as a single-family house.

The property in which the unit owner has an undivided interest is the *common area.* Common areas include the land on which the structure is built; any facilities that are not part of the individually owned units (i.e., swimming pools, tennis courts, playgrounds; and hallways, basements, elevators, lobbies, boilers, air vents, exterior walls, and all other structural and mechanical elements).

Historical Perspective

The shift toward condominium housing in the United States has been motivated by two factors. First, as profits from residential rental property development have dwindled, condominiums have become more profitable for developers than rental properties. As added evidence of this fact, thousands of rental units have been converted to condominiums.

Second, condominium owners enjoy the same advantages as owners of single-family homes. With the onset of high inflation, tenants feared that rentals would be raised drastically and desired the protection of owning the units they occupied. Moreover, the prices of houses were increasing rapidly, confirming their suspicions that they should buy homes as soon as possible. The fact that the same tax subsidy that is extended to owners of single-family homes is extended to condominium owners, namely, the deductibility of property taxes and mortgage interest from income tax payments, further encouraged purchase of condominium units. More recently, especially as increasing numbers of rental units are converted to condominiums and the stock of rental housing is decreasing, condominium ownership is viewed by the consumer as surety of a place to live.

Types of Condominiums

The several classes of residental condominiums are based on their use. The most popular are the *primary housing units,* or those condominium units that are the basic homes of their occupants. It has been in these housing units that condominium buyers have found the primary financial benefit.

The second most popular use of condominium ownership is found in *second-home,* or *resort, condominiums,* most prominent in resort and ski areas, such as Hawaii, Florida, Arizona, and Colorado. Here, developers have built multifamily units by the thousands. Owners occupy them for a part of the resort season and sublease them to tenants for either part of the season or in off-season periods. By renting such a unit, the owner may be entitled to claim it as an income-producing property and take the tax benefits of depreciation (in addition to the interest and property tax deductions).

In some cases, this trend has been carried to the extreme by creation of so-called *condhotels.* Hotel rooms are sold to seasonal occupants on a contract under which the owner occupies the room for one month and agrees to sublease it for the remaining 11 months at resort rates. In these cases, the management provides full hotel service, including maids and hotel amenities.

The Governing Structure

The organization that is responsible for the operation of a condominium development is the *condominium,* or *home owners', association.* This association, to which every unit owner automatically belongs, acts as a small government to settle differences of opinion among residents, establish and collect funds to operate the project, enforce rules and regulations, and make all decisions that are vital to the unit owners.

The real work of the association is carried on by a *board of directors,* which is the association's official governing body. The directors are elected from among the condominium unit owners. In turn, the board elects its officers. Usually there are a president, vice president, secretary, and treasurer.

The duties of the board of directors, as well as the rights and responsibilities of all unit owners, are expressed in a set of governing documents. These documents are recorded by the developer and, in effect, create the condominium. The kinds of documents required vary from state to state. Most common are the declaration, bylaws, individual unit deed, articles of incorporation, and rules and regulations. A brief description of each follows.

- *Declaration.* The most important legal document, the declaration commits the land to condominium use, creates the association, defines the method of determining each unit owner's share of the association's expenses, and outlines each owner's responsibilities to the association and the association's responsibilities to the owner. It is, in effect, the association's constitution.
- *Bylaws.* Whereas the declaration establishes a broad administrative framework for the association, the bylaws provide specific procedures for handling routine matters.
- *Unit deed.* The individual unit deed is the document that legally transfers the title of a condominium unit and its undivided portion of the common areas to the owner.
- *Articles of incorporation.* The articles of incorporation set up the condominium association as a corporation (usually a nonprofit one) under the laws of the state.
- *Rules and regulations.* The house rules and regulations are the guidelines for day-to-day personal behavior. They tell the residents how they must conduct themselves in the common areas and may include measures that affect relations among neighbors.

Cooperative Ownership

The cooperative form of ownership was employed widely from about 1920 to 1950 but has diminished in importance during recent years as condominium development has flourished. To a limited extent, cooperative ownership is employed in commercial properties and those occupied by agribusiness but is most commonly found in residential structures.

A *cooperative* is a corporation that owns real estate, including the building and the land on which it is built. Unlike the condominium owner, the person who purchases housing in a cooperative does not actually own either the individual unit or a share in the common areas. Instead, the owner becomes a shareholder in the corporation and is given a *proprietary lease* on a unit within the building.

Reasons for the development of cooperative apartments are varied. Initially, cooperative ventures were formed when the apartment market did not offer the type of space being sought. For example, people who wanted large, luxury units often banded together to develop a building with large units simply because they were not offered by conventional builders. Cooperatives also were bought because they enabled the owner-shareholder to participate in the advantages of home ownership through deduction of mortgage interest and property taxes.

As is true of all corporations, the cooperative apartment has an elected board of directors, which represents the owners. The board establishes a set of rules under which the project is to be operated. These rules should cover the conduct of the building's occupants and their guests in every possible area—including such items as personal behavior, criteria of occupancy, payment of assessments, and conditions under which units can be leased and sold.

One of the major disadvantages of the cooperative form of ownership lies in its method of financing and the impact this has on resale. Since the building is owned by a corporation, which is the borrower under a mortgage, each apartment theoretically owes a portion of the total mortgage. The amount of money the individual occupant owes is decided on by the cooperative's board of directors when the building is new. The occupant is not given the option to arrange his own financing. As the mortgage is paid down, subsequent owners must have more cash to cover the mortgage—for instance, a new owner would have to come up with 75 percent if the total mortgage was paid down to 25 percent of its value—as well as any increase in the value of the unit. For this reason, it may be difficult to resell cooperative units, and they often are priced lower than otherwise would be expected.

This is beginning to change. Measures are being enacted that permit certain lending institutions to consider a share in a cooperative on the same basis as a condominium unit or single-family home when financing is being arranged. This should correct the major deficiency in the cooperative form of ownership.

Role of Management

Although some condominiums and cooperatives choose to manage themselves, others turn to professional property management agencies to supervise their operations.

The manager's responsibility regarding cooperative and condominium properties is to maintain the integrity of the corporate aims on behalf of the owners and stockholders. Often this extends beyond the routine matter of maintenance to include efforts to guarantee the exclusive nature of the property. A doctor's cooperative building, for example, has a purpose which the owners will be reluctant to see compromised by poor management. Likewise, a condominium must guard the interests of those who remain as units are bought and sold.

Services provided by property managers can range between extremes. A 20-unit building is not likely to need a full-time manager, but the unit owners may wish to retain a management consultant on a fixed-fee basis. In slightly larger properties, fiscal management services may be needed, so that assessments can be collected regularly and a budget plan followed. With very large properties, full management services will be needed. In all situations, a condominium (or cooperative) management agreement should detail the managing agent's level of activity.

The problems encountered in condominium and cooperative management are unique because owner relationships replace those of tenants, common areas create new responsibilities, and fiscal matters require management on behalf of the owners' association. While the condominium manager will not, as a rule, be concerned with maintenance of unit interiors or establishing a rental schedule, other responsibilities, and the skills to meet them, remain the same as for rental housing. Some of the differences in management techniques between rental properties and multiowned properties are noted here. For a more complete description of the role of condominium management, *The Condominium Community,* published by the Institute of Real Estate Management (Chicago: 1978), is suggested.

Resident Relations

There is a psychological distinction between an owner and a tenant. Success in managing a condominium or a cooperative rests on the ability to recognize this difference and act accordingly.

The ability to work with owners depends on being familiar with the policies and procedures outlined in the governing documents and the development of decisions made by the association's board of directors. A property manager should read and be familiar with the governing documents before accepting a property's management, since these documents indicate the responsibilities of each condominium owner, the management entity, and the association.

The management of cooperatives and condominiums is complicated by the fact that, with owners living on the premises, unintended
mistakes and flaws in service are seen and reported quickly. The result
is that more time will be spent by managers per unit space, and more
follow-up will be required to meet owner demands.

Further, with owners living on the property, there is a likelihood that each owner will feel qualified to give instructions to the
property manager. One solution to this problem is to include a provision in the management agreement that the manager is to take
instructions from only one person, usually the president of the board
of directors.

Many of the decisions made by the board of directors, and by
the association as a whole, are made during business meetings which
are authorized by the governing documents. Many times the property
manager is expected to prepare for and attend all meetings. This
can result in a heavy imposition on the manager. The management
agreement provides the solution to this problem. For example, many
agreements limit the agent's required attendance to one meeting per
month or impose an additional charge if attendance is necessary. Not
every meeting will involve the manager's input, and a levy can
encourage the board to use the agent's meeting time wisely.

Sound resident relations can be established if the manager
adopts a viable communications program. One means of achieving
this is through publication of a monthly association newsletter. The
newsletter can be used to transmit official information from the
board, announce proposed policy changes and rules and regulations, and act as a community bulletin board to promote a sense of
neighborliness.

Maintenance

Properly, a unit owner is responsible for all physical maintenance
relating to the individual premises and its physical equipment. The
association assumes the responsibility for the maintenance and servicing of common areas and all matters relating to structural elements,
such as exteriors, roofs, elevators, grounds, and lobbies. These dis-
tinctions should be clearly defined by the documents that govern the
association. Managing a multiowned building without specific instructions creates serious problems. For this reason, a manager should
be familiar with a condominium's governing documents before em-
barking on its management.

The level of maintenance and repair figures importantly to
unit owners. In an apartment building, adequate maintenance is

essential to producing a constant flow of rental income. In a condominium or cooperative, adequate maintenance is essential to preserving and perhaps increasing the value of the property owned by the association members. Therefore, much of management's attention must be concentrated on the repair, cleaning, and upkeep of the common areas.

The difficulty in maintaining condominiums and cooperatives is closely linked with the resident relations problem—there are many owners, each with his own maintenance priorities. The person who enjoys being outdoors may be adamant about having the lawn meticulously manicured, while another resident may be indifferent to the landscaping but become upset if the building is not repainted annually. The property manager must work through the board of directors to resolve these problems.

One of the problems the manager faces is that employees of the condominium are paid by all the owners; any service given to one must be given to all without discrimination. The manager should work out employees' duties to make certain that all owners are treated alike and that services of an extraordinary nature are charged to the individual owner. Evidence of favoritism can create much friction.

Fiscal Affairs

Most condominiums and cooperatives that engage professional management make the manager responsible for the fiscal matters of the property. Basic to this function is the preparation of the operating budget.

Since the bulk of the property's operating expenses pertain to the maintenance of the property, the budget can be a reflection of how the unit owners want the common areas to be maintained and serviced. Consequently, to prepare a budget, the property manager must define the common areas the association is charged with repairing and maintaining, outline a program for implementation and the costs thereof, and ascertain if any additions or major improvements are to be made. A good source of information regarding condominium operating expenses is the *Expense Analysis for Condominiums, Cooperatives, and Planned Unit Developments,* published annually by the Institute of Real Estate Management. For itemizing expenses, IREM has adopted the chart of accounts shown in figure 11.1.

The budget is significant to the unit owners because it is used to establish each owner's share of the *common expenses* (i.e., the

FIGURE 11.1

CHART OF ACCOUNTS: CONDOMINIUMS AND COOPERATIVES

Administrative Expenses
  Office Salaries
  Office Expense
  Management Fee
  Legal
  Audit
  Telephone
  Other

Operating Expenses
  Elevator
  Heating Fuel
  Electricity
  Water/Sewer
  Natural Gas
  Exterminating
  Rubbish Removal
  Window Washing
  Miscellaneous

Repair and Maintenance
  Security
  Grounds Maintenance
  Custodial
  General Maintenance
  HVAC
  Painting—Interior Common Areas
  Painting—Exterior
  Recreational
  Other

Fixed Expenses
  Real Estate Tax
  Other Tax
  Insurance
  Recreation Facilities Leased
  Ground Rent

Replacement Reserve

Amenities
  Pool
  Recreation Building
  Outdoor Recreation Facility
  Other

costs of operating, managing, maintaining, repairing, and replacing the common areas and administering the association). An owner's share of the common expenses is determined by the owner's interest in the condominium itself. This usually is based either on the area covered by the unit as compared to the total area of all units, or the original value of the unit as compared to the total original value. The method of allocation should be spelled out in the governing documents. Each unit owner's share of the cost of operating the property is referred to as an *assessment*. A unit owner's annual assessment is equal to the percentage of ownership interest multiplied by the yearly estimated common expenses. If all units are of equal size and value, common expenses are divided equally.

In addition, a program must be adopted for collecting and recording assessments and handling delinquencies. Typically, the board of directors establishes the collection policy, and the manager then implements it.

The property manager also may be charged with paying taxes,

insurance, and payroll; seeing that the property is adequately insured; and filing necessary reports. In any case, the management agreement should contain a detailed description of the manager's fiscal duties and responsibilities.

Summary

Condominiums and cooperatives represent two alternatives to single-family home ownership in the United States. While cooperative ownership has existed longer, condominium ownership undoubtedly is the more popular. Many of the problems encountered in managing condominiums and cooperatives are the same as those faced in managing rental housing. However, there are significant differences. These stem largely from the form of ownership and tenancy involved.

Condominium refers to the fee simple absolute ownership of an apartment-like unit and undivided interest in a development's common areas. The unit owner enjoys the same advantages as the owner of a single-family home, including tax benefits and protection against inflation and loss of a dwelling unit. Condominiums also offer advantages to developers, since they are more profitable to develop than rental properties, as evidenced by the increasing number of conversions.

A condominium community is governed by a condominium association, which in turn works through an elected board of directors. The duties and responsibilities of the association and the board are outlined in a set of governing documents. Condominiums are created according to state law, and the documents that must be filed vary from state to state. The most common governing documents are the declaration, bylaws, articles of incorporation, unit deed, and rules and regulations.

A cooperative is a corporation that owns real estate, usually a multifamily dwelling and the land on which it is built. Unlike the condominium unit owner, the person who purchases a share of the cooperative does not own the unit but rather is a stockholder who has a proprietary lease on the unit. Like the condominium, the cooperative is administered by an elected board of directors.

Although some condominiums and cooperatives manage themselves, others rely on professional property managers. The scope of management activity ranges from simple consultation to full-service supervision and administration.

The key difference between managing rental housing and managing a condominium or cooperative lies in the psychological distinction between owners and tenants. There are many property owners; their reasons for owning their units, their priorities in maintaining the common areas, and their philosophies toward budgeting for common expenses may differ. The property manager who succeeds in managing multiowner properties must learn to accommodate all of the owners and assure the integrity of the property, while working under the supervision of the board of directors.

REVIEW QUESTIONS

1. Write an essay about the differences and similarities between full management duties for condominiums, cooperatives, and multifamily rental dwellings.
2. Under what circumstances would condominium owners merely want occasional management consulting services? Full property management services?
3. Define *condominium, condominium unit,* and *common area.*
4. How is the common space owned in condominium arrangements? In cooperative arrangements? How do these differences affect property management (if at all)?
5. Can a property manager offer maintenance services to a condominium unit owner? If so, under what conditions?
6. How does a condominium management agreement differ from the management agreement negotiated with the owner of a rental property? What factors enter into the pricing of condominium management service?
7. What is the chief drawback of cooperative ownership? How is the deficiency being corrected?
8. What means can a property manager use to promote internal communications within a large condominium or cooperative development?
9. Define *assessment.* How is an assessment established?

Office Buildings and Special-Purpose Properties

MANAGING OFFICE BUILDINGS is a specialized field, demanding the increasing attention of real estate practitioners. Developers and owners must plan to meet a building's management requirements even before the cornerstone is laid, and management service should be initiated long before the first tenant moves in.

An *office building* is defined as a structure in which a service is provided, in contrast to structures in which products are manufactured or sold or people reside. The policies and procedures for managing properties in which people provide services frequently differ from those used to manage other property types. Nevertheless, the property manager still needs to adopt certain operating guidelines.

In order to supervise office buildings more efficiently, the property manager should be familiar with their chronological and financial development.

Historical Perspective

Office buildings originally were built almost exclusively in the central business districts (CBDs) of metropolitan areas. And, because of limited construction techniques, these buildings were only a few stories. With the development of the steel-frame structure and vertical transportation to serve it, however, high-rise buildings appeared and now are commonplace in suburban and urban locales.

Constructing office buildings usually occurs in the last phase of a real estate boom. With high prosperity levels, businesses thrive and the demands for office space increase. Businesses and financial institutions and professional people can pay the high rentals created by inflated building costs (the result of a number of factors: expensive urban land; high costs of construction, largely due to use of unionized tradesmen; utility relocation and installation; energy restrictions; and building code compliance). This occurred in the late twenties, when there was a boom in new high-rise office building construction throughout the nation. However, when the real estate cycle declined in the depression of 1929 to 1933, these new office buildings were forced to reduce rents or face foreclosure and high vacancies or, often, both. Consequently, there was no new office building construction for more than two decades, except in New York City. In Chicago, no major office structures were built between 1930 and 1957.

When construction finally resumed, the new buildings were built almost exclusively by bulk space users. Because the construction of office buildings involved costs that their rentals could not support, institutional owners alone could afford their development. Only since the mid-seventies have annual per-square-foot rental rates soared into double-digit figures in many cities (and to as high as $25 and even $45 per square foot in New York City), allowing traditional entrepreneurs to realize profits from office building development.

Another significant change that has increased the demand for office space is the shift in employment away from agriculture and industry. Today, less than 25 percent of the work force is involved in manufacturing, and less than five percent is employed to grow food. More than two-thirds of the nation's labor force, then, is found in office settings, and it is expected that this proportion will become still larger.

Although most major buildings are and will continue to be located in the downtown centers of larger metropolitan districts, an increased share of new office space will be found in smaller structures in outlying suburban areas. More construction of commercial buildings in these outlying locations is due to eight factors:

1. The rapid development of interstate highway systems surrounding major cities, which have reduced traveling time into minutes from central business districts to suburban sites.
2. The attractive park-like settings and employee amenities that many office parks provide.

3. The frequently lower rentals due to lower suburban tax rates, greater availability of less expensive land, and the diminution of services offered to tenants. (There are, however, exceptions to this, particularly in the South and Southwest).
4. More major companies desire accessibility to airports (usually located in suburban areas), in contrast to proximity to a major railroad terminal. (Exceptions do exist, such as in Manhattan.)
5. The greater level of security usually found in suburban settings.
6. Greater corporate identity and tax benefits that accompany ownership, made possible by suburban sites.
7. The increased labor force available in suburban areas.
8. Lower-cost, ground-level parking (as opposed to multidecked parking garages usually necessary in central business districts).

Regardless of the size or type of building or its location, the principles of office building management, while more complicated in larger buildings, remain the same.

Property Analysis

The first procedure in assuming the management of an office building is to carefully inspect the property itself, or, if the structure is a proposed new building, the plans and specifications. In fact, it is now customary for knowledgeable developers to consult a property manager in the planning process. The developer can benefit from management's expertise in correcting potential operating problems before construction, which will increase the building's economies and efficiencies. After all, a building's design should not only enhance its desirability as a physical project but also should maximize net earnings, assuring its financial success.

Office buildings must have maximum flexibility to offer their tenants. It is especially important to measure gross and net floor areas, ceiling height, column spacing, space depths (from windows to corridors), and bay widths. The following features should be inspected, corrected or repaired if necessary, and then described to tenants as selling points: window treatment, provision for wiring and communications, corridors, washrooms, floor coverings, types of partitions, plans for security, cleaning services, window washing, utility capacity, freight delivery, periodic painting and decorating, parking, heating and air-conditioning, and whether such service is available in evenings and on weekends. Vertical transportation (i.e., elevator systems) and the scope of building-wide amenities (conference rooms and refreshment facilities) also contribute to a building's marketability.

If the property is an ongoing enterprise, the manager must compile this information and also make a detailed examination of the physical condition of the building and its mechanical and electrical equipment. The manager should become familiar with the building's staff, its tenancy, and the terms and conditions of its leases as well. Only in this way can the manager evaluate the building's standing in the office space market and appraise its rental value.

Market Analysis

A thorough market analysis for an office building will determine its desirability compared to other buildings in the office space market. As with most standards, the ranking of office buildings changes constantly—not so much in the actual gradings as in the application of those grades. Most office buildings are placed in categories, Grades A to D, on the basis of the following:

Grade A   These properties usually command the highest rentals because they are the most prestigious in their tenancy, loca- cation, and overall desirability.

Grade B   These buildings are yesterday's Grade A structures and are priced slightly below those that qualify as Grade A.

Grade C   These properties (once Grade A or B) are older and reasonably well maintained but are definitely below current standards. They are priced to match the rent-paying ability of a lower-income tenancy.

Grade D   Older and poorly maintained, these buildings are still habitable. They are usually located near the CBD.

The ranking of an office building, compared with other buildings, is determined by 12 criteria, which are explained here in detail.

Location

The value of an office building is largely measured by its location to other business facilities. However, the desirability of specific urban locations is constantly changing. This nation always has given special value to anything new. With the high density of downtown development, much of the land in formerly desirable locations has been built on and the improvements are still too sound and recent to be demolished. Consequently, new sites must be found for succeeding developments. Because the newest location is likely to be—or at least appear to be—the best, it is the most desirable.

When a locational analysis for an office building is being performed, trends must be noted. In most American cities, there has been a significant shift in the location of office buildings enjoying a Grade A rank: the automobile has done much to create another (i.e., suburban) market for office space, and developers no longer are limited to sites near rail transit for the convenience of visitors, commuters, and patrons. Yet despite these trends, there is still pressure to locate major office buildings in central business districts because of the accessibility to banks, lawyers, accountants, government offices, clubs, and other businesses in the same or competitive lines. Therefore, new desirable locations are still within central business districts.

The most suitable locations for outlying office buildings are most frequently close to local airports, regional shopping centers, or the core of suburban communities and near heavily traveled highways and mass transit terminals. Professional buildings and clinics are often clustered around "campuses" or at focal points of consumer traffic. As examples, medical office buildings frequently are located near hospitals, and buildings that market to attorneys are located near local and state courts. A new trend that developed in the late 1970s was to locate office buildings adjacent to regional shopping centers.

A relatively new factor in this era of multinational and giant corporations is the clout that is evident in these corporations' ability to determine the office locations for many of their associating firms. These giants of commerce and trade include regional banks, especially those that support the major firms. In many cases, this clout is effective in obtaining tenants for the large and prestigious office buildings.

Location is more a matter of prestige and convenience rather than geography. Amenities and their availability have become important in where firms situate their headquarters. A strategic location near transportation, within walking distance of major business and financial centers, or adjacent to government services can make a 100-year-old building in sound condition as desirable to the office user as a modern skyscraper.

Neighborhood

The value of office space definitely is affected by the building's immediate neighborhood. Obsolete and dilapidated buildings detract from an area and reduce the value of even the most beautiful structure. Streets strewn with litter, unsightly vacant land, and careless occupants also reduce values. If such conditions predominate in an area, it is impossible for any single building to overcome a poor image.

On the other hand, attractive surroundings raise the value of older but less desirable adjacent properties. The age of an office building, then, is not as important to prestige or desirability as neighborhood appearance.

Transportation

Multistory buildings house hundreds of persons who must travel to their offices to transact business; therefore, transportation facilities vitally affect the value of such buildings.

It is unlikely that a multistory office building would be erected on a location without adequate transportation facilities; still, a manager's analysis should review transportation facilities. If the building enjoys excellent service, this can be used as a selling point in marketing its space. Greater use of private vehicles has created parking and accessibility requirements that are important in measuring an office building's desirability.

The energy shortage, too, may be part of the nation's problems indefinitely. This creates a heavy demand for buildings with direct access to urban transportation systems, such as rapid transit, bus, subway, or, as in San Francisco, the cable car.

Prestige

Class-conscious attitudes are not unknown in the commercial world, image being an important factor in business. Sometimes it can be attained by close association with established businesses that enjoy prestige. A budding, ambitious lawyer may want an office in the same building as the city's leading law firms or, at least, on the same street or in the same area. A financial institution will want to locate in the most desirable building in the financial district or as close as possible to such a center. In this way, the building with a prestige address and reputation ranks high on the desirability scale.

Appearance

When appraising an office building's standing within the market, a manager must consider its physical appearance. Although most new buildings will have an attractive appearance, this does not imply that older buildings will be unattractive. In most office markets, well-maintained, older buildings can be occupied at high levels throughout their lives, if the location and surrounding neighborhood do not deteriorate or reduce necessary supportive services. In fact, the uniqueness of many older buildings often makes them desirable throughout their lives.

Lobby

An important factor in grading an office building's desirability is the central lobby, specifically, its appearance, style, character, and lighting. The entrance to any building forms the setting in which each tenant's business is conducted. The lobby should be rated not only on architectural quality and the effectiveness of the lighting but also on its management. Poor management will be shown by a lack of cleanliness and improper maintenance or by tenants who do not reflect the building's high standards. Unsightly newsstands, a poorly operated cigar stand, or an ill-kept and disorganized directory can mar the appearance of an otherwise attractive lobby.

Elevators

Since vertical transportation is vital to the modern multistory office building—low-rises as well as high-rises—the quality of elevator equipment and service are extremely important in measuring overall desirability.

The first factor in grading elevators is their location within the building. If it is necessary to walk a long distance from the main entrance to the elevator banks, tenants will dislike occupancy and lower their estimation of the building's space. This is particularly true if tenants must walk equally long distances after arriving on their own floors to reach their offices.

A second factor in appraising elevators is the appearance of the entrances, cabs, and, in some cases, operators. If the cab is modern in styling and adequately lighted and ventilated and equipped with understandable manual controls and a well-maintained floor covering, then the appearance is judged to be excellent. Any lessening of visual desirability in any one of these factors detracts from the value of the office building as a whole.

The third standard by which elevator service is measured is the newness and operating speed of the equipment. People often grade a building on the quality of the elevator equipment. Key-controlled lighting, automatic hatchway doors, and high-speed signal-control elevators are among the standards by which systems are judged.

Elevator speed does not necessarily mean only the rate of travel in feet per minute but also includes the interval between the departures of elevators from the ground floor and other floors in the building (i.e., the waiting time). Service that is synchronized to provide an elevator at each floor in each direction every 25 seconds at a speed of 600 feet per minute is superior to elevator service at 800 feet per minute but with an interval between cars of 50 seconds.

Corridors

A quiet good taste in building corridors is important to an office building's desirability. Floors and floor coverings, corridor walls, entrance doors, and illumination are basic factors in a comparison with other structures. Clashing colors, poorly supervised tenant advertising and entry signs, mismatched floor coverings, carpet–tile–marble mixtures, all detract from appearance and, ultimately, rental value. Many tenants and prospective tenants are conscious of good design and color coordination, and their tastes should be considered.

Office Interiors

Unlike apartment units, office suites usually are renovated to accommodate new tenant needs and aesthetic choices. In appraising office space, then, desirability depends not so much on the existing interior design but rather on the possible layout that is provided. The possibilities center on the number of windows and the view and light, the depth of the office from corridor to wall, and the width of the office between supporting columns. While newer office buildings usually have wide column spacing, permitting efficient use of space, most structures built before 1945 have a great deal of load-bearing material that severely limits design efficiency.

In addition to the layout factors, desirability also depends on the quality of decoration, interior wall finish, light fixtures and illumination, and ceiling height. All of these will be judged by their conformity, or lack of conformity, to the "ideal" office interior, which is generally represented by the most prestigious building in town. Indeed, the rental value of an office building is ultimately based on comparability.

Tenant Services

Prospective tenants judge an office building by the quality and adequacy of the various services that either are included in the rent or can be obtained. Most important among these services are office cleaning, janitor service, protection and security services, responses to service requests by on-site maintenance personnel, after-hours access to the building, and after-hours heating and air conditioning service.

Some office buildings provide special amenities for tenant use, such as auditoriums or meeting places. These facilities, and any charges made for them, are noted by the selective tenant who is definitely shopping for office space or is simply considering a move. Often these amenities will decide the question.

Management

The quality of a building's management adds to the value of its space. Businesses are very aware of the influence management has on the overall desirability of an office building and the efficiency of its services.

Of special importance is the level of maintenance, often provided as a building service and a direct and visible reflection of management's professionalism. A well-ordered building with bright wood, polished floors, clean washrooms, dust-free cornices, and general cleanliness is a high-yielding investment. The prospective tenant, discovering anything less, will select the better-maintained of two buildings under consideration. The level of management affects not only the building's desirability but it also reflects the reputations of the firms located within the building.

Tenant Mix

In discussing a building's value as an "address," the fact that office buildings are rated by their prestige was introduced. This prestige is established by the surroundings, transportation, physical appearance, equipment, and maintenance. It is enhanced, too, by the character of its tenants.

Office buildings are rated by the size, financial standing, and general reputation of their tenant mix. Professional office buildings are rated according to the standing and reputation of the professionals who have offices there. Financial office buildings frequently are rated by the prestige of the bank centered on the lower floors or the character of the financial institutions located in the property. In appraising an office building's space value, then, one must examine the tenancy list and determine what impact the tenant mix has on its rental value.

FIGURE 12.1

STANDARD METHOD OF FLOOR MEASUREMENT FOR OFFICE BUILDINGS

RENTABLE AREA—MULTIPLE TENANCY FLOOR

RENTABLE AREA — MULTIPLE TENANCY FLOOR

The Net Rentable Area of a multiple tenancy floor, whether above or below grade, shall be the sum of all rentable areas on that floor.

The rentable area of an office on a multiple tenancy floor shall be computed by measuring to the inside finish of permanent outer building walls, or to the glass line if at least 50% of the outer building wall is glass, to the office side of corridors and/or other permanent partitions, and to the center of partitions that separate the premises from adjoining rentable areas.

No deductions shall be made for columns and projections necessary to the building.

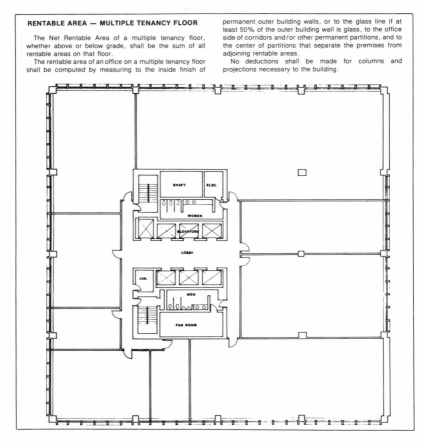

Rental Schedule

Based on the physical, locational, and psychological influences in the ratings of buildings from Grades A to D and the application of this ranking system to a particular building, the property manager sets prices on the building's space.

Measuring Rentable Space

The manager first must measure the space within the office building. This is not so simple, as there are several acceptable methods of mea-

FIGURE 12.1—*Continued*

RENTABLE AREA—SINGLE TENANCY FLOOR

RENTABLE AREA — SINGLE TENANCY FLOOR

Rentable area of a single tenancy floor, whether above or below grade, shall be computed by measuring to the inside finish of permanent outer building walls, or from the glass line where at least 50% of the outer building wall is glass. Rentable area shall include all area within outside walls, less stairs, elevator shafts, flues, pipe shafts, vertical ducts, air-conditioning rooms, fan rooms, janitor closets, electrical closets — and such other rooms not actually available to the tenant for his furnishings and personnel — and their enclosing walls. Toilet rooms within and exclusively serving only that floor shall be included in rentable area.

No deductions shall be made for columns and projections necessary to the building.

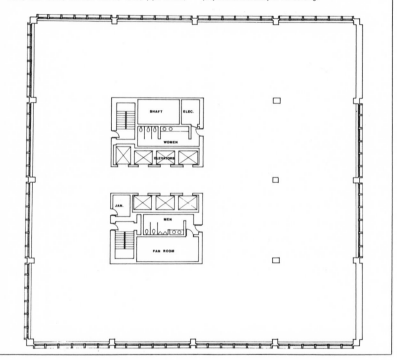

suring space. The most commonly used method of floor measurement is the one adopted by the Building Owners and Managers Association (BOMA), a trade association that supports and represents the needs and interests of the high-rise office building industry. The BOMA standard method of measuring office space is used by owners, managers, tenants, appraisers, architects, lending institutions, and others active in office building investments. According to BOMA:

> . . . this standard can and should be used in measuring office space in old as well as new buildings. It is applicable to any architectural design or type of construction because it is based

on the premise that the area being measured is that which the tenant may occupy and use for his furnishings and his people.

The Standard Method of measuring office space . . . measures only occupiable space, undistorted by variances in design from one building to another. It measures the area of an office building that actually has rental value and, therefore, as a standard can be used by all parties with confidence and with a clear understanding of what is being measured. (*Standard Method of Floor Measurement for Office Buildings*, 1977)

According to the BOMA measurement method, *rentable space* on a single-tenant floor consists of the total area minus an allowance for the shell and core of the building. On a multiple-tenancy floor, a tenant's rentable area is measured from outer walls to demising partitions. In neither case are deductions made for columns and projections necessary to the building. (A detailed explanation of the BOMA method of measuring office space appears in figure 12.1.)

Measuring the rentable area accurately is extremely important. To prove this, assume an error of one percent is made in measuring a building's space. Rather than arriving at an accurate measurement of 100,000 rentable square feet, the property manager determines that it has 99,000 square feet. A sizable loss of income can result from this mistake, with a negative effect on the property's value. If the space in the building is renting for $9.00 per square foot, the error would mean a $9,000 loss of income annually; the estimate of value, computed at a ten percent capitalization rate, would be miscalculated by $90,000.

Establishing Rates

The property manager bases the rental schedule on the rentable area, with the rates expressed in either dollars per square foot per year or dollars per square foot per month, depending on local custom.

In determining rental rates for an office building, it first is necessary to establish the base rate that the average space will command. There are several procedures in establishing the actual base rate. First, an economic analysis is needed to determine the minimum rate that will offset debt service, real estate taxes, operating costs, vacancy loss, and the owner's desired return on the investment. This analysis should yield the lower limits of an acceptable rental schedule. Hopefully, the market rental rates will be higher than those necessary to meet the owner's financial requirements. If the rate required to offset these items is greater than the market rate, the manager will face problems.

Implied, then, is that an economic analysis alone is not sufficient to set rental rates. The rental schedule, whether for new or existing space, must be based on the realistically estimated current market. For example, if the manager determines that a building's space is in the Grade A category and that the base rate for this grade ranges from $14 to $16 per square foot, the manager must select the rate at which it is believed (after analyzing the facts) the property can be rented to a satisfactory occupancy level.

From this base rate, all other spaces in the building are priced on a plus or minus basis, depending on their location within the building, with emphasis on height and exposure. In a 20-story office building, for example, the space on the top floor probably commands a higher rental rate than space on the second floor. Similarly, a suite with an attractive view, such as a city skyline, a lake, or mountains, is more desirable and should be priced at a higher rate than space overlooking a parking lot.

Critics sometimes complain that luxury offices with spectacular views and prestigious top-floor locations are overrated. Nevertheless, businesses pay higher rentals to occupy these offices, and the space should be priced according to current market value.

A formula for applying a rental schedule to office space was devised in the 1930s by two Chicago building managers and named for them. Although regional in application and seldom used today, the *Sheridan-Karkow formula* was a major step in systematically analyzing rentable area and assigning rates. Before this time, space within a typical office building was priced the same throughout. This created a situation in which desirable space was leased quickly, and undesirable space remained vacant.

Even when a scientific method of setting rental rates has been followed, the property manager still must ensure that rents offset rising costs. The most common means of accomplishing this is a lease escalation clause, under which some or all operating expenses are passed on to tenants on a pro rata basis. Each tenant's share of increased operating expenses is usually based on the relationship between the area occupied by the tenant and the building's total rentable area. (A more detailed explanation of escalation clauses appears later in this chapter.)

Marketing Office Space

For as long as occupancy statistics have been available on the nation's office buildings, the managers of these properties have faced the problem of space merchandising. Although 100-percent occupancy in some buildings has been attained for brief periods, general business activity, in the long term, has not demanded all of the nation's office space. Moreover, new office buildings are built whenever high average occupancy is reached, which then introduces new space.

Renting office space in periods of normal business activity first involves searching for prospective space users, and then creating a desire in them to view the available space, demonstrating the adaptability of the space to the prospective client's needs, establishing in the prospect's mind a conviction that the space represents good value, and inducing the prospect to close a lease arrangement. From an operational point of view, renting office space also requires considerable planning by the manager. With planning, tenant growth can be handled without major expense to the owner and without losing tenants because of a lack of space flexibility.

There is a great advantage in appointing the manager of a new building as soon as construction plans are formed. In this way, a promotional campaign can be designed that will maximize the initial occupancy level. As *preleasing* office buildings becomes more commonplace, this type of merchandising increases in importance. During construction, certain occasions can be utilized for publicity purposes, i.e., ground breaking, the topping-off ceremony (which marks the completion of the structural frame of the building), and the official opening of the building. Attractive brochures describing the new building and its facilities are useful promotional items. These can be supplemented by point-of-sale printed matter, such as floor plans and instructions to new tenants.

Because of the unique problems and opportunities associated with marketing any office space, and especially new space, a new field within the property management industry has developed—office leasing. The *leasing agent* is the overall organizer and administrator of the marketing program, which includes coordinating the advertising campaign, setting rental rates and rental achievement targets, searching for and qualifying tenants, and coordinating and planning for move-ins. Above all, the leasing agent must be an effective salesman, able to convince prospective tenants that a given building is the most desirable for the rental dollar.

Despite the large role played by the leasing agent, the property manager, however, should remain highly involved in the process. While the leasing agent handles tenant transactions until the lease is signed, the property manager assumes total responsibility throughout the lease term and any renewal period. To ignore leasing activity could create serious problems for the property manager.

Obtaining Prospects

Locational proximity is often advantageous to businesses in related activities. In almost every city large enough to support more than one or two office buildings, grouping of tenants results in certain buildings housing mostly lawyers, or insurance companies, or financial houses, or other businesses or professions.

Considering this factor, the first step in obtaining prospects for an office building is to determine if it is suited to a specific use. To classify potential categories of office users, the property manager may use the Yellow Pages. In some cases, the building's purpose will be established before the manager assumes its administration. If the building houses a bank and is located in the heart of the financial district, it will be tenanted largely by brokerage houses, investment companies, corporation lawyers, and reputable commercial establishments. If the building is directly across the street from the main courthouse, it probably will attract lawyers, court attachés, and mortgage firms. When a concentration of one business activity is indicated, the manager should create centers of similar attraction in the building.

Every building, of course, cannot become a center for a particular type of business. In most cities, the number of individual firms forming a specialty is not large enough to fill an office building. However, the same market analysis should be prepared. It may be assumed that every individual, firm, or government agency in the community is a possible prospect for any office building, although one particular building may be more desirable for some potential space users than for others. If this assumption is valid, the marketing effort can be directed to those prospects who are the most logical users of space. Preparing a *prospect list,* then, is a qualitative and quantitative task.

There are also other ways of preparing prospect lists. For instance, in a new building, if the property is constructed by a prestigious institutional owner (such as a bank, an insurance company, or a major commercial operation), it is likely that the owner can influence a substantial number of tenants to locate within the building. Since the owner will have connections with a law firm or an advertising agency, these or any of a number of other firms possibly can be persuaded to become tenants. All these prospective tenants should be listed and then invited to become charter tenants of the building. A list also should be prepared of other logical prospects, determined by the location and other advantages of the proposed property. Courtesy calls may be made to these prospective tenants—in the hope of closing a deal before the property opens, or, at least, to acquaint them with its advantages.

Many office building management firms initiate other canvassing programs by discovering the expiration dates of occupants of competitive buildings. In fact, most office building tenants (especially large space users) review their quarters long before lease expiration, sometimes by as much as two or three years. While this practice has been frowned on in some areas as raiding, it is employed in intensely competitive situations. Some property managers even create a "rival file" of all competitive buildings that lists all tenants floor-by-floor and notes those that might need to expand, as well as those who might block such expansion. The property manager also must remember that satisfied tenants prefer to remain in their existing quarters, while the disenchanted can hardly wait to move. Finding those who are unhappy with their current space, then, may provide some prospective tenants.

However obtained, a list of prospective tenants, complete with the amount of space they occupy, lease expiration dates, and other pertinent information, is invaluable.

Arousing Interest

Many inquiries for space will reach the office building manager or leasing agent either by telephone calls or written requests for information or in person from prospects who want to see space and learn its prices. However, except in unusual periods or for buildings that enjoy unusually high, specialized consumer pressure, voluntary inquiry is not enough to achieve high occupancy. A substantial portion of the renting activity must be generated through solicitation and by canvassing.

Since a prospective tenant would never rent existing space sight unseen, the first objective is to interest the prospect sufficiently to encourage a visit to the building. If the building is under construction, an artist's rendering should be prepared that accurately portrays the completed structure and its interior spaces.

To draw the attention of office users, promotional activities should be planned in the form of eye-catching signs and billboards, attractive brochures that describe the building, classified advertising in appropriate newspapers and periodicals, and direct mail programs that focus on the target market. The following arguments should be used in promotional pieces designed to attract otherwise disinterested prospects:

- **Price advantage.** Well-managed businesses are always striving to improve net profits. If the leasing agent can prove a price advantage in an alternate location that fully meets a prospect's requirements, the likelihood of stimulating at least preliminary action is great. However, a substantial price advantage in an economy beset by double-digit inflation is rare.
- **Increased efficiency.** If the agent can prove that by moving to another building a prospect noticeably will increase efficiency, positive results are likely. Increased efficiency is really another form of price advantage, yet it assumes a different approach and broadens opportunities for prospect response. The promise of increased efficiency should be illustrated, if possible, with office space plans and layouts demonstrating to a prospective client specifically how the new location will achieve this efficiency. A demonstration of space adaptability is an especially strong factor in arousing the prospect's interest. For example, if a tenant can increase efficiency by ten percent in a new, better-designed office, the savings may justify a move. In fact, a higher rental for efficient space usage may be economically preferable to a lower rental for inefficiently used space.
- **Increased prestige.** Prestige is an important factor in determining office space value. A careful evaluation of prospects will identify those businesses that can benefit most from increasing the prestige of their locations. Effectively presenting this value to a qualified prospective client should stimulate interest.
- **Economy.** The above reference to price advantage suggests comparable space at a savings. Solicitations based on economy refer to lower-priced space, but not necessarily space that is equal to that currently occupied by the prospect. For example, many businesses are located in Grade A buildings in major commercial districts but could just as well be situated in less expensive space in another grade of property. Especially during inflationary periods, many businesses are squeezed by high expenses that may make them consider less luxurious space at lower rentals.

The leasing agent should not call on a prospect unless familiar with the business being conducted, the customers of that business, and all other pertinent information. Preparation is needed for a detailed discussion of the advantages of the building's location (if these advantages exist) as they relate to the prospect's business. The agent also should be able to mention any other advantages, such as available transportation for the customer's clients, other neighborhood facilities (i.e., restaurants, shopping, and clubs), an attached parking garage, and building security.

No building is perfect. In discussing an office building with a prospective tenant, the manager should focus on its best features in order to reduce the inadequacies. For example, if the building does not have a prestige address, then it may be helpful to discuss the economy of operation. Many businesses that operate on small profit margins are vitally interested in holding their office costs to the lowest possible levels. Whenever an objective seems important to the client and the building could fulfill it, the manager should explore it in detail.

Personal contact is the only effective method of leasing office space. Although inquiries for space can be stimulated through advertising, the real action-getting sales work is effected by personal solicitation and personal selling efforts.

It is quite possible that a potential tenant for a given building may not, for one reason or another, want to rent space in that building. The structure may not accommodate the tenant's space requirements. In order to earn a personal commission and one for the firm, the leasing agent should try to locate space for the tenant in another building operated by the agency. If this is not possible, efforts should be made to find space in another facility, even if one leased and managed by another agency.

Facilitating Space Inspection

In an office building that is actively recruiting new tenants, personnel must be prepared for the prospect who comes unannounced, even though the leasing agency will try to see that appointments are made first. It is essential to the sales effort that the rental office personnel be acquainted with the prospects who have been contacted. Then, if a prospective client appears when the agent is absent, the person whose duty it is to show the space can do so effectively. The prospect's needs can be discussed adequately while the suitable space is shown.

In buildings with high vacancy levels, management should consider a model office or offices for exhibit purposes. If this is impractical, management can make arrangements with tenants whose offices are attractively laid out and decorated for prospects to be shown this finished space. It is important in any kind of merchandising to exhibit products only in their most attractive form. Displaying unprepared, vacant office space to prospective clients is a poor merchandising practice. Although major decorating is not called for, housekeeping should be performed to make vacant space presentable for showing. If a building is under construction, color renderings of typical office interiors that accurately represent the finished product could be prepared.

Tenant Qualification

Commercial tenant qualification is similar in nature to the selection of residential tenants outlined in chapter 10. However, the procedure takes a somewhat different direction. Prospective commercial tenants must be judged from the standpoint of business acumen, aggressiveness, and progressiveness. Measurement of tenant desirability is not concerned with the personal traits of the tenant (since many are corporations or large groups of individuals) but is based on factors created by the commercial situation. Hence, a direct inquiry into the background of commercial tenants is easier than checking on individuals, which must be done in the residential sector.

The more important criteria for qualifying a prospective commercial tenant are discussed below.

Business Reputation and Strength

The value of office space is partly established by the business reputations of its tenants and the atmosphere that prevails in the building. The manager must recognize the impact of the individual reputation of a commercial tenant on a given building and measure this reputation from a personal as well as a professional standpoint.

In addition to the potential tenant's business reputation, its stability also should be evaluated. The manager must take steps to ensure that the tenant is capable of performing under the terms of the lease—that it can pay the rent on time. Although a large national firm or respected local company may not require a formal credit check, the procedure should not be ignored when smaller, unknown firms apply to rent office space.

Service Requirements

A prospective tenant may be perfectly acceptable in ability, aggressiveness, and reputation factors and yet not be accepted because of special service requirements. For example, if a prospective tenant is being considered for a building in which there are limited freight loading and elevator facilities and an inquiry indicates that accepting this tenant would strain these facilities enough to deny their value to other tenants, then perhaps this particular tenant should not be admitted.

Consideration, in this respect, should be given to excessive security needs, extra electrical or HVAC requirements, and the need for extended hours of operation. Buildings owners and managers always are seeking ways to conserve energy. Often, this means limiting the operational hours of HVAC systems and lighting. If a prospective tenant must have 24-hour-a-day service, including weekends, this could force a building to operate all systems beyond normal business hours. The extra expense of having such a tenant may cause the building to lose money from operations.

In any case, the property manager must study a prospective tenant's service requirements and balance them with the building's operation, simply as part of the qualification process. If the two sides are incompatible, disqualification of the tenant may be the best decision.

Space Requirements

Space requirements are one of the basic criteria in determining if a prospective commercial tenant qualifies for a particular office building. The amount of space the business requires and the organization of that space must be assessed. In doing this, many property managers adopt standards that enable them to predict with relative accuracy the amount of space occupied by the various business departments, such as private offices, secretarial areas, areas that accommodate large numbers of personnel, and special-purpose facilities (i.e., conference rooms, reception areas, and storage areas).

In qualifying tenants, the manager must be aware of current space needs and also possible future expansion requirements. Successful businesses are growing businesses. Buildings, however, are static and cannot always accommodate tenants' growth. This must be considered when qualifying a tenant. At the same time, the manager must think about present tenants who may need to expand to adjoining space. It is often unwise for a manager to approve the application of a prospective tenant whose growing business indicates that occupancy will be temporary.

Space Planning and Tenant Improvements

As long as the office environment is an important factor in attracting and keeping quality employees, more businesses will be concerned about the appearance of the work areas they provide for employees. At the same time, companies are more aware of the need for greater efficiency of space usage. This is especially true when rental rates are climbing. Based on these trends, property managers have found that marketing office space successfully depends on planning coordinated office interiors that combine functional efficiency and effectiveness with a pleasing appearance. The process of creating office interiors is referred to as *space planning.*

As has been pointed out, in qualifying a prospective tenant, one criterion is the office user's space requirements and the building's ability to satisfy them. In any new building, and all but the smallest suites in older buildings, it is necessary to construct or alter the existing space to meet these requirements. Through the space-planning process, the manager translates the prospect's square footage needs, organizational structure, aesthetic preferences, and financial limitations into a three-dimensional office. The data for planning the office interior is gathered during an in-depth interview with the prospect and an inspection tour of the prospect's current space. Based on this information, preliminary plans are prepared, usually by a specialist in space planning, and submitted for approval to the prospect. After this, detailed plans are formed.

New techniques in office design have had a great impact on space planning. Chief among these is *open-space planning,* which eliminates fixed partitions and permits the tenant to rearrange work stations easily, as changing needs require. *Office landscaping* is another new concept in space planning that utilizes floor space in an open manner.

Most office buildings have *standard tenant improvement allowances,* which concern items that may be installed on the leased premises at no charge to the tenant (e.g., one telephone jack every 125 square feet of rentable area, one door per 300 square feet). The landlord's generosity in granting allowances depends on building policy, as does responsibility for tenant improvements that exceed allowances. Building policies vary with the state of the market. When demand is low and vacancy high, owners are more generous in their allowances for space alterations. But, when demand is brisk and occupancies tight, owners will be conservative in observing their market-related policies regarding these allowances.

Managers of modern office buildings (especially for the larger space users) often encounter complex situations in preparing tenant quarters. The use of computers and the employment of high-technology office equipment and communications systems have

greatly complicated the space-planning process. Skills of highly experienced personnel often are required, and the construction of
leasehold improvements may become a major undertaking. The
situation calls for a longer-term lease commitment for both landlord
and tenant.

Leases and Lease Negotiation

The rights and obligations of the office tenant and the building owner
are defined in a written office lease, which is subject to the requirements of a legal contract (outlined in chapter 7). A property management firm often uses a standard lease form for renting space in office
buildings under its management. This standard rental agreement
initiates lease term negotiations with tenants.

Negotiation is the technique of concluding a rental agreement
that satisfies both the tenant and the owner. It involves give and take,
with the property manager acting for the property ownership and as
mediator between it and the tenant. Although nearly every lease
clause is subject to at least some negotiation, debate usually centers on
a few specific clauses. One provision that is negotiated automatically
is that of tenant improvements. Other clauses receiving special attention here are those related to rental adjustments, services, and
tenant options.

Rental Adjustment

As a result of rapidly rising operating costs and spiraling inflation,
office building owners and managers consider it mandatory to include
in leases of longer than one year clauses that permit rental rates to be
adjusted. These clauses, discussed briefly earlier in this chapter, are
referred to as *escalation clauses*.

Escalation clauses may be structured in various ways. One of
the most common is an operating cost escalation clause under which
increases in a building's operating expenses, usually including property taxes, are added to tenants' rents on a pro rata basis. Another
frequently used rent adjustment clause is the index escalation clause.
This calls for the rent to be adjusted in an amount equal to the annual change in a specified index, usually the Consumer Price Index,
although others are used. Other clauses may base rental adjustments
on changes in wage levels, utility costs, property taxes, and similar factors.

Regardless of the type of escalation clause used, such a provision
is necessary to protect the real estate investment. Without a means of

adjusting rents, income remains the same while costs climb. As a result, services probably will be curtailed and the overall value of the building, to the tenant as well as the owner, will decline.

Utilities and Services

Any and all services that will be provided by the owner should be detailed in the lease. Customary services and utilities include air conditioning and heating, janitorial service, elevator service, and electricity. Especially important in this portion of the lease is an assignment of the financial responsibility for these services and any special restrictions on their use.

For example, as mentioned earlier, many landlords have established a policy of providing heating and air conditioning only during regular working hours. However, a tenant might need this service at other times (such as a company with a computer whose temperature must be maintained). If this additional service is to be provided, the agreement, and the allocation of expenses connected with it, must be expressed in the lease.

Options

Some office tenants will try to negotiate certain *options* that will grant them specific rights or privileges not otherwise stated within the standard rental agreement. The most common options are: the option to expand, which might be sought if the tenant anticipates growth; the option to renew the lease on expiration for an additional term, under the same conditions, and at a stated rental rate (usually the basic rate plus escalation increases); and the option to cancel, which permits the tenant to cancel the lease before expiration, usually under a penalty.

When negotiating options to a lease as the owner's agent, the property manager should base any decisions to grant them on current market conditions. Options are one-sided: with few exceptions they favor the tenant, not the landlord. For this reason, tenant options must be weighed against the objectives of ownership in terms of the marketplace.

Maintenance

While many aspects of office building maintenence are identical with other properties, commercial properties can present unusual maintenance problems and consequently have special maintenance services.

These special services usually are concerned with elevator operation and general cleaning.

Elevator Operation

Elevators in office buildings must provide good service. Unfortunately, management usually has no decision in the number of elevators originally installed or the design of the equipment. Too frequently, builders do not provide adequate equipment. (This emphasizes the importance of management participation in planning new structures.)

Generally, office buildings with elevators are higher than residential buildings with elevator service. The miles traveled by a typical office building elevator, therefore, are considerably greater, and the elevators require more constant maintenance. In residential buildings, elevators are operated only when there is a call for service, while, in many office buildings, elevators are positioned at varying locations in the shaft to anticipate service calls.

Maintaining a satisfactory schedule that sets a minimum time between available elevators and the satisfactory movement of the public during peak traffic hours are the two principal problems.

Cleaning

An office building's cleaning problems differ from those found in other types of buildings. The relatively heavier traffic in these structures creates a greater need for cleaning the public areas. And, because cleaning crews cannot be permitted to interfere with office work, most cleaning activity is performed at night.

Many office buildings in recent years have employed specialized cleaning firms. This is especially true in smaller, outlying developments. This can be more efficient and more economical, but the chief advantages are in recruiting help, scheduling, and replacing absent employees. If a contract is negotiated with a cleaning firm, that contract should include detailed cleaning specifications. These specifications should be used throughout the term of the agreement as a checklist to ensure that the cleaning firm is providing the service for which it is being paid.

Cleaning public and tenant areas in office buildings is chiefly the work of the night crew, but an adequate staff of janitors and cleaners must be on hand to maintain the cleanliness of the property at all times. Daytime cleaning activities involve maintaining the cleanliness of lobby floors, elevator cabs, front walks and entrances, and special areas and windows. Since the main cleaning crew works the night shift, only those cleaning activities that must be performed during the day should be handled by the day crew.

Night cleaning in office buildings traditionally began at 9:00 p.m. or later and was done by employees of the building itself, under the direction of a night superintendent. In most buildings today, however, cleaning activities begin as early as 6:00 p.m. This practice takes advantage of the remaining daylight and reduces the hours during which the building must be heated or cooled. Also, in recent years, there has been a shortage of night workers. Thus, the practice of contracting for union-affiliated night cleaning with companies specializing in this field has grown significantly.

Cleaning has become more mechanized and less strenuous for the individual; a well-trained janitorial employee should have a thorough knowledge of new materials, equipment, and techniques. The numbers of poorly trained and equipped cleaning personnel diminished after World War II, when minimum wage demands and union-organized cleaning crews were prevalent. The militancy of hourly rate employees increased during the 1960s and 1970s.

Too many property managers have overlooked hourly employee concerns for too long. This is no longer true of the modern manager, who understands how to work with people to achieve maximum results for everyone.

Life-Support Systems

Office buildings in metropolitan areas are exposed more than ever to all types of personal and security risks ranging from crime to terrorism to fire. To combat these, it is necessary to provide security personnel and other measures to protect tenants and their property. Security is now an important facet of competent office building management.

When assuming the management of an office building, the property manager should inspect and evaluate its security system. If the manager is not equipped to perform this survey, a security consultant can make the inspection. Most important to the evaluation is the traffic within the building, with special attention to all exits and entrances (windows and shipping docks as well as doorways). Management then should tighten security measures at any weak points revealed in the survey.

A security system involves such precautions as locking washrooms, observing those entering and exiting the building, converting certain employees to auxiliary policemen, and issuing special identification for after-hours personnel. Television screens and cameras may be located strategically to monitor vulnerable areas. Electronic access systems may be installed at exit points, not only to tighten security but also to reduce labor costs. Eliminating elevator operations has complicated security problems; now, lobbies must be under complete observation at all times.

Besides adopting an ongoing security program, plans for dealing with emergency situations (i.e., bomb threats and fires) should be prepared. This takes on added importance in high-rise office buildings, which complicate evacuation. By working closely with local police and fire departments, the property manager can form evacuation plans and be prepared to deal with any emergency that may occur. These plans should be distributed to all tenants and their employees and also posted permanently in key locations. If necessary, a meeting with tenants can be held to discuss all security procedures and the importance of upholding them.

The property manager also should develop a standard procedure for reporting all breaches of security and other threats to the safety of the building and its users. In fact, this must be done for insurance purposes. By maintaining detailed records, and subsequently analyzing losses and the circumstances surrounding them, weaknesses in the security system may be revealed and tighter security measures can be suggested.

Special-Purpose Buildings

Some buildings are designed for the specialized needs of their occupants and are called *special-purpose buildings*. Most special-purpose properties are leased to individual tenants on net leases, which stipulate that the occupants will assume responsibility for maintenance, insurance, property taxes, and other operating expenses and needs. Usually these buildings are not supervised by property management firms.

There are, however, some special-purpose properties that engage property management. Owners of professional buildings, for instance, often hire property managers, as do owners of some industrial, loft, and mart buildings.

Medical and Dental Arts Buildings

Before the development of outlying areas where many physicians and dentists relocated, medical facilities were situated in the downtown areas of most communities. More recently, however, they have located within the campuses of hospitals or in major outlying commercial centers.

While many techniques in managing these buildings are similar to those for general office buildings, certain differences must be mentioned. The factor of tenant improvements is a main area of concern. In dentistry, for example, facilities require specially designed plumbing for water, gas, compressed air, and drainage, which also affect the electrical facilities. Sometimes these installations are included in the building's original design, but custom work frequently is required. Ideally, all costs for custom alterations are sustained by the tenant, but that is subject to the market, space demand, and the owner's policy.

Maintenance of medical and dental arts buildings also must be given special attention. By the very nature of the services that are provided in these buildings, cleanliness is of utmost importance. In addition, hours of operation may need to be extended in emergency situations, and parking demands may be greater than for other office buildings. Staff adjustments naturally must correspond to service demands.

Higher maintenance costs, longer operating hours, and special staff and security requirements dictate higher-than-normal rental rates. Although the level will depend on the marketplace, the point of variation must be considered.

In marketing office space in a medical office building, prospective tenants, other than doctors and dentists, are pharmacies, laboratories, technicians, physical therapists, and optical services. More than that, depending on the facility's size, most buildings would prefer a balance of specialties for complete medical coverage.

Legal Arts Buildings

Although most law firms are established in prestige office buildings, there are a few properties that may attract tenants because of such convenient facilities as law libraries, bar association headquarters, special conference rooms, and secretarial services. In supervising a legal arts building, the property manager must accommodate the needs of the legal profession by providing after-hours accessibility and other supportive services.

Industrial Properties

Industrial real estate can be defined as property that is used for the processing and manufacture of goods. For the most part, industrial plants and buildings are owned, operated, and managed by their occupants. They ordinarily are not considered as real estate investments but as part of the plant and equipment capital needed to conduct business. However, there are a few instances in which industrial real estate will represent a management opportunity.

The location of an industrial property is a significant factor. Locating industrial real estate entails analysis of labor, raw materials, utilities, distribution, and taxes. In order to assess the requirements of locating a specific type of industry, the manager must be familiar with the special problems relating to these criteria. It is seldom possible for an industry to find a location that is ideal from all points of view; hence, site selection must represent the most favorable compromise.

So-called *industrial parks* have become popular in recent years. These parks are merely industrial subdivisions designed to accommodate light manufacturing, warehouses, research, assembly, and industrial office buildings. Virtually all industrial parks offer land to comparatively small land users (one to 15 acres) in restricted surroundings. In most cases the land is sold to users who either build or lease back their buildings. Seldom do these properties require the services of a professional property manager.

Loft Buildings

The type of industrial property most frequently managed by the professional property manager is the *loft building,* a structure of two or more stories designed for industrial use. Loft buildings originally were developed to accommodate the needs of small manufacturers who had to be near urban rail transportation. They are now largely obsolete economically, and few loft buildings have been built in the past 25 years.

Loft buildings have been occupied less and less by firms actually manufacturing goods and more and more by quasicommercial establishments that do not need to be housed in finished office buildings. A large part of this new occupancy consists of printing and allied arts, semiwarehousing and distribution activities, and bulk office spaces. One factor in the changed occupancy of loft buildings has been the sharp increase in office space rental rates. Logical office space users who cannot afford the rentals charged for conventional office space have turned to less desirable quarters in less prestigious locations. The loft building adjacent to a commercial area is ideal for this type of tenant. With minor alterations, many loft buildings have been converted into office space suitable for those who do not require luxury quarters.

The rental value of loft space is set by the level of demand and the quality of the space itself. The manager's analysis should be based on a study of the competitive market for loft space weighed against the advantages of the building's location. Rental value also may be influenced by the services and facilities of the property, although usually these are quite limited and not as important as in other types of buildings.

Miniwarehouses

A recent development in the real estate industry is the *miniwarehouse,* a facility that provides secure, self-storage units to private individuals and businesses on a rental basis.

The storage units range from closet-size to room-size. The monthly rental rate, which depends on the unit size, usually is much lower than the cost of leasing space in a moving and storage warehouse.

The demand for this type of storage space stems from several factors. First, more people are living in apartments and condominiums, which usually have little storage space. Second, as a result of today's affluent society, many people have more personal and household items than can be stored at home. Third, with increased emphasis on record keeping, many businesses have need for more storage space than their offices provide. Further, with high office rental rates, it makes sense economically to store materials in less expensive miniwarehouse units.

Management's role in miniwarehouses ideally begins in the development stage and involves marketing the storage units, budgeting operations, and accounting for income and operating expenses. The property manager also is charged with establishing applicable policies and procedures, such as the hours renters may have access to their units and the level of security provided.

Mart Buildings

Mart buildings have been developed in most larger cities since World War I. A *mart building* is a multistory, finished-interior property that is a cross between a retail arcade and a loft building. It is used principally by wholesalers and jobbers to display sample merchandise. The management problems peculiar to mart buildings revolve around traffic, renting, and special maintenance.

Most mart buildings are faced with the problem of occupancy peaks which occur seasonally for special market periods. Large numbers of buyers gather: elevators are crowded, restaurants are overtaxed, and entry control is difficult. Mart buildings must be designed to accommodate these busy periods—adequate corridor width, elevator capacity, etc.

Most mart buildings are promoted around a nucleus of specialized occupancy. There are furniture marts, merchandise marts, clothing marts. To succeed, a mart property must serve a broad trading area and attract a volume of buyers to the events staged by the tenants. Leasing this type of property requires a high degree of creative talent and a high level of public relations skill in establishing relationships with the trade groups involved.

Summary

An office building is a structure in which services are provided, as opposed to one in which products are manufactured or sold or people reside. Traditionally, office buildings were located solely in downtown centers. While many office buildings still have sites in central business districts, increasing numbers of office buildings in outlying locations—i.e., suburban office buildings—are representing a share of the office market.

The objective in analyzing an office building and its market is to determine how it compares with the competition. Office buildings are ranked as Grade A, B, C, or D according to 12 criteria: (1) location; (2) neighborhood; (3) transportation; (4) prestige; (5) appearance; (6) lobby; (7) elevators; (8) corridors; (9) office interiors; (10) tenant services; (11) management; and (12) tenant mix.

Based on an office building's rating and a study of current market rents, a rental schedule for the building's space can be established. This rental schedule is applied to the building's rentable area, which may differ from its total area. The most accepted means of measuring rental area is the method adopted by the Building Owners and Managers Association (i.e., the BOMA method).

The marketing of office space is, essentially, a four-step process. First, the property manager develops a list of logical prospective tenants. Second, the interest of these prospects is aroused through a promotional campaign that emphasizes the building's price advantage, the increased efficiency and prestige it offers, and its economic advantage. Third, the space is shown, either in the form of a model office, a vacant office interior, or, in the case of a building under construction, color renderings of office interiors. Fourth, the prospective office user is qualified as to its business reputation, service requirements, and space requirements.

Assuming the office space meets the needs of the prospective tenant and the prospect meets the selection criteria, the property manager proceeds with the space planning process. Here, the office user's space and service requirements, financial restrictions, and aesthetic preferences are interpreted as a functional office interior. When the plans are approved, a lease can be negotiated.

Most office leases are long term and contain escalation clauses. An escalation clause permits rental rates to be adjusted, usually once a year, throughout the term of the lease in proportion to increases in operating expenses. The lease also should state the utilities and services that are to be provided by the landlord and assign responsibility for expenses connected with these services. Most office tenants try to negotiate options; options to expand, renew, and cancel are most common. Options benefit the tenant, not the landlord, and should be granted only if market conditions force them.

Of special concern to the office building manager are maintenance and security. The principal tasks associated with these two management functions are: cleaning elevator equipment and keeping it in working condition; arranging for night cleaning crews; establishing an ongoing security program; and implementing emergency plans for fires and bomb threats.

There is a wide range of opportunities in the office building management field. For example, some office buildings are designed for a very narrow tenant mix; medical and dental arts buildings, legal arts buildings, industrial and loft buildings, miniwarehouses, and mart buildings are key examples of structures that require specialized management.

REVIEW QUESTIONS

1. Define *bulk space user*.
2. Define *suburban office building*. What factors have led to development of these buildings? List them by importance.
3. Why are office buildings ranked by grade?
4. What 12 points would a property manager check in evaluating the desirability of an office building?
5. How are the following buildings rated for prestige: financial, professional, jewelers, advertising agencies? Justify the answer.
6. What is meant by *physical proximity*, and how does this affect an office building?
7. On what points would a property manager grade a building's elevator system?

8. Define *tenant mix*. What impact does this have on the building's rental value?

9. What is the *BOMA method*? What is *rentable space*? Why is it important to measure space accurately?

10. Can a property manager expect to keep an office building 100-percent occupied during normal market conditions through unsolicited inquiries for space? Why or why not?

11. How important is the preparation of a list of prospects for the rental of office space? Explain.

12. How could a property manager stimulate the curiosity of a prospect who had expressed no previous interest in an office building?

13. There is a vacancy in an office building that is 80-percent occupied by wholesale jewelers. The property manager is approached by a luggage jobber, a furrier who sells at retail, and a wholesale optical concern. There are no present tenants in any of these classifications. All need the same amount of space. What desirable features does the building possess for each? Which is the most desirable? Why?

14. Define *space planning*. What bearing does this have on the marketing program?

15. Give two specific ways of convincing an office user to lease a particular space.

16. When should a tenant be expected to pay for alterations?

17. When might it be necessary to turn down a prospective office tenant because of space reasons? Because of service requirements? Give three examples of each.

18. Define *standard tenant improvement allowance*. What effect can this allowance have on lease negotiations?

19. Define *option*. When is an option to the landlord's advantage? When is it to the tenant's advantage?

20. Describe the problems associated with cleaning an office building.

21. Define *special-purpose property*. Name three kinds of special-purpose properties. What factors make their management easy? What makes it difficult?

Chapter
Thirteen

Shopping Centers
and Retail Properties

CHANGES IN ECONOMIC, social, and political attitudes create changes in the types of properties that are developed. In no other category of real estate have these changes been more noticeable than in *retail properties,* in which goods and services are sold directly to individuals and households. Consequently, retail property management, and specifically the management of shopping centers and strip stores, has acquired a new dimension.

Historical Perspective

Aside from purchasing simple necessities (food and household items), shopping is a multipurpose activity. A shopper usually plans several purchases for one trip rather than a single item. There is an advantage, therefore, to a center that offers commodities and services. As a result of shopping habits and the retailer's need to be accessible to the greatest number of shoppers, retail districts first were developed in downtown business areas and near public transportation facilities. But urban *decentralization*—the decline of the original urban core and simultaneous suburban growth—altered this trend.

Cities expand as their populations increase. Growth patterns reflect the topography of the area and assume one of three general shapes: (1) the *square city,* which develops approximately the same distance in each direction (e.g., Indianapolis or Dallas); (2) the *fan-shaped city,* in which growth is concentrated behind a natural barrier, such as a lake or river (e.g., Chicago or St. Louis); and (3) the

rectangular city, in which geographical conditions prevent growth
in two directions but encourage it in the other two (e.g., Manhattan
or Birmingham).

In all of these types of cities, major retail districts remained
largely in downtown areas until several developments affected
retailing:

- The development of the automobile enabled Americans to move
  farther from downtown business districts and rely less on public
  transportation.
- The emergence of chain stores allowed smaller retail units to
  offer merchandise on a competitive basis with large downtown
  stores and in more convenient locations.
- Advances in electronic technology created an almost unlimited
  distribution of power and permitted growth away from central
  cities.
- The widespread use of consumer credit encouraged the purchase of consumer goods.
- The construction of highways gave both public and private
  transportation greater accessibility and flexibility, a fact that
  opened up large land areas for improvement.
- A developing mass-production and mass-distribution economy
  introduced standard brands that could be purchased anywhere
  at similar prices. This factor provided the background for the
  decentralization trend referred to as *trade inception.* It applies
  to the technique of locating a new point of retail supply that
  lies between the consumer and the existing source of supply
  and thus is more convenient to the consumer.
- A wide variety of recently introduced goods and services desirable to society as a whole (i.e., automobiles, radios, cosmetics,
  ready-made clothes, laundry service) strained the family budget
  and forced retailers to reduce prices. One means of accomplishing this was by introducing self-service, which decreased labor
  costs by allowing the consumer to select merchandise. The
  supermarket was the most obvious outgrowth of this trend.

From these occurrences, and the tendency to cluster retail establishments, the modern shopping center developed. The first shopping
centers were freestanding groups of stores, with limited parking,
located on the outskirts of urban areas. They were convenient retail
outlets for the new suburban neighborhoods. A typical center would

contain a grocery store, drugstore, and several small shops offering other goods. Most of these were *strip developments,* which were straight lines of stores quite narrow in proportion to their length. After World War II, larger, more comprehensive projects were planned. Soon major retail and department stores, long established in downtown areas, relocated in the suburbs for economic survival. Shopping areas continued to develop in the suburbs, and larger projects were constructed.

Property Analysis

A shopping center is more than a group of retail establishments. A shopping center differs from a retail district in that it is usually located in a suburban area, it is planned as a single project, on-site parking is provided, and there is a unified image. According to the Urban Land Institute, the term *shopping center* refers to:

> A group of architecturally unified commercial establishments built on a site which is planned, developed, owned, and managed as an operating unit related in its location, size, and type of shops to the trade area that the unit serves. The unit provides on-site parking in definite relationship to the types and total size of the stores. (*Shopping Center Development Handbook* [Washington, D.C.: Urban Land Institute, 1977])

Shopping Center Classification

Shopping centers are classified according to their function. These classifications are based on the nature and variety of merchandise they offer and the size of the trading areas of the individual stores. There are four primary categories of shopping centers:

- *Neighborhood center.* The neighborhood shopping center is designed to provide convenience shopping to satisfy the day-to-day needs of consumers in the immediate area. Although shopping center classifications are based on function, not size, the convenience center usually is the smallest of the three types, with approximately 25,000 to 75,000 square feet. It serves a population of 2,500 to 40,000 shoppers. Typically, the neighborhood center takes the strip form.
- *Community center.* A better selection of merchandise is offered in the community shopping center. In addition to certain convenience items, it also offers apparel and home furnishings and

often has a department or variety store. Its size is approximately 100,000 to 250,000 square feet, and it serves a population of 40,000 to 150,000.

- *Regional center.* The regional shopping center, frequently designed as a mall, is supported by at least one major department store and includes other stores that, together, offer a broad selection of general merchandise. It serves a large residential sector and requires from 300,000 to 1,000,000 square feet. When its area is greater than 750,000 square feet, this center is referred to as a *super-regional.*
- *Specialty center.* In recent years, specialty or theme shopping centers have become popular. These centers offer fashion goods, atmospheric restaurants, gift items, and other specialty merchandise and cater to upper-income discretionary spending. Specialty centers are usually small (rarely more than 250,000 square feet) but attract shoppers from a wide business area.

Evaluation of Facilities

Determining a shopping center's classification is only the first step in performing the detailed property analysis that is so essential to its management. The procedure in performing a shopping center analysis is similar to that for other property types. There are some special considerations, however.

For instance, the property manager must be able to compute the total floor area of the center according to industry standards. The term *gross leasable area (GLA)* has been adopted as a measurement of the total floor area designed for tenant occupancy and their exclusive use.

The property manager should note that gross leasable area differs from *gross floor area,* which includes space that is not used and occupied exclusively by individual tenants. This space is termed the center's *common area.* Common areas include public washrooms, corridors, stairways, equipment rooms, management offices, storage areas, lobbies and mall areas (enclosed or not), and parking areas. Common areas are not leasable to tenants but are necessary to a center's operation.

The property manager also must consider the center's parking facilities, especially as they relate to the gross leasable area. Parking is an essential facility for shopping centers, and sufficient spaces, compatible with the size and function of the center, are necessary. In this respect, it is helpful if the property manager is familiar with the term *parking index,* which is the number of parking spaces per 1,000 square feet of gross leasable area. The parking index is useful in comparing the shopping area with the parking demand. According to the Urban Land Institute, the commonly accepted standard parking index for shopping centers is 5.5 (or 5.5 parking spaces per 1,000 square feet of gross leasable area).

Factors other than adequate space must be considered, too: parking facilities should be well maintained, free of litter, and marked with easily understood traffic signs. Access to the shopping center's parking facility is also important to its overall success. To attract retail traffic, a center must be available and safe and easy to enter and leave.

Location Analysis

A complete property analysis must contain an evaluation of the shopping center's location. All merchants prefer to locate where the highest volume of profitable business can be obtained. Traditionally, this would be an established site where the most consumer-minded traffic already exists.

Obviously, the volume of traffic that passes by a retail site indicates the volume of sales that can be realistically estimated. Yet, traffic volume alone does not necessarily ensure an attractive retail market. Traffic must be qualified in its volume and also in its attitude. For example, thousands of persons pass through commuter railroad stations in major cities each day. However, areas near these terminals are not always profitable for prospective store proprietors. People are in a hurry, and their shopping is confined to impulse purchases, such as last-minute buying of liquor, groceries, and flowers. In order to benefit the merchant, people must be in a mood for shopping and come to the location primarily for this reason.

Aside from a few isolated merchants whose success did not depend on their location, retail sites originally were established because of consumer, rather than merchant, preference. Traditionally, if a storekeeper desired to do a large volume of business, the required rental for a location in an established urban retail district had to be paid, and traffic assured success.

The principle behind the development of the first shopping centers was that, instead of relying on established locations that enjoyed consumer pressure, a group of retailers could select an appropriate place to create a cluster of stores. These would, in themselves, attract numerous buyers away from existing retail establishments.

Developers first experimented with one-of-a-kind shopping centers. They persuaded one department store (usually a major local establishment), one mass-market chain department store, one local and one chain women's store, one men's wear store, one sportswear store, and one sporting goods store to join in the plan to create heavy consumer pressure by combining their drawing power. Some developers, who believed more incentive was needed, also included one supermarket and another convenience goods store.

When locations were chosen carefully, this theory proved extremely profitable. Not only did developers earn satisfactory returns on their investments, but the yield on land (usually bought at acreage prices) soared tremendously. In fact, some major local and national chains soon realized that their contributions to the centers' attraction were sufficiently profitable for them to buy their own land and develop centers themselves.

While the first centers claimed one or two major department stores as anchor units and a one-of-a-kind assortment, the newer mall-type regional centers are planned around as many as five anchor establishments and a wide variety of both chain and local support stores, all of the *primary-goods* type (i.e., clothing, shoes). In many cases, developers acquire more land than is needed for the center itself, and then facilities for *secondary goods* (i.e., furniture, appliances), as well as cinemas and apartment and office buildings, are constructed. Regional shopping centers often attract other types of development.

Trading Area Analysis

The analysis of a shopping center's *trading area* is a study of the traffic habits and purchasing power of the people living within the given area. Since new centers do not create new buying power but, instead, attract customers from other shopping facilities, it is important to evaluate competing businesses in the area.

Given a shopping center to manage, the property manager should obtain a map of the community on a scale large enough to show the individual blocks. The next step in the analysis is to locate all competitive enterprises. For example, if the object is to judge a neighborhood strip center's success at a given location, the map should include all competitive operations. Notations about parking and probable volume are helpful, too. After these competitive operations have been identified, the map should define the principal traffic arteries for private transportation and all public transportation lines serving the area.

As a rule, consumers will shop at the subject site when they are closer to it than to other competitive establishments of equal attraction. A boundary line can be drawn on the map to outline the trading area formed.

Analyzing the trading area also requires estimating the number of potential consumers located within this bounded area. The manager should obtain a copy of the latest census and identify the census tracts that lie within the area. By analyzing the census data, information can be learned about the number and composition of families located in the area. If the area's rapid growth has made the data obsolete, then the manager must interpret growth that has occurred since the last census.

A measurement of the income level of the population within the trading area is desirable, not only in terms of total available dollars but also in terms of expendable income by retail categories. Just as it was important to perform a locational analysis to evaluate shopper's attitudes, it is also important that potential customers can afford the available merchandise. The purchasing level of consumer traffic and the quality of merchandise must match. It is a poor merchandise practice to locate a high-quality center in a mass-market shopping area or to locate a mass-market center in a sparsely populated, high-quality shopping area.

Market Analysis

While families must have homes and businesses must have offices from which to operate, retailers are more difficult to quantify and qualify as users of space. There is a retail market, just as there is a housing market and an office space market. Yet, one can imagine a housing unit and a square foot of office space but find it difficult to picture a standard unit of retail space.

The latest Census of Business lists 1,934,500 retail establishments, ranging from one-man, mom-and-pop stores to giants such as Sears, Roebuck and Company. However, the average retail establishment employs only nine people.

The market for stores cannot be measured exactly, since it is impossible to determine the number of potential proprietors who are considering becoming store tenants or owners at any given time. However, analyzing two factors may be helpful: first, the occupancy of store spaces (community-wide or in specific neighborhoods), and, second, the general trends in the retail business. Data on the former can be obtained by a survey, and on the latter from business statistics relating to local or national operations. Retail trade reflects consumer numerical presence, earning power, employment, and attitude. Fortunately, these statistics usually are available. Occupancy ratios for store properties are obtained easily, since vacant stores are visually discernible, and, therefore, vacancy can be estimated with some degree of accuracy.

Marketing Retail Space

Under normal circumstances, marketing space in a shopping center is the job of its developer. Because getting the financing for a project often depends on a sufficient number of tenants committing to leases, a developer must obtain the most significant leases before proceeding.

Two criteria must be met before most *anchor tenants* can be induced into making a lease commitment. First, the developer must have a successful background. While it is not essential for the developer to have succeeded with a shopping center, an established managerial record is necessary. Second, the proposed center's location must be acceptable on three bases: (1) It must be a point of high traffic concentration, served by major highways and with direct access to them. (2) It must be in the center of a trading area with sufficient population density, purchasing power, and growth potential to support the planned retail facilities. And (3) competitive retail establishments must not pose a serious threat to its success.

Once the center's construction is assured by enough leases to obtain financing, the developer usually engages a property manager to assume its routine administration and the rest of its marketing.

The process of acquiring tenants for any kind of shopping center—even those in established facilities—requires diligence and determination. Prospects must be selected who would most benefit the owner from the standpoints of their rent-paying ability, their potential contribution to consumer traffic, and their willingness to cooperate in the center's overall objectives. After initial identification, prospects must be contacted routinely, either by mail or telephone or personal visit, until a realistically qualified prospect list is formed, which is comprised of retailers who would benefit by becoming tenants.

Marketing retail space, on a practical basis, means presenting an opportunity to those already in a particular kind of business. There really is no way to identify or contact people who may consider becoming merchants other than to advertise, hoping that they will identify themselves.

While display advertising in newspapers and general magazines may attract the attention of some prospective retail tenants, most people interested in this space do not check for retail sites in the newspaper. More often, they drive through desirable areas and look for signs on available locations. Displaying attractive and readable billboards and "for rent" signs, therefore, is important in merchandising available space in shopping centers. Also to be considered in planning marketing strategy are concise and tastefully designed brochures for distribution to potential tenants, direct mail campaigns directed to retailers who are potential tenants, and the placement of advertisements in trade journals that reach specific groups of prospective tenants (e.g., laundry industry journals).

Shopping Center Tenancy

Tenants are the chief factor in making the shopping center a profitable investment. For this reason, securing strong key tenants and suitable supplementary tenants cannot be stressed too much.

Tenant Mix

In assuming responsibility for a new shopping center, the property manager's duty is to select a combination of tenants who will make the center the most complete shopping facility possible. This collection of tenants is known as the *tenant mix* and is composed of one or several anchor tenants plus a number of *satellite tenants.*

The most desirable key tenant for a shopping center depends on its type. In a neighborhood center, a supermarket is an ideal key tenant. In community centers, key tenants include variety stores, junior department stores, and discount stores. For large regional centers, major department stores are desirable anchors. The market analysis will indicate which kind of anchor tenant has the most drawing power.

In determining the ideal tenant mix, the manager also must consider the supplementary retail tenants. Again, the center's classification will affect directly the type of tenants needed to increase the center's business. A neighborhood center will offer mostly convenience goods stores, while the community center's tenant mix will have more variety. Figure 13.1 includes the types of tenants usually

FIGURE 13.1

Tenants Most Frequently Found in Community Shopping Centers

General Merchandise	Gifts/Specialty
Junior department store	Cards and gifts
Variety store	Jewelry and Cosmetics
Food	Jewelry
Supermarket	Drugs
Food Service	Drug store
Restaurant without liquor	Other Retail
Restaurant with liquor	Yard goods
Fast food/Carry out	Personal Services
Clothing	Beauty
Ladies' specialty	Barber
Ladies' ready-to-wear	Cleaner and dyers
Men's wear	Financial
Shoes	Banks
Family shoes	Offices
Home Appliances/Music	Medical and dental
Radio, Tv, Hi-Fi	

found in community shopping centers. (Figure 13.1 is taken from *Dollars and Cents of Shopping Centers: 1978,* an analytical report on income and expenses in shopping center operations published by the Urban Land Institute, Washington, D.C., and invaluable to the shopping center manager.)

Ideally, the property manager assumes the management of a shopping center when it is new. But, this does not always happen. In assuming management of an existing facility already tenanted, the manager may have no immediate opportunity to restructure the tenant mix. However, as leases come up for renewal, or in the unfortunate event that tenants default on their leases, the property manager can replace these tenants with retailers who will create a more profitable tenant composition.

Tenant Selection

Certain criteria for accepting retail tenants should be imposed, as they are in all tenant selection. One of these is the retail business's history of success. This is especially important for a new shopping center. There may be a slow period until the center is recognized in the marketplace, and the retailer must be financially sound enough to get through the initial slump.

Selection also should be based on the tenant's compatibility with the other tenants, the design of the center, and the consumer market; the estimated drawing power of the tenant; its merchandising and advertising policy; the parking facilities that are needed by the tenant; and the tenant's housekeeping ability and special maintenance requirements.

Tenant Placement

Not only must the property manager carefully select the appropriate retail tenants for a given shopping center, but there also must be careful consideration in locating these tenants within the facility.

The tenant placement process ideally should ensure a maximum interaction among the various tenants. One way to achieve this is to place key tenants so that shoppers must walk past the other, smaller retail establishments in order to reach them. This is the reason that major department stores are located at either end of a mall. Anchors have drawing power, and walking from one major store to another exposes shoppers to the other tenants.

Tenant placement also requires the property manager to weigh the effect of specific tenants on parking. A supermarket in a neighborhood center, for example, creates a heavy demand for parking spaces. This is also true of personal service businesses, such as beauty shops and coin laundries. These kinds of tenants should be located as close to parking facilities as possible.

The clustering of tenants active in the same type of retail operation is another factor for the manager to consider. According to *Shopping Center Development Handbook* (Washington, D.C.: Urban Land Institute, 1977):

> Seasoned leasing brokers, appraisers, landlords, and shopping center operators have learned many things about grouping certain kinds of businesses:
> - Men's stores—shoes, clothing and haberdashery, sporting goods—tend to swell each other's volume.
> - Similarly, women's apparel, shoes, and millinery and children's clothes and toys—the soft lines—prosper in proximity to one another.
> - Food products do well when grouped together—groceries, meat and fish markets, delicatessens, bakeries, doughnut shops, and confectioners.
> - Stores which sell personal services and conveniences naturally go together, but in shopping centers they should be as close as possible to the parking area.

Rental Rates

Although the cost of creating and maintaining any kind of space does not in itself determine its current rental value, it does figure importantly in an investor's decision to erect a building. If these costs plus the cost of land cannot produce a satisfactory return on the invested capital, the investor obviously will not proceed with construction.

Once the decision to proceed has been made, or if the structure already exists, rental rates must be set for the space. Various methods are employed in establishing rates for retail operations. The most common are space rental, franchise rental, percentage rental, and fixed-dollar rental.

Space Rental

One of the methods property managers use to establish rental rates on retail space is termed *space rental*. If, for example, a store were built in a location never before used for retail purposes, its rental will be fixed by the cost of the land purchased, the construction cost of improvements and depreciation, and the cost of maintaining the finished property. If this works out as "X" dollars per square foot, then "X" is the cost of renting the space. The program must determine if a store in this location can produce "X" dollars of sales per square foot; the sales must be sufficient to justify the investment involved.

Franchise Rental

In most cases, retail rent values are not space rentals but belong to a second type that shall be called *franchise rentals*. The price of the retail location does not have a direct relationship with the space involved but rather with the location of that space and the potential customers who pass by it.

This franchise principle operates in a retail unit located in an established shopping center, in which adjoining units have established a large volume of consumer traffic. If the volume of consumer traffic represents a high business potential to a prospective tenant, then leasing the store does not stem from an abstract desire to possess a certain area of floor space but results instead from a desire to profit from this potential business volume. The franchise, then, sets the value, not the space. It is a characteristic of the location of the store building and is not a quality of the improvement. A prospective tenant who only needs space accommodation rarely will pay a rental higher than can be justified by an adequate return on current construction costs plus land value.

A commercial tenant's first objective is to obtain volume business. This volume of business must stem from the consumer pressure created by the traffic concentration.

In analyzing a location, a prospective tenant must appraise the value of consumer traffic in terms of its cost. The tenant may decide that it is not necessary to pay a high rental in order to obtain a satisfactory traffic volume, that spending less on advertising will produce customers at a lower cost per person. Operators of larger national chains may decide that their reputations, along with current advertising, make it unnecessary to pay franchise rentals. In typical situations, however, franchise rentals produce the highest consumer pressure for a business, and most prospective tenants must pay this higher rental to attain a large sales volume.

Percentage Rental

Especially because of the inflation in recent years, space valuation has been determined more often by a fluctuating franchise payment method, known as the *percentage rent* and negotiated in the percentage lease.

Percentage rent (based on a percentage of the gross income of the business, often with a guaranteed minimum rent) is a means of continually adjusting the franchise value of a given location according to its business worth to a retail merchant. Under the percentage lease, the landlord, in a way, is a partner of the tenant. If the tenant's business succeeds, then the landlord's rental is high. If the tenant's business declines, then the landlord's income declines. The fixed minimum rent protects the landlord to some extent from a serious loss of rental income due to the tenant's poor sales performance.

The percentage lease, however, does not eliminate the manager's responsibility to produce the highest possible net revenue from the property. In order to be acceptable from the landlord's standpoint, a percentage lease should be made only after two factors have been considered carefully.

First, the type of business scheduled for occupancy must have the best chance to attain the highest possible volume under the most favorable percentage terms. The manager cannot simply locate a tenant in a given place at a percentage rental that is currently acceptable for that type of tenancy. For example, a store has been leased to a tavern at an eight-percent rental, which is in line with what taverns ordinarily pay. The manager may well believe that this situation is satisfactory. But, maybe the highest potential use of this store is not a tavern but rather a men's clothing store, in which an established percentage rental of six percent would produce a substantially higher net income. It is the manager's responsibility, then, to continually review all retail space and the type of tenancy, in order to obtain the maximum income.

A second factor to be considered is that the leasing of space on percentage to a given tenant results in a limited partnership, at least to the extent that the landlord's rental income depends on the tenant's ability and resources. If the store operator is an alert and resourceful merchandiser with sound financing and aggressive methods, then the landlord's income will be substantially higher than if the tenant lacks the ability to produce at the highest potential level. It is the manager's responsibility, then, to examine operations of percentage-base tenants to be sure they are obtaining the maximum sales volume.

The actual percentage of gross business income that is charged depends largely on how that type of business relates to business volume, the cost of doing business, profit margin, and inventory turnover rates. Slower turnover usually indicates lower business volume but a higher profit margin. An automobile dealer, for instance, generally experiences slower turnover than a liquor store. Consequently, the automobile dealer would be charged a lower percentage rate than the liquor dealer. Percentage tables have been published by various real estate management organizations, which serve as general guides when negotiating lease terms.

While most percentage lesase are based on gross income, one method, adopted only on occasion, bases the value of the space on the net revenue of the lessee. This special form of lease has been used so far when the space rental is virtually nil, and the franchise rental is highly questionable.

An example involves a bank lease in a large midwestern city. The ground floors of a multistory office building were designed to accommodate a major bank. The entrance to the property contained a stairway to large banking rooms, and it was not practical for these quarters to be used for another purpose. The bank for which the space was designed no longer occupied the space, which became vacant. Obviously, the only prospective tenant would be a new bank. It was equally apparent, however, that no new financial institution initially could afford a space rental that would allow the building owners an adequate return on their investment. Moreover, from judging economic trends, it was determined that percentage rentals are not reasonable for banking institutions, since the fluctuating gross deposits produce rentals that are either too low or too high in relation to space values.

In this instance, a lease based on a percentage of net profits of the financial institution was an equitable solution. The landlord agreed, after study, to base the rental on the bank's chances for success. The space was valueless without such a tenant, and in order to induce the bank to lease, it was necessary to offer an attractive rent.

Many real estate professionals believe the percentage lease will continue to gain acceptance and resolve the space merchandising problems of many special-purpose buildings.

Fixed-Dollar Rental

For many secondary store properties, the value of store space cannot be determined by space rental computation or by a fluctuating franchise. There is no necessary relationship between the capital invested in building space and the competitive rent value at any given time. Also, percentage leases are impractical for certain types of tenants, either because it is too difficult for the tenant to maintain adequate sales records or because of the possible fraud on the part of the tenant. In these cases, ordinary store rentals are based on three factors: first, comparability with other store rentals in the neighborhood; second, adjustments upward or downward according to their relationship to traffic-producing adjacent stores; and third, adjustments upward or downward to reflect retail trends in the economy.

Certain trends have increased vacancy in obsolete store buildings; they are no longer suitable for retail trade but often useful as offices, repair services, storage, or other nonretail occupancy. In the case of obsolescent retail space, value is set by comparing with uses for office space, store, maintenance space, or other purposes, minus the lack of design conformity.

Lease Document

The lease is a legal record of the conditions of a retail property's operation and management. As such, it clarifies how the property is to function by defining the responsibilities of the landlord to the tenant and the responsibilities of the tenant to the landlord.

If the lease is based on a percentage rental, the document should outline how rentals are to be collected. Monthly collection of percentage rentals, with minimum rents paid in advance and year-end adjustments, are popular. In addition, a percentage lease should allow the property owner to check the tenant's books at any time. Most leases specify that the cost of this audit is the landlord's, except if the audit indicates that the tenant's actual sales vary in excess of a given percentage (usually two percent) of reported sales.

The provisions within shopping center leases are negotiable. A tenant's bargaining position depends on the class to which it belongs. A major department store may be able to dictate to the landlord, since the tenant offers the prestige needed to attract shoppers and other satellite tenants. The anchor's rents are usually very low while satellite tenants, on the other hand, are in a much less favorable bargaining position and usually pay a higher rent.

The terms for which shopping center leases are negotiable likewise vary according to the tenant. For an anchor tenant in a large shopping center, a term of 20 years would not be unreasonable; leases with smaller chain stores or local tenants, however, might extend for only five years. The advantage of shorter-term leases lies in the fact that they provide greater opportunity to negotiate for a higher minimum rental or terminate tenants that do not perform as expected. Neither options nor extensions are common in retail property leases, except with anchor tenants and possibly with restaurants.

Other lease clauses that apply specifically to shopping centers and outline the basis of their operations usually are needed, too. Descriptions of some of the most common clauses follow:

- *Use clause.* A shopping center lease must contain a clause that explicity states how the area being leased will be used. Without this clause, it would be impossible to maintain control over the tenant mix. Often, retailers will request an *exclusive* or *noncompetition clause* that forbids the landlord from leasing space in the center to a competitor. This clause should be avoided for two reasons: first, many property managers believe that competition is healthy and encourages retail activity; second, this type of clause may violate the antitrust provisions of the Sherman Antitrust Act.
- *Radius clause.* A radius clause is a kind of noncompetition clause imposed on the tenant to protect the landlord. Under a radius clause, the tenant agrees not to own or operate another outlet within a specified distance of the center.

- *Escalation clause.* Many shopping center leases (also true of most office building leases) contain rent escalation clauses. This clause permits the rental rate to be adjusted to reflect changes in the operating costs of the property or in the general cost of living. Escalation clauses may be formed in various ways: rental adjustments may be tied to increases in property taxes, operating costs, or a cost-of-living or other index. Increases usually are passed on to tenants on a pro rata basis. Regardless of the type of rent escalation clause used, it should be explained fully in the lease.
- *Common area maintenance clause.* A shopping center's common area includes any area not actually occupied and used by the individual tenants. The center's tenants are still responsible for maintaining this area. A lease clause is necessary to clarify that the tenant must pay a share of the cost of operating and maintaining the center's common area and to state just how these charges will be assessed. Usually, the charges are based on the relationship of the gross leasable area occupied by a given tenant to the total gross leasable area. Fixed charges are imposed in some situations.
- *Merchants' association clause.* The promotional activities of most shopping centers are handled by merchants' associations. When applicable, a lease should contain a clause that establishes this association, provides for mandatory membership by all tenants, and specifies the tenant's contribution to the association's budget. (More on the merchants' association follows.)
- *Sign restriction clause.* Control of promotional signs at a shopping center is essential in creating a unified image. Each lease should contain a clause that restricts the use of outdoor signs (and, for enclosed malls, indoor signs) and other graphic displays.

Depending on the leasehold arrangement, other lease clauses may be needed. Certainly, if the tenant is responsible for any other charges in addition to the base rent these should be noted. For example, some retail tenants pay the property taxes and insurance on the space they lease.

Tenant Relations

Tenant relations as it affects retail properties has a special function within the field of real estate management. One characteristic of retail properties is that individual tenants must attract consumers for their products. In most shopping centers, tenants organize into *merchants' associations* in order to advance their common interest. Based on an equitable allocation of expenses among the tenants, they plan advertising, stage promotional events, book entertainment, plan appropriate interior and exterior decorations, and strive to widen and intensify the center's trading area penetration. While these associations may vary from center to center according to original tenancy arrangements, management is usually a strong ally to their efforts. Often, management is a dues-paying member of the merchants' association, contributes as much as 25 percent of the association's budget, and directs its activities.

When percentage leases are employed, the greater the revenue to the tenants, the greater the income to the property. If the property manager is to maximize the property's income—and in turn the management fee—becoming involved in the shopping center's promotion and publicity is necessary. This is why many property managers have assumed more control in promoting the shopping center and its tenants. They encourage balanced promotional events to meet market demands, give financial direction, and actually participate in the promotional activities that are planned. Often, a promotion director is hired to function as an integral part of the management team. At other times, the promotion director is employed and paid by the merchants' association.

Another tenant-related matter the property manager encounters is store hours. Many retail landlord-tenant problems center on this issue. Since, with a percentage lease, the rental is related to the sales volume, the landlord will encourage maximum store hours to obtain the highest gross sales. The merchant, on the other hand, is keenly aware that the store's operating expenses are directly related to the hours of operation. If traffic is not heavy enough during late night and Sunday hours, the tenant may lose money at an increasing rate as the volume per hour declines. One solution to the problem is for the lease to state the minimum hours the store must be open. Usually, smaller tenants are required to maintain the same business hours as anchor tenants.

Maintenance and Security

While tenants are responsible for maintaining their individual interior areas, the manager must recruit and supervise whatever staff are required, or employ the necessary independent contractors, for maintaining, cleaning, and servicing public areas and parking lots and providing interior and exterior landscaping, cleaning, snow removal, lighting, and security. It is important for these spaces to be under continual observation to preserve cleanliness and order.

Certainly, the complexity of maintaining the retail property varies with the center's size, as well as its geographic location and the type of leases that are in effect. While strip centers usually need only exterior building maintenance and upkeep of parking facilities, enclosed regional malls need attention for heating, air conditioning, and waste disposal systems. There also is a need for interior housekeeping.

In providing security for a shopping center, the property manager must satisfy various interests. The property owner is concerned with preserving the real estate investment. The tenant requires protection of employees and merchandise, as well as assurance that the center will maintain a high image. The shopper is concerned with personal safety. How the manager handles these problems depends on the type of community in which the center is located and the size of the center. The solutions range from a full-time, armed, and uniformed security force—to electronic security and communication devices—to plainclothes detectives.

Shopping centers are regarded more frequently by the public as public property. This attitude has resulted in new security problems. Social and labor demonstrators, political candidates, and charitable solicitors see shopping centers (especially enclosed malls) as a prime place for their views to be heard. Young people regard centers as a place to congregate, and the result often is disorderliness. These problems must be handled tactfully. The property manager may consider establishing guidelines to assure that all groups who wish to use the center are treated equally. The policies could include use of loudspeakers, harassment of shoppers, and general conduct that might disrupt business or offend the public.

Summary

Retail trade, as a general rule, follows consumers. As the population has moved to outlying suburban areas, shopping centers have developed, creating a new opportunity for property managers.

A shopping center is a facility in which a number of retail establishments are located and many consumer needs may be satisfied.

There are four principal categories of shopping centers: (1) neighborhood center; (2) community center; (3) regional center; and (4) specialty center. A center's classification depends on the nature and variety of merchandise it offers and the size of its trading area.

In undertaking a shopping center account, the property manager must perform a property analysis. This includes computing its gross leasable area (the total floor area designed for tenant use and occupancy) and the gross floor area (which includes common areas as well as tenant areas). Complementing this study is an evaluation of the facility's parking facilities, with emphasis on the relationship between the gross leasable area and the number of parking spaces. Also important to the shopping center analysis is an evaluation of its location. The desirable retail site has a high volume of consumer-minded traffic passing by regularly.

Another evaluation also is required—a trading area analysis. This is a study of the traffic habits and purchasing power of the people who live within the area served by the center. The size of the trading area depends on the classification of the center. This analysis should reveal the center's likelihood of success.

The task of marketing shopping center space often is assumed before the project is off the drawing board, since few lenders will make mortgage commitments until anchor tenants have agreed to sign leases. Once these anchors are committed, the job of securing satellite tenants gets underway. All of these tenants must meet criteria regarding their business history and compatibility with the center's design and the other tenants that make up the tenant mix. Once selected, tenants also must be placed thoughtfully. Tenants should be located within the center with the idea of ensuring maximum interaction among them.

There are four principal types of retail property rentals: (1) space rental; (2) franchise rental; (3) percentage rental; and (4) fixed-dollar rental. The most common is the percentage rent method, under which the rent is based on a flat fee plus a percentage of either the tenant's gross or net income.

In negotiating the rent, as well as other lease terms, the large anchor tenant has more bargaining power than the small satellite tenant. Still, most landlords will insist on clauses that: define the use of the rental area; prohibit competition; permit rents to be adjusted; make membership to a merchants' association mandatory; require tenants to share in the cost of common area maintenance; and restrict the use of promotional signs.

Tenant and public relations assume more importance to the manager of a shopping center. With percentage leases in effect, the manager's ability to maximize the owner's objectives depends on the retail success of the center's stores. Merchants' associations are designed to advance the interests of the tenants and, hence, the property owner. Similarly, the property manager must strive to establish a reputable community image in order to obtain the community's support.

REVIEW QUESTIONS

1. What are meant by *square, rectangular,* and *fan-shaped cities?* How did they arise?

2. What occasioned the development of suburbia? List the causes in order of importance. What impact has this had on the retail property industry?

3. What are the four principal types of shopping centers? Why does a property manager need to determine a center's classification?

4. Define *gross leasable area, gross floor area,* and *parking index.* What is the relationship between the three terms?

5. What is the object of store location? What is meant by a *multipurpose shopper?* In seeking a location, what does a merchant consider of greatest importance?

6. Define *trading area.* In analyzing a trading area, what data does the property manager need? Where can this information be obtained?

7. Define *anchor tenant* and *satellite tenant.* How do the two tenants interrelate? Why is tenant placement important to the shopping center management process?

8. List shopping center tenant selection criteria in order of importance. Justify the order.

9. Explain the theory behind the *percentage rent.* What are its advantages and disadvantages to the tenant? To the landlord?

10. Why is the anchor tenant in a strong bargaining position when a lease is negotiated? What effect does this have on the satellite tenant?

11. What caused the wide usage of the percentage lease? How does it differ from a residential lease?

12. Explain the difference between a percentage rental agreement and a partnership.

13. What is the role of the property manager with respect to the merchants' association?

14. A group of social protestors have gathered inside a regional mall and are disrupting business. How does the property manager handle this problem?

15. Define *radius clause, escalation clause, common area maintenance clause,* and *sign control clause.* Why does the landlord insist on these provisions? Why would the tenant not want them?

Entrepreneurial Role of Real Estate Management

The Real Estate
Management Office

To HAVE A BUSINESS of one's own is the common ambition of most American workers. Although not all property managers will have the opportunity to form their own firms, there is an accepted course of action for those who will.

Obviously, the mechanics of forming and operating a property management business depend on size and resources. An individual property manager starting a business will encounter very different problems than a corporation forming a property management department. However, while the techniques must be adjusted to the situation, the principles are the same. First, a base of operation must be established, and a formula for computing the management fee must be determined. Then, the property manager is faced with the most difficult part of opening a real estate management office—obtaining that first management contract.

Establishing the Management Firm

Although the practice of real estate management is a profession, when a firm is created for this purpose, it is a business. A first step in establishing a firm is selecting its name, style, and size of operation.

In forming a property management company, a decision must be made about its legal form of business organization. The principal organizational forms are the sole proprietorship, partnership, and corporation. Each has both advantages and disadvantages that should be related to the individual situation before a decision is reached.

The chief factors to be weighed are income tax considerations, exposure to liability, and the ability of each form of ownership to achieve the owner's goals.

The corporate form of ownership is advantageous because it limits the liability of the owners and extends ownership through the sale of shares of stock. On the other hand, because, for income tax purposes, the corporation is a separate taxable entity, the effect is double taxation on the dividend income paid to the shareholders.

Partnerships often are formed when two or more property managers want to start a management company together. They enter into a partnership agreement that defines the purpose of the business and how it is to be managed. A disadvantage to a partnership is that the partners have unlimited liability; an advantage is that, for income tax purposes, the partnership is a conduit. Thus, income generated by it is not taxable at the partnership level but passed directly to the partners as taxable income on the individual level.

For an individual property manager who is forming a management company, the sole proprietorship probably is most suitable. The sole proprietorship is easy to form: usually it can be arranged if the property manager has a state real estate broker's license and obtains a business license from the city in which business is to be conducted. It is easy to administer and advantageous from an income tax standpoint: the firm and its sole proprietor are considered a single taxable entity. And it is simple to operate: few restrictions and regulations are imposed on sole proprietorships. However, this form of organization has its disadvantages, too. The chief drawback is that the proprietor is fully and personally liable for the debts of the firm.

Until recently, most firms adopted the names of their owners and operators (i.e., Joe Smith Property Management). While this is an option of its founders, there is an advantage to choosing a title that describes the business operation, such as Real Estate Management Company. If the proprietor should wish to sell the business, this can be accomplished without disrupting the firm's image or operational continuity. Although this may not seem important to the property manager at the time the firm is established, it is never too early to consider such matters.

Setting Up the Management Office

The second decision in forming a management business is selecting a site for the office. The office of a successful property management firm is a vital center for the operation of all properties under the agency's supervision. It is where policies are established, business is transacted, and records are maintained and stored. For this reason, careful attention must be given to site selection and then to the layout and equipment of the office.

Location

The location of the real estate management office depends primarily on the type of the individual operation. Every property manager would prefer to have an office at a prestigious address, but, for the property management firm that is just beginning, this probably is not economically possible. (Unless, of course, the manager can obtain the management of such a building.) Still, there are certain principles in site selection that are always applicable.

A ground-floor location usually is preferable—either in store space or a building specifically designed and constructed for this purpose. If the management office does a large business with the public, it should be located as close as possible to a center of consumer activity. Since real estate offices cannot pay high rents for being situated on major commercial streets, they are usually found on side streets adjacent to shopping areas.

The management company's rent collection policy affects selection of the office location. A manager of small residential properties that do not have rent-collecting resident managers should have a street-level office with ample, convenient parking in an accessible location. This is especially important in dealing with low-income tenants who do not have checking accounts and must pay with cash.

In large cities, management offices frequently are located on upper floors of downtown office buildings. The firms trade the advantages of more favorable consumer locations for the prestige that stems from the downtown sites. However, few management firms that are starting out can afford luxury, high-rise offices. Usually, this is the goal of an established management company whose portfolio has increased to 1,000 or more units.

As the management company grows, it may be necessary to have branch offices as well as a central office. Branch offices usually are located in outlying neighborhoods to attract more consumers. For this reason, almost all branch operations are situated in ground-floor locations.

Selecting an office location involves different considerations if the manager assumes supervision of a single, large property or is establishing an institutional real estate management office.

When an office is located in a building under management, the only concern is the selection of a specific area within the building. The ideal location provides maximum convenience for present and prospective tenants and clients, without using space that has high rental value. In a high-rise office building, for example, the building manager's office usually is located somewhere other than in prime, top-floor space or valuable, ground-floor space.

The location of the institutional real estate management office often is dictated by the institution itself. For banks and insurance companies, the property management department is usually a part of the central office. In the case of other institutions, it is frequently desirable to locate their management offices in one or another of the institution's buildings—preferably in the one closest to the center of the holdings—to provide maximum convenience for the firm's customers.

Before selecting an office location, a property manager should contact the local real estate board. All CERTIFIED PROPERTY MANAGERS® must be members of their local boards. Restrictions may be imposed on site selection: in a few cases, for example, these boards require all main real estate offices to be located in commercially zoned areas. Therefore, even if a property manager specializes in managing high-rise apartment buildings, the board may prevent the manager from locating the firm's main office in one of these buildings.

Layout and Design

An attractive, modern office is an important factor in acquiring new business. It is also true that well-designed offices provide a genuine savings, both through increasing the efficiency of operation and in recruiting desirable employees. In the past several years, many real estate organizations have constructed their own office buildings in prominent locations. These buildings have been developed not only as desirable investments but also have added substantially to the owner's all-important image and, therefore, to the volume of business. It is necessary, however, for the property management executive to build up to this level; it cannot be achieved instantly.

Although the management office need not be luxuriously appointed, it should be clean and attractive and a symbol of the manager's professional ability. The management office should demonstrate the manager's good taste in interior design. It should be artistically colorful and adequately illuminated, and office furnishings should be simple, in good style, and uniform throughout. In a modern agency, the tasteful use of decorator plants may be appropriate.

The office layout, above all, should be efficient and depict this efficiency. To a degree, the design of a management office reflects the efficiency of the firm's operations. Office arrangements and procedures, therefore, should be scrutinized by the management executive. The office must provide adequate space for its accounting operations in an atmosphere conducive to concentration and accuracy. Most of all, the layout should accommodate the basic functions of the property management firm. These include receiving the renting public; dealing with suppliers, architects, tradesmen, and others; and meeting present and prospective clients.

For example, if tenants pay their rents at the management office, this service should be accommodated. There should be an elbow-high counter where rents can be paid and receipts made. This counter also is a barrier to prevent tenants and other visitors from wandering through the office, which gives the person collecting rents, often a receptionist, a feeling of security.

Whenever possible, the real estate management executive should be available to the public. A luxurious private office can result in the envy of clients and hinder public relations and accessibility. Conference rooms can accommodate interviews that require special privacy.

Equipment

The property manager creates no product, has no inventory, and usually has no substantial plant investment. Since there is comparatively little equipment, it should be the best obtainable. The average real estate management office today is faced with one of two certainties—either the cost of operation must be reduced, or the net earnings of the office will decline. If the volume of work cannot be lessened, lower costs must be sought by reducing personnel through increased efficiency. In an efficiently operated management office the personnel are always busy, and their productivity can be increased only by using modern, well-maintained labor-saving devices.

Equipment that increases productivity and lowers labor requirements has been introduced in many professional real estate management companies. These organizations have benefited from installing machines that pay for themselves many times over by increasing business volume.

When a property management firm is established, often the only piece of equipment in the office will be a used typewriter. As the number of management accounts increases and the company expands, more sophisticated equipment will be necessary. Yet, regardless of the company's stage of growth, the property manager's main concern should be to set up an accounting system and obtain the appropriate bookkeeping equipment to implement it.

Accounting Systems.   The most basic and simple bookkeeping system is a *hand-posted,* or *manual, system.* Most property managers starting their own firms will adopt a manual system because it needs little skill and can be performed easily and efficiently by a bookkeeper. Collections are posted by hand on ledger cards, and operating reports are prepared manually with the help of a calculator.

As management firms grow, most replace manual account keeping with one or more of the wide variety of mechanized or computerized accounting systems that are available.

The *mechanized system* relies on a bookkeeping machine for posting accounts and uses one trust fund account with a subsidiary ledger for each property. The major advantage of this system is that the operator always knows the balance in each property's account. The chief disadvantage is that it is difficult to balance the accounts of larger properties and to track posting errors. Also, it is harder to find experienced operators of bookkeeping machines.

Computerized, or *electronic data processing (EDP), systems* increasingly are becoming a part of professional management operations. A computerized system permits accurate, timely records to be kept; establishes controls over income and expenses; and prepares sophisticated reports for analysis by management and presentation to property owners. The primary drawback to a computerized system is its expense, which can be quite high.

William Walters Jr., CPM®, in *The Practice of Real Estate Management for the Experienced Property Manager* (Chicago: Institute of Real Estate Management, 1979), suggests guidelines that are useful in determining which bookkeeping system is most suitable. According to Walters, a hand-posted system is sufficient until a firm's portfolio grows to 800 to 1,000 units or 20 to 30 buildings; a mechanized system is effective for a company managing 30 to 100 properties; and an EDP system may be used efficiently by a company managing as few as 1,500 units and generally is regarded as necessary for any firm managing more than 4,000 units.

Computer application is a separate science that is both complex and expensive. When a property management organization outgrows its existing mechanized or manual system, computer experts should be consulted to analyze the advantages and disadvantages of EDP equipment.

Furnishings and Supplies.   Other types of labor-saving equipment also are found in a fully outfitted management office. Descriptions follow of some items that often are needed when a management company acquires a business volume of 800 to 1,000 units. In all cases, equipment should be selected to produce operational efficiency.

- Typewriter. The typewriter remains the basic office machine Improvements that have been made permit better performance, both in the amount of work produced and the efficiency of the operator. Any property management executive analyzing operations should obtain the best available typewriter (typically an electric model) and be sure that it satisfies the clerical employees.
- Dictating machine. Dictating machines can increase office efficiency and thereby reduce personnel through the establishment of secretarial pools. Some property managers also use portable dictating machines as aids in making on-site property inspections.
- Telephone recorder. This instrument is useful in recording important conversations. If a warning signal advises participants that a telephone conversation is being recorded, as required by federal law, there is no ethical disadvantage to these recordings.
- Intercom. An intercom system increases efficiency by eliminating interoffice visits and constant telephone communication.
- Addressing machine. Not only does it save labor, an addressing machine also is essential to a mechanized sales program, which is vital to steady business growth. It can be used for recurring correspondence, direct-mail advertising, and accounting department notices.
- Mailing machine. Simple or sophisticated, mailing devices not only speed general mailing but also may be used for direct-mail advertising.
- Postage scales. These eliminate improperly stamped mail that either wastes postage or is a nuisance to those who must pay for "postage due."

- Duplicating or copying machine. From the simple mimeograph machine to the more expensive photocopier, these devices eliminate tedious, time-consuming retyping. They can produce limitless numbers of copies—often exact copies—for all uses, including record keeping.
- Microfilm machine. Microfilm allows the management office to retain records from many years in a space smaller than would be needed for a few days' papers in their original forms.
- Other equipment. Devices such as check-writing and payroll machines may be worthwhile to consider. In many offices, calculating machines also have proved sound investments.

Regardless of the type of office equipment needed, security precautions require that serial numbers be engraved on all items. A record of these numbers should be kept in a safe place, and a description of each machine listing any identifiable marks and photocopies of original invoices from purchase also should be maintained.

Labor efficiency definitely is not confined to the use of equipment. Management records that are clearly labeled, properly maintained, appropriately stored, and systematically disposed of when no longer needed can increase office efficiency. Similarly, business forms that permit consistent communications and uniform reporting encourage expediency.

Scientific studies have shown that productivity is vitally affected by the comfort and design of chairs, the height and width of desks, the type of floor covering, and the type of lighting. Improper seating and desks that are too high lead to fatigue and decrease efficiency in the latter part of each day. These discomforts often cost the proprietor in lost work hours—more than if new equipment were purchased.

Identifying Prospective Clients

The real estate management firm is not a functioning organization until its principal has secured one or more properties to manage. Traditionally, professionals "hang out their shingles" and await the arrival of clients. Property managers who organize a business, however, do so only when they have clients who wish to turn their business over to them.

Anyone who owns urban real estate is a prospective client for a fledgling management firm. Obviously, however, it would be impossible for a property manager to solicit business from all the property owners in the area. A more sophisticated technique for developing new business is needed.

Nearly all property management business is created by problem situations. For example, the owner of an 80-unit apartment building experiencing a 35-percent vacancy rate probably would benefit from a professional property manager's advice. Similarly, an over-financed office building and a shopping center whose anchor tenant went out of business represent problem situations that require management expertise.

Efforts to obtain management business, then, should focus on owners of problem properties. Those persons or organizations most likely to engage professional managers to solve their properties' problems comprise four categories.

Individuals and Limited Partnerships

Individuals who are active in their own enterprises consider their income properties strictly as investments. Most of these property owners have neither the time nor ability to assume the responsibilities of management nor the inclination to collect rents, handle rental inquiries, show space to prospective tenants, listen to service complaints, or supervise maintenance. Individuals most likely to need property management for these duties are accountants, architects, builders, developers, lawyers, doctors, and other professionals.

Absentee landlords do not work or reside in the immediate area of the property they own. They almost always require the services of local managers and are excellent prospect sources.

Limited partnerships usually are formed by groups of businessmen, stimulated by a desire for either profit or yield, who need professional guidance and attentive property administration. Often, these syndicates are created by management firms that have, as a chief objective, the management of properties owned by such syndicates.

Lawyers represent either owners or estates that have properties requiring administration. While some law firms will assume the management of these properties as a sideline, most lawyers engage professional management.

Corporations

As noted earlier, only recently have corporations become common owners of investment real estate. Like individuals, these corporations are divided into several major groups.

First, there are corporations that own and have the responsibility for operating income properties but are not large enough to create an organization for that purpose. These corporations almost always engage the services of professional property managers.

Second, there are corporations that are formed through cooperative or condominium properties. In these cases, most of the stockholders are active in businesses of their own and have neither the inclination nor the capability to supervise the property in which they have an interest. Moreover, there is an advantage in having an outside management firm, rather than the residents, manage the property.

Third, there are what are called bulk users of space (mostly commercial), who erect buildings primarily to house their own enterprises. However, either for prestige or future expansion, these corporations often construct buildings considerably larger than their own space needs. The building, then, not only requires administration, but renting as well. Some of these corporations hire individual managers on their payrolls to administer their property. Others—the majority—engage management firms for this work.

Fourth, there are institutional owners, such as colleges and universities, which frequently hire managers to supervise their buildings.

Financial Institutions

Financial institutions represent a large market for professional management services. Banks, insurance companies, trust companies, savings and loan associations, mortgage bankers, and investment houses almost inevitably acquire properties for administration—either because individual owners name them to that responsibility through trusts and estates or because of mortgage foreclosures. As has been mentioned before, acquisitions by financial institutions are likely to be high during periods of recession and depression and low during periods of peak prosperity. However, they are always excellent sources of property management business.

Government Agencies

Government—federal, state, and local—is an imporant factor in the local real estate economy and an important prospective client for the property manager. With the present level of federal agency participation in apartment financing, it is inevitable that these agencies will acquire properties for management. Most government agencies will engage private professional managers rather than set up their own management departments. Obviously, it is essential that property managers be fully aware of and responsive to all government regulations about the type of property being managed.

Many government agencies are presented with income property needing management. Litigation in the courts involves naming receivers, trustees, and so forth. For all of these posts, the private property manager is qualified. A wise manager will be well acquainted with the heads of local federal agencies and in good standing with the courts having jurisdiction over such matters.

Acquiring Management Business

Converting prospects into active clients results from six major aspects of a firm's operation: direct solicitation, favorable referral, reputation, influence, institutional advertising, and public relations.

Direct Solicitation

The best way to acquire business is to ask for it. However, in asking for the management of a particular building, the manager must ensure that a thorough study has been made of the property and a management plan for its operation has been prepared. In this way, the manager's ability to improve the property's results can be shown to the owner.

Anything as important as soliciting an owner for the management of a property deserves adequate preparation. The manager should know as much about the owner as possible. Complete familiarity with the building for which management is being solicited is also necessary. Ideally, a brief proposal for managing the building should be prepared to outline the advantages of professional management generally and the specific advantages in this particular management. This means that before calling on the prospective client, the manager will have made a careful examination of the building and will have analyzed it to justify its need of the manager's service. Certainly, the manager also should have a well-prepared sales kit through which the prospective client can be acquainted with the kind of services offered by the management organization and its qualifications.

The manager who directly solicits for new business must recognize that it is most unlikely that any property owner will turn over management as the result of one call. The property involved usually is a major investment of the prospective client, and its administration is, therefore, extremely important. For this reason, solicitation often requires many calls, much persuasion, and perseverance. Only through constant and dedicated efforts in direct solicitation can continuous new business be obtained.

Referral

Recommendation by a satisfied client is the best source of new business. Other important references include the prospective clients' bankers, lawyers, accountants, or tax counsels. The manager may consider contacting these individuals before the first interview with the owner.

Reputation

For the property manager who is starting a management firm, reputation probably is the most important requirement for business success. *Professional reputation* may be defined as the overall opinion of the business community as to the character and capability of the property manager. Much of the new firm's business will result from the achievement record the property manager has built with properties operated for other management firms.

When an owner turns a property over to a management firm, it is because of trust in the integrity and capability of that firm. Establishing the worthiness of that trust should rank uppermost in the property manager's efforts to obtain business. This can be accomplished by obtaining as many solid credentials (e.g., CERTIFIED PROPERTY MANAGER® designation) and good references as possible.

Institutional Advertising

Advertising can be employed effectively in selling management services. Such advertising is usually institutional in character, designed to build the reputation of the organization. Three types of institutional advertising have proved to be most effective.

Display advertising in community newspapers reaches a wide circulation and, if well handled, enhances institutional prestige. It is generally advantageous to place these advertisements on the financial page of local or national newspapers, although this preference has not been proved to be most effective. When a management firm buys newspaper advertising, it is paying for circulation of which only a

FIGURE 14.1

INSTITUTIONAL ADVERTISEMENT FOR PROMOTING MANAGEMENT FIRM

small part represents potential customers. (A sample institutional ad appears as figure 14.1.)

Direct-mail advertising for new management business has the benefit of being addressed solely to likely prospects. Direct-mail advertising is sent only to those persons who have been qualified as logical prospects and who actually own buildings that represent profitable management business. As with all direct-mail advertising, the care with which mailing lists are prepared and maintained, to a large degree, determines the success of the effort.

Signs on buildings are a significant source of new business. Prospective clients are influenced by the judgment of their fellow building owners. Every time they see a building on which there is a sign "Managed by John Jones," it is helpful to the cause of John Jones. All signs displaying the name of the manager or management firm should be designed carefully and maintained meticulously. Nothing will destroy confidence in a management organization's ability more than a sign that has been allowed to deteriorate and testifies to careless management. On the other hand, well-designed, strategically placed, and attractively maintained signs are an extremely effective institutional advertising medium.

Public Relations

In addition to purchased advertising, a thoughtfully conceived *public relations* program is a valuable aid in selling management services. Public relations means public knowledge, approval, confidence, and preference. The primary object of a public relations program is to acquaint as many people as possible in the community with the existence of the company, with what it does and what it stands for, and to encourage general acceptance of the company. Public relations means making friends for oneself and the organization and establishing a desire for the service offered.

Developing a sound public relations program is extremely important to the real estate manager, whose product is service. The responsibility of establishing public acceptance rests on the personnel of the organization. The business is entirely one of stewardship, and, finally, the business advances in proportion to the reputation of the steward.

A successful public relations program is not accidental; instead, it is the result of careful planning and constant updating. Every management organization, and every property manager as an individual, should have a planned public relations program designed to attain for the firm or individual the goals of public knowledge, approval, and acceptance. If public knowledge of a manager's performance is to be established among a wide circle in the community, then the manager, junior executives, and all employees must be encouraged to increase their activity among creditable groups within the community.

Individuals within the organization should be encouraged to participate in professional activities and establish themselves as respected authorities in their particular fields. They should be helped to write and speak well and perform duties that will bring credit on themselves and the organization they represent. Members of the organization must be encouraged to seek leadership in civic affairs and then perform the duties they are assigned. Frequently, the public image is harmed rather than helped by those who accept positions of civic responsibility but fail to measure up to the responsibilities involved. Only those assignments should be accepted that can be fulfilled with distinction, adding to the general reputation of the organization. Each individual in an organization must be fully aware of the public relations objectives of the firm and understand that the attainment of these objectives is as important to each employee as it is to the firm's founders.

Publicity is, perhaps, one of the most effective methods of building reputation. Most people believe what they read in the newspapers, although they may question the truth in advertising. Organizations should take advantage of every opportunity for favorable publicity. One staff member should be responsible for regularly submitting publicity ideas; if possible, a publicity agent should be retained to examine the operation from the standpoint of publicity potential.

A successful public relations program also requires critical examination of the firm and a willingness to make changes. The property manager regularly should study the operation of the business. Employees should be viewed in terms of fulfillment of their public relations responsibilities. The office should be examined with the idea of making it more attractive, efficient, and receptive. Buildings should be considered as to whether they reflect credit on the organization and win public approval.

Beyond examining the firm internally, the manager also should measure the enterprise's level of public acceptance. If necessary, interviews with residents in a representative cross section of the community can be conducted to ask if they have heard about the company. Only by sampling public opinion can the manager determine whether or not the public relations program is effective.

One of the best methods of measuring public relations effectiveness—and advertising effectiveness as well—is to determine the source of each business contact. Building agents should ask prospective tenants how they happened to come to the property. Clerks should ask those who come to the office why they selected the company. If certain media are succeeding well, efforts and expenditures in these media should be increased; if other media are failing to produce desired results, their use should be reduced or discontinued.

Critical examination can help establish a course of action. It is useless for the manager to discover deficiencies in the organization unless there is a willingness to remedy the conditions responsible for these deficiencies. Too often, a business operates in a well-defined rut. People sink into routines from which it is very difficult to remove themselves.

Determining Management Fees

Many people engaged in property management are direct employees of individuals or corporations. Their compensation is either a straight salary or based on a percentage of the profits from the building managed. Concern here, however, is with those real estate managers who manage a number of properties on an agency basis for a contract fee. The profits from the management operation represent the difference between the gross revenue received in management fees and the costs of providing the service.

Drawbacks of Standard Rates

Management fees for income-producing properties are related to the income collected from those properties. Real estate boards in urban areas often establish fee schedules that are accepted locally as standards but are not adopted universally. These fees vary considerably, according to the locality. Occasionally, managers are paid an additional percentage of expenditure if extra service is required. In most cases, however, the percentage-of-gross fee is considered full payment for management service, and no additional compensation is necessary.

The basis for the management fee for commercial buildings is often the same as that for residential buildings. In the case of large income properties, the rate may be reduced as the gross revenue rises. The property manager always must remember, however, that the rate of compensation is a matter of negotiation between agent and principal.

The standardization of rates based on gross income is often an unsatisfactory, impractical, and undesirable method of compensation. Management is a professional activity, and a guideline of professionalism is to relate compensation to ability and performance and to shun any form of standardization. It might be assumed that the rewards for management ability are found in an increased business volume, but this assumption is incorrect and explains why some managers build large organizations as false measures of ability.

Recently, there has been a greater tendency to base fees for management service on the manager's performance. In these cases, a minimum fee is agreed on with the understanding that the manager will share in increasing net profits.

Establishing Cost of Management Service

The operator of the management business initially should study the costs of supervising various types of properties and accept only business that will be profitable. In general, the expenses involved in providing management service fall into five main classifications: (1) rent; (2) payroll; (3) equipment and supplies; (4) advertising and promotion; and (5) insurance. With the exception of rent and insurance, these expense factors are controllable and can be maintained in a satisfactory relationship to gross revenue. The operating problem, then, is to obtain a satisfactory volume of basically profitable business and to establish and maintain a fixed-level relationship between gross revenue and operating expenses.

A management pricing form, illustrated in figure 14.2, will be helpful in computing a realistic management fee that is based on the actual cost of doing business.

General real estate offices, which offer collateral services, often assume the management of buildings at rates that produce less than satisfactory profits on the belief that these buildings will at some time produce collateral revenue. If the ownership decides to sell the property, for example, the real estate office probably will earn a brokerage fee. If a mortgage becomes due, the real estate office may profit from placing a new loan. It is also possible that the real estate office may write the insurance on the property or perform other services for which additional fees may be charged.

This type of reasoning, however, does not always apply. In certain periods of the real estate cycle, the income from other departments of the real estate operation declines to a point at which the bulk of overhead must be assumed from the management operation. If a volume of management business has been undertaken with fees that will not in themselves produce a reasonable profit, the organization, then, must raise fees at the most difficult time in the cycle.

The profits from real estate management are by no means uniform, even in identical properties. Unreasonable building owners frequently require amounts of attention entirely unjustified by the level of the fee for management service; this is especially true in condominium management. Properties with extremely heavy tenant turnover or poor physical equipment demand more staff time than can be paid for from standard fees. Properties located in remote areas require much staff travel time, plus transportation expenses. Although the manager must expect some deviation from normal costs, each business opportunity should be reviewed from the standpoint of operating expenses. Accepting a management account should come only when there is evidence that it will create profitable business.

In small towns and cities, the manager faces a limited market and must be diligent in obtaining any type of profitable business. In larger cities, however, where many large and small buildings exist, the manager should remember that it is as easy to sell service on a large property as on a small property. In fact, the owners of larger

FIGURE 14.2

MANAGEMENT PRICING WORKSHEET

Property _____ Date _____

Address _____ Owner _____

Number of Units _____ Gross Possible Income $ _____

Age and condition of property and improvements _____

_____

_____

Miles from Management Office _____ Number of On-Site Employees _____

	Times Per Month	Hours Each Time	Total Hours	Cost
I. Account Manager's Services (Rate per hour $ _____)				
A. Inspections				
B. Site Visits				
C. Capital Improvement Supervision				
D. Owner/Investor/Association Meeting				
E. Travel Time: $ _____ per hour x _____ hours				
F. Office Hours Per Month				
G. Travel Expense _____ ¢ per mile x _____ miles				
Total Cost				
II. Executive Services (Rate per hour $ _____)				
A. Owner/Investor/Association Meeting				
B. Site Visits				
C. Surveys/Consultations				
D. Inspections				
E. Statement Review				
F. Budget Preparation				
G. Office Hours Per Month				
H. Travel Time: $ _____ per hour x _____ hours				
I. Travel Expense _____ ¢ per mile x _____ miles				
Total Cost				

properties frequently are easier to work with than the owners of smaller properties. The former usually have a higher level of business comprehension, make quicker decisions, and require less coddling. The owners of small properties, on the other hand, often have their entire interests centered in a single property, and they require much personal attention.

The property manager who is engaged in—or plans to engage in—the administration of government-assisted housing is faced with

FIGURE 14.2—*Continued*

	Times Per Month	Hours Each Time	Total Hours	Cost
III. Accounting and Clerical Services (Rate per hour $ _____)				
A. Receipts Accounted For				
B. Disbursements: Invoices, Payments				
C. Monthly Billing				
D. Payroll: Checks Issued				
E. Owner/Association Statement Preparation				
F. Resident Statement Preparation				
G. Duplication				
H. Owner Consultation				
Total Cost				
IV. Subtotal Before Overhead and Profit				
V. Overhead and Profit			Percent of Total	
A. General Overhead				
B. Marketing				
C. Profit and Contingencies				
VI. Total Monthly Fee				

$ _____ Fee ÷ _____ Units = $ _____ Per Unit Per Month

$ _____ Fee ÷ $ _____ Gross Possible Income = _____ Percent

Prepared by _____

Approved by _____

special problems when setting a management fee. Since there is not, in the conventional sense, gross income against which a percentage can be applied, other factors must take precedence. Specifically, the cost of providing management service must be weighed with extreme care.

The U.S. Department of Housing and Urban Development (HUD) is debating the structure of management fees for its properties. On one side are those who support the establishment of a formula, which would be the basis for computing the management fee for any HUD property in the United States. On the other side are those who argue that any formula unfairly assumes that the cost of providing management service is uniform throughout the country; they believe that qualified, competitive bidding is far superior. The outcome has yet to be determined, but any property management company becoming involved in government-assisted housing must stay informed on the issue.

Summary

Many property managers, after gaining experience working for others, often choose to form their own management firms. The first step in doing this is twofold. First, the property manager determines the legal organizational form for the company—sole proprietorship, partnership, or corporation; and second, a firm name is selected.

The next concern of the property manager who is establishing a management company is the office itself. The management office is where daily business is transacted, records are maintained, and policies are effected. Its location, layout, design, and equipment should accommodate the scope and nature of the management business. The property manager may want a luxurious high-rise suite, but a storefront office on a downtown side street may be preferable—both to the rent-paying public and to the fledgling company's financial capacity. Likewise, it is not necessary for the office to be luxuriously appointed, but it must be clean and attractive and symbolize organizational efficiency and professional ability.

The first piece of equipment the property manager must acquire is the bookkeeping equipment. While smaller offices can be run manually by the manager and an assistant bookkeeper/secretary, larger firms will require either machine assistance or a computerized system. The size of the firm's portfolio determines the sophistication of the accounting system required. Other equipment—typewriters, dictating machines, telephone equipment, addressing and mailing machines, and copying machines—should be added to increase efficiency as the company expands.

The management firm is not a functioning organization until owners have turned over their properties to be managed. Most management business results from problem situations, and the property manager should focus efforts on identifying problem properties and their owners. Those who might have such problems are: (1) individuals and limited partnerships; (2) corporations; (3) financial institutions; and (4) government agencies.

Having recognized the prime prospects for management business, a plan of action for converting prospects into clients then must be adopted. For the property manager just starting a business, referrals from previous clients, reputation in the real business community, and direct solicitation of property owners are most productive. As the firm grows, more formal approaches to obtaining new business—i.e., institutional advertising and public relations—can be employed.

An integral part of entering the management business is knowing what to charge for providing management service. Most management fees for income properties are quoted as a percentage of income collected. However, standardization of fees is unsatisfactory, since it does not take into account the cost of doing business. Rather than simply quoting a percentage, the property manager is advised to study the costs of doing business and accept for management only properties that will be profitable.

REVIEW QUESTIONS

1. Why is office equipment important? Support the answer.
2. What factors are involved in selecting an office location for the real estate manager or management firm? Give examples.
3. A property manager is opening an office, and staff must be limited to two employees. Outline the duties that would be assigned to each.
4. What services are performed in the property management office that must be considered in planning the office space?
5. To what extent are computers being used in property management offices today? Based on experience and projection, to what extent will they be used five years from now?
6. In opening a new property management firm, what types of people and organizations should be solicited for business? Why?
7. What methods are used in obtaining management business? List them in order of importance and practicality to the property manager who is forming a new management firm. Justify the answer.
8. Name one way to measure the effectiveness of a public relations program.

9. Of what value is publicity? What are the best methods of obtaining publicity?
10. A property manager is managing an apartment complex in a suburban area with a gross monthly income of $24,500. What income could the property manager expect for services? Explain how the answer was reached.
11. Why do some real estate firms assume the management of properties that do not pay adequate profits or give an adequate net return? Should this be a common practice? Justify the answer.
12. What factors must be weighed in determining the cost of providing management service? What effect does this have on the management fee?

Chapter Fifteen

Creative Property Management

MOST PEOPLE SPEND the better part of their lives pursuing relatively common goals. Professional real estate managers are no exception. Usually they are seeking:

1. A comfortable living standard for themselves and their families.
2. An education for their children.
3. A reasonable security for their retirement.
4. The creation of an estate for their chosen beneficiaries.

While these goals often are reached through diverse means, wealth in the form of money, or its equivalent in convertible property, is the first requirement. The property manager is fortunate to be in a business that offers many opportunities to acquire personal wealth and, at the same time, increase the current income of the management firm. Indeed, the ambition of the property management business is to create and preserve wealth in the form of real estate.

The object of creative property management is to employ the skills and knowledge that have been described throughout this text in performing a broad range of duties that will result in a sufficient volume of business to attain the above goals. Included here are the undertaking of related real estate activities and the application of property management principles to developing opportunities in new and existing properties. Both can provide the entrepreneurial property manager with a broader base of profitable business.

Related Services

By offering specialized services in connection with real estate management, entrepreneurial ability is displayed. It is impossible, however, for any manager to be an expert in all the specialized fields within the real estate industry. In operating an office singlehandedly, the property manager is limited by the amount of time available for study and the amount of detailed knowledge that can be acquired and retained by one person. Nevertheless, the manager should accumulate enough knowledge in each of the specialty areas to be able to discuss problems with clients and appropriately select specialists. In large real estate management organizations, it is possible to have several specialists as part of the firm's operations. There should be a group of experts in various fields, each of whom has had thorough specialized training, study, and experience.

According to a study conducted in 1979 by the Institute of Real Estate Management, 68 percent of the average CERTIFIED PROPERTY MANAGER's® time is spent managing real estate. The remainder is spent in other real estate activities, as indicated by figure 15.1.

Within the scope of specialized services that the property manager can provide clients, the most important are: appraising, consulting, and syndication. The corporate fiscal, tax, and insurance

FIGURE 15.1

TIME SPENT IN REAL ESTATE ACTIVITIES BY
CERTIFIED PROPERTY MANAGERS®

Activity	Average Percent of Time (If Involved)	Weighted Average Percent of Time (All CPMs®)
Property Management	68%	64.0%
Brokerage	28%	11.5%
Appraising	24%	3.8%
Development	26%	8.1%
Counseling/Consulting	16%	5.0%
Syndications	16%	2.2%
Other Activities	38%	5.4%
		Total 100.0%

services that can be provided by the property manager also need explanation.

Appraisal

Real estate management and real estate appraisal are interdependent activities. Property managers increasingly are expected to exercise business and economic judgment in the interest of property owners. Owners ask about the future of their properties and wonder what they should do with their real estate investments. To answer these questions, the manager must be an appraiser. The manager should gather information to determine the highest and best use for a property and outline an operating program that will produce the greatest net profit from the property. Basically, appraisal is a way to measure the manager's judgment.

The procedures taken in appraising real estate are similar to those the property manager uses in forming a management plan. An *appraisal* is an estimate of a property's value. To arrive at this estimate, competitive data, economic information, population movement figures, neighborhood trends, and market conditions must be reviewed, and an in-depth analysis of the property must be made. The information needed by the appraiser is much the same as that needed by the property manager to perform regional, neighborhood, market, and property analyses.

There are three common methods of estimating value: (1) cost approach, which bases value on the value of the land plus the cost of reproducing improvements; (2) market approach, which establishes value by comparing the property being investigated with comparable properties that have been sold recently; and (3) income approach, which bases the value on the flow of income that can be anticipated from the property. The income method is the most important of the three approaches in appraising income properties. The value estimated by applying the income method is a significant factor in a manager's recommendation to rehabilitate, alter, convert, or modernize a building.

Because the techniques used by the property manager and the appraiser are similar, it can be profitable to operate a management business and an appraisal business from the same office. The two activities support one another. For example, the need for tax work, condemnation appraisal, estate tax appraisal, and other special-purpose appraisals arises frequently for managed real estate. The manager, then, has many opportunties to solicit appraisal jobs. On the other hand, an essential part of an appraisal is an analysis of operations and the selection of a new operating program. The opportunity to obtain management business following such an analysis is obvious.

Consultation

Many times property owners do not need ongoing management service but do need professional advice on specific problems. Property managers can accommodate these clients by offering consulting services.

Based on experience in the real estate industry, a property manager can advise owners on ways to manage their properties to achieve maximum profits. Most consulting work concerns recommendations on rehabilitation, modernization, and the conversion of existing properties to other uses. At other times, an owner who wishes to buy, sell, or refinance a property may request a management plan. Developers, too, call on property managers as consultants to assist them in determining a project's feasibility. A property manager also may be hired by a developer to recommend rental schedules, marketing programs, and leasing policies for proposed projects. In all cases, the recommendation made by a consultant depends on a thorough analysis of the problem being studied and the information that is available.

As the economy expands and real estate problems become more complicated, consultation is likely to grow as a specialization that the property manager can practice. Potential clients include buyers and sellers, investors, developers, corporate owners of real estate, and financial institutions.

Syndication

A *syndication* is an association of investors who provide the necessary funds to engage in a real estate enterprise. A syndication can be formed to acquire, develop, manage, operate, or market real estate or undertake any combination of these activities. It provides investors with an opportunity to participate in a substantial real estate venture that otherwise might be inaccessible to them. The investors are passive; the entity that organizes the venture, known as the *syndicator,* oversees the operation of the property.

The property manager who would act as a syndicator must make several decisions. First, the manager must be convinced that the individual property is desirable both from a personal standpoint and the client's standpoint. This requires the same type of in-depth analysis employed in creating a management plan. In addition, the property should be appraised to confirm the manager's personal opinion as to the soundness of the investment.

The second major decision involves the type of organization used to accomplish the venture. Syndication does not describe a form of legal organization but is merely an association of many like-minded investors. A real estate syndicate can take any legal organizational form, but the limited partnership is the most frequent choice.

In a limited partnership, the liability of the limited partners for the debts of the partnership is confined to the capital invested in the business. Limited partners cannot have a voice in the management of the partnership. They merely invest money and receive their share of the profits, usually on an equal basis. It is the general partner or partners who manage the real estate operation and are liable for all of the debts.

Many property managers form and promote limited partnerships to participate in the business venture and stabilize their management firms' business activity. The property manager becomes the general partner, usually with the flexibility needed to supervise the real estate investment without interference so long as honesty and capability are proven. The limited partners must have the highest opinion of the manager and the management firm if they are to grant the kind of authority the partnership requires.

One major disadvantage in the real estate management business is that the manager may lose management accounts for reasons not in any way related to the quality of the management service being performed. This loss of business often results from the sale of property, the death of one or more owners, or the dissolution of a partnership. In some especially discouraging instances, the very efforts of the manager are responsible for the loss of business. If, for example, the level of property income is raised to a point at which its value makes liquidation attractive to the owner, the manager may lose the management account as a direct result of an excellent management job. In any event, stabilizing management accounts is a problem the property manager can solve through the formation of an adequately financed and properly organized limited partnership.

When forming a limited partnership, the manager must be familiar with the laws (both federal and state) that govern investment activity and may apply to the proposed operation. Once a suitable property has been found and has withstood a careful analysis, the manager is ready to solicit prospective limited partners. The promotional plan should be examined by an attorney who can verify that the activities are entirely legal and outline the manager's personal liabilities in the promotion. A prospectus, listing the basic facts of the investment, should be reviewed with prospective limited partners so that all are completely familiar with the nature of the investment. A prospectus must be an exact statement of the facts as revealed by a feasibility study and should not contain exaggerations.

Once the partnership has been formed, the manager should stress the need for a conservative program of operation. If possible, the limited partners should be persuaded to accept limited dividends on their ownership, reserving excess funds for contingencies or application against the debt on the property. When a partnership is in operation, the only threat to continued management of the property is the possibility of a default on the debt obligation. In case of a default, the syndicate would be frozen out of ownership, and the management probably would be terminated by the lender. This must be avoided at all costs.

Operating a limited partnership requires a special type of public relations, for the limited partners become clients of the manager. Reports of operations should be sent to members regularly, and periodic meetings should be held to inform them of the progress of the investment. If possible, the manager who has formed a partnership should seek alternative investors who can replace individual partners who may wish to liquidate their shares in the investment. This provides flexibility and, at the same time, protects the continuity of the partnership and assures the permanence of the account.

Conditions are not always favorable for forming limited partnerships. During a major downswing in the real estate cycle, the manager may have to withdraw completely from this type of activity, since it is risky to purchase real estate on a thin margin. If partnerships are formed in such periods, property ownership should be outright and not subject to debt that might endanger the investment position.

It is worth noting that the term "syndication" has become tarnished recently. In the early 1970s, as competition among syndicators became fierce, higher and higher returns were promised to investors. A number of syndications failed to meet their promises, and the problem syndicates were highly publicized. Despite this, most ventures were sound, and syndication remains a worthwhile option for the property manager who wishes to participate in real estate investments.

Joint Ventures

There is every reason for the property manager to initiate real estate investments. After all, who is better qualified for such activity than a manager whose professional career has been built on skills, experience, and investments in real estate?

Another means by which the manager can participate in the ownership of a property being managed is a *joint venture,* which is an association of two or more persons or legal entities conducting a single business enterprise for profit.

Real estate enterprises that require large amounts of investment capital frequently are operated as joint ventures. Often such an arrangement is designed to pool not only financial resources but equipment, skill, knowledge, and talent as well. A property manager may enter into this business arrangement by offering professional management skills in exchange for sharing in the property's success.

For income tax purposes, a joint venture is considered similar to a partnership, acting as a conduit to pass income directly through to those participating in the venture. Unlike a partnership, the coventurers join together for a specific purpose—e.g., development of an income property—rather than in a continuing, ongoing business relationship.

Corporate Fiscal Service

During the comparatively brief period in which corporate ownership of real estate has been allowed, its popularity has increased steadily. The real estate manager often must be prepared to administer not only property owned by a corporation but other corporate affairs as well.

Managing corporate affairs involves responsibilities over and above those entailed by the management of real property. These extra duties of corporate management are called *fiscal services.* The availability of these services through one agency—the property management organization—is an advantage to the corporation and, for this reason, an asset to the management firm in soliciting management of buildings under corporate control. Because the percentage of buildings owned by corporations is increasing steadily, it is expedient for the management organization to be able to provide these fiscal services.

The affairs of most corporations that own real estate are administered by a board of directors. The management firm that is providing complete fiscal service may be called on to plan board meetings and to send a representative to the meetings who will furnish information and advice on a property's operations. Often, this management representative performs all routine duties usually performed by the secretary of the corporation, such as distributing minutes of the meeting. Annual corporation meetings may require the same type of activity.

Stockholders in real-estate-owning corporations often have inquiries about the properties. These questions may be handled by the management firm that is providing fiscal service. For this reason, the account executive must keep up-to-date with the affairs of the corporation and its real estate holdings.

The management firm also may be placed in complete charge of the books and records of the corporation. This is an accounting department activity that transcends simply maintaining operating records on the building owned by the corporation. It may involve supervising the filing of capital stock tax returns, the preparation of income tax returns, and the preparation and filing of social security and other government forms. Summary reports of these activities are prepared for presentation to the board of directors, so that it may know the financial condition of the corporation as well as the operating statistics on individual buildings.

Tax Service

The property manager's scope of activity has expanded throughout the history of real estate management. Investors are more inclined to turn properties over to managers for complete administration, including collateral services related to ownership. As more personal and financial decisions hinge on tax implications, property management may be faced with administering a tax program for the real estate involved.

The manager of income properties has a complex series of tax problems that require special skills. The first of these skills is administrative in nature. Appropriate records must be kept so that tax reports may be filed for clients, and tax calendars must be prepared to ensure prompt payment of the taxes involved. The second skill is analytical in nature. The management firm's tax department must understand tax law if savings are to be realized.

The scope of the tax service to clients will vary with the company's size. The small management firm is concerned mainly with basic routines and engaging special tax counsel when needed. In a large organization, however, this counsel may be handled directly by the management firm. In any event, an awareness—if not an in-depth knowledge—of tax regulations on all levels is necessary to complete management.

Real Estate Tax. The primary duty of the real estate manager who has complete responsibility for the administration of a given property is to ensure that adequate funds are available to pay real estate taxes on or before the due date. Wherever possible, reserve funds should be set up for this purpose.

In addition to this important duty, the manager also should analyze the tax bill, especially if there is any change. The valuation placed on an individual property by the local assessor is the basis of the real estate tax. The manager first must check the measurement, age of the property, amount of depreciation allowed, classification of the property, and unit replacement cost. Second, the computations by which the total tax was determined must be validated. This involves applying the tax rate to the assessed valuation. If this analysis indicates reason for a protest because of excessive assessment, the property manager should prepare and submit the protest to the assessor. If the protest is disallowed, an appeal to the next higher authority may be in order. Similar steps should be followed for state property taxes.

Personal Property Tax. If personal property taxes are imposed locally, it may be necessary for the manager to file a schedule of personal property subject to tax with the assessor. The real estate manager must be familiar with local laws in order to take advantage of accepted practices. Here again, the manager is responsible for the timely payment of the tax.

Social Security Tax. As the nominal employer or employer's agent, the management office is responsible for collecting and paying social security taxes and for representing the property owner's interests.

Contributions to federal old age insurance must be arranged through the collection of employer and employee contributions, and accurate records must be kept. Much of this activity involves accounting department details. The same is true of state unemployment compensation taxes.

Federal excise taxes on wages must be compiled where these taxes are payable, and annual returns must be filed along with the tax payment.

Federal Income Tax.   Most individual property owners handle their own income tax matters based on the inclusion of property income in their personal returns. Many corporations, however, are represented by property management firms and rely on the manager's accounting department to prepare and file federal income tax schedules.

The greatest service to property owners is in advice concerning decisions that may be strongly influenced by income tax regulations. Such advice is extremely helpful to owners who do not have an opportunity to become familiar with complex income tax laws and the tax shelters offered by real estate investments. Careful study of federal income tax regulations (and state income taxes, where they exist) is an important part of the competent manager's job. In larger management organizations, one member of the firm should be responsible for staying fully informed about federal income tax laws.

Excise Tax.   In the operation of office buildings and other large properties, the real estate manager may have to collect federal excise taxes—i.e., taxes on dues and admissions, the sale of electric light bulbs, and charges for telephone messages. When the management of a building includes the operation of separate merchandise or service departments (such as restaurants, bars, drugstores, or telephone switchboards), management should investigate its responsibility concerning the levy and collection of excise taxes. Frequently, managers have been embarrassed to find, after operating an enterprise for several months, that they are obligated for taxes that they failed to collect because of ignorance of the law.

Sales Tax.   In states having a sales tax law, a return must be prepared and the tax paid when taxable sales are transacted. The property manager may find it necessary to collect sales tax on electricity resale, newspapers, hotel food and beverage operations, gasoline and oil sales—on all taxable goods sold in subsidiary operations under the manager's direct administration. Here again, sales tax regulations should be checked when assuming management of property in which goods are sold.

Insurance Service

Another feature of the trend toward complete property administration is the provision of insurance protection. One of the main problems of ownership is the matter of fully underwriting the risks as much as possible. Since these risks vary in different localities and under different operating conditions, it is customary to expect the real estate management firm not only to appraise the extent of the risks involved but also to know with whom these risks may be safely and adequately insured. In keeping with this trend, some managers have begun writing insurance as a service to clients.

The real estate manager also has been motivated to enter the insurance field as a service to tenants as well. Over the years it has proved desirable for the real estate manager to enlarge the service nature of the management office to include the needs of the community. Certainly, writing insurance for tenants is a logical outgrowth of the manager's close contact with the public.

The position of the real estate manager is one of a broker who represents the insurance buyer. In this capacity, the manager determines the risk from the buyer's point of view, scans the insurance market for the best and most economical protection, then places an order for the proper insurance on behalf of the client. The insurance company or agency usually pays the broker's commission, but the broker still represents the buyer, not the insurance company or agency.

Any extra activity brings with it extra responsibility. Insurance underwriting is no exception—in fact, the duties of representing a client in insurance matters are extremely important and must be carried out meticulously.

The responsibilities related to insurance underwriting fall in two general categories. The first of these imposes on the real estate manager the need for an adequate knowledge of all aspects of insurance underwriting. The second responsibility entails keeping records of policies so that expirations are handled in ample time.

This responsibility also requires a continuous review of the risks involved in order to assure the client constant and adequate coverage. The property manager also must be sure that schedules are set up for inspecting tenants' properties to determine whether changes have taken place that might increase the risk to be underwritten. This is especially true in the case of commercial and industrial tenants, where changes in types of merchandise carried or kinds of goods manufactured may alter materially the cost or jeopardize the effectiveness of insurance coverage.

Opportunities in New and Existing Properties

The ability to identify and anticipate trends that increase or decrease values in the real estate field cannot be overlooked. While the entrepreneur may find profitable opportunities by participating in real estate ventures or offering a broader scope of services than usually is associated with the management profession, there are significant possibilities for new business in real estate management itself.

A prime example of the profits to be made through foresight is found in the condominium, which was developed as a remedy to inflation. Condominium management has become one of the most profitable trends of the 1970s for those who not only realized the growing role condominiums would play in the housing market but also acted on this realization.

Another opportunity for management appeared in the expanding retail business and with it the development of shopping malls, fast food establishments, and discount chains.

One opportunity still emerging is in current rental housing demand, which is calling for smaller units to match the declining birth rate and shrinking household size.

Likewise, the trend toward a higher percentage of employees in office settings presents greater opportunities in the property manager's plans for the future.

The real estate industry reacts quickly to changes in a variety of factors—national and local economics, demographics, interest rates, government intervention, inflation, supply and demand, social mores, and lifestyles. The property manager who is aware of these changes, no matter how subtle, and acts on them immediately is likely to succeed in the real estate management profession.

Among the activities in which far-sighted property managers become involved are: rehabilitation of neglected properties, recycling of old buildings, conversion of rental apartment buildings into condominiums, implementation of energy conservation measures, and management of mixed-use projects.

Rehabilitation

Professional property managers have found unlimited opportunity in the field of real estate rehabilitation. Not only does this serve the community by halting urban blight, but it also has proven to be a profitable business venture.

Rehabilitation means restoring neglected properties to a well-maintained condition and attractiveness without changing their use.

The major cost of new construction is in building materials. As these costs continue to rise, the value of rehabilitating existing structures will become more apparent. The shells and foundations of older buildings represent a substantial investment in money and time. Upgrading these buildings is a labor-intensive activity. While labor costs are high, they have not risen as rapidly as the costs of materials.

There are many older buildings that are structurally sound and can be modernized to make them competitive with new buildings and, often, realize a profit on considerably lower rentals. In some cases, because of the intrinsic value of old buildings (i.e., high ceilings, ornate woodwork) the marketability of rehabilitated properties is improved drastically.

Any type of building—loft building, office building, retail establishment—is a possible subject for rehabilitation. Still, the nation's most acute real estate need is in the housing sector. The federal government has recognized the potential of rehabilitation in solving some of the nation's housing problems. Grants are available through HUD's Section 8 program for rehabilitating housing to be made available to low- and moderate-income households.

The increasingly popular consumer attitude that frowns on new development has heightened the need to examine older buildings with the idea of improving and modernizing them. A rehabilitation project requires selecting a building that is structurally sound and for which there is a market, outlining the most advisable procedure, determining the amount of money to be spent and financing available, and presenting the findings—all activities that can reinforce the property manager's business judgment and reputation.

Recycling

Although still in its infancy, *recycling* real estate is becoming more and more practical as the cost of new construction rises. Preservationists long have been committed to the idea of recycling, which refers to the process of reclaiming old buildings for adaptive use. They believe that recycling permits the real estate needs of a community to be met without destroying the community itself. Now, real estate managers are aware that recycling represents a profitable business opportunity and is a viable alternative to maximize investors' objectives.

The success of a recycling project depends on realistic planning in five areas. First, the building under consideration must be in a location appropriate for its adaptive use. Second, the building needs close examination by a real estate professional who can determine the possibilities for reuse. Third, advice on the rental potential of the building and its marketability is needed. Fourth, a professional opinion is needed on the structural condition of the building and what is needed to bring it into conformity with code requirements. And, fifth, appropriate financing arrangements for the rehabilitation must be made. The professional property manager is qualified to offer recommendations in all phases of the decision making.

The lives of many old buildings can be extended when modernized to meet current standards and recycled to new use. Although it was not the first recycling project, Ghirardelli Square in San Francisco is recognized by many as a prototype. Built as a chocolate factory in the late nineteenth century, Ghirardelli Square was recycled into a charming complex of specialty shops, restaurants, and theatres.

While recycling is a business opportunity that should not be overlooked, the manager also should recognize that the completed project itself represents an opportunity. Recycled income properties need ongoing management if their viability is to be maintained. In fact, because of the importance of preventive maintenance in dealing with older buildings, ongoing professional management is especially important.

Condominium Conversion

Property managers have become leaders in the trend to convert rental apartments to condominium ownership. Two factors contribute to this trend. First, there is definitely a market for condominium units. As the average household becomes smaller (more childless couples, empty nesters, and one-person households), condominiums, usually smaller than single-family homes and often in attractive locations, are appealing. Second, because of the potential profit that may be earned over a relatively short period, conversion appeals to developers and investors. This is especially true when high financing costs result in negative cash flows and when rent controls restrict landlords' ability to increase rents to market levels.

The success of a conversion depends largely on a building's ability to accommodate condominium use. A person buying a condominium unit and making a long-term financial commitment is more selective than a person looking for an apartment to rent. Many apartment buildings do not have the amenities sought by condominium owners or have fallen into disrepair. Location also is important; sites close to shopping, transportation, and business facilities are desirable.

To reduce the risks involved in a conversion, expert advice should be obtained. The property manager is in an excellent position to recommend buildings suited to condominium conversion and to prepare feasibility studies on proposed projects. This study should compare the value of the property as a rental building with its value as a condominium, taking into account the market value of each condominium unit. The fact that most multifamily buildings are more valuable as condominiums than as rental properties has contributed to the conversion trend.

The age of the structure, condition of the physical plant, and the extent of renovation are important considerations when evaluating a property for conversion. For this reason, the cost of performing restoration or making improvements necessary to make the project marketable should be indicated in the manager's feasibility study.

Conversions have been the object of much criticism, the most frequent opposition coming from tenant and consumer advocate groups. Numerous problems have been associated with the conversion process. Two of the most significant are: (1) the displacement of tenants, often the elderly and low-income families; and (2) the depletion of rental housing stock, lowering vacancy rates and reducing housing opportunities for many segments of the population. This problem has been compounded by the recent low level of new rental housing construction.

Perhaps the most publicized issue has been the situation of tenants who cannot afford or do not choose to purchase their units. The problem is compounded in a tight market. The property manager involved in a conversion should take every step necessary to treat tenants fairly. They should be fully and formally told about the conversion project as soon as possible. Legislation has been enacted that is designed to protect tenants in conversion buildings by requiring an adequate notification period. Moreover, the property manager should consider tenants as the primary market to purchase the converted units. Possibly, tenants can be offered a better deal than nontenants; for instance, they might be given the option to purchase their units on an as-is basis at a reduced cost.

Although there are negative consequences to condominium conversions, they do provide benefits to communities, too. The lower price of many condominiums, when compared with the price of single-family homes, has made home ownership possible for many households. More importantly, the conversion of older apartments, especially in inner-city neighborhoods, has resulted in the upgrading of the affected housing inventory. Substantial rehabilitation and subsequent conversion of older apartments have extended the life of existing housing resources and stimulated neighborhood improvement. Condominium conversions also have represented a fiscal windfall for local governments by significantly increasing real property tax revenues. This is attributed to the difference between assessment practices for rental apartments (on an income-stream basis) and condominiums (on a market-value basis).

Energy Conservation

There is little doubt that the energy crisis is both real and permanent. Rising energy costs can be translated into rising operating expenses. This has a negative effect on the value of all properties, but especially inefficient buildings constructed during the pre-energy crisis period. Property managers responsible for these buildings—in both the residential and commercial sectors—recognize the need to upgrade the efficiency of their heating and cooling systems in order to maximize the objectives of the property owners.

According to a joint study by the Institute of Real Estate Management and the Federal Energy Administration (now the U.S. Department of Energy), in 1975, energy costs for apartment buildings nationwide averaged about 27 percent of total operating costs. And, these costs are rising. In one two-year period alone, utilities increased 48 percent and heating fuel shot up 98 percent. The result is that managers increasingly are becoming concerned about reducing energy costs. It is not necessary for major capital investments to be made or new technology implemented in order to realize a savings. Better maintenance, minor modifications of environmental controls, and a positive tenant attitude about energy conservation are effective procedures.

Figure 15.2, taken from *Energy Cost Reduction for Apartment Owners and Managers* (Chicago: Institute of Real Estate Management, 1977), summarizes potential dollar savings that can be realized if certain retrofitting techniques are implemented. For example, by installing storm windows that keep heated air inside the building from escaping, heating costs can be cut back by 10 to 20 percent. A savings also will be realized in summer months, when the storm windows keep cool air inside.

FIGURE 15.2
ENERGY SAVINGS SUMMARY

Recommendation	Cost to Implement	Payback Period (years)	First-Year Energy Cost Reduction	10-Year Savings
Savings on Hot Water:				
1. Replace Showerheads and Sink Aerators	$ 1,094	.1	$ 9,570	$147,818
2. Reduce Hot Water Temperature	No Cost	Immediate	7,837	121,946
3. Install Timer on Hot Water Circulating Pump	16	.3	61	911
Savings on Lighting:				
4. Relamp Apartments	1,623	.6	3,215	39,632
Relamp Common Areas	98	.1	1,886	29,249
Savings on Heating and Cooling:				
5. Correct Overheating	39,000	.8	48,583	715,616
6. Limit Temperature	5,465	.8	6,522	96,019
7. Set Back Temperature (1)	6,000	1.1	5,558	80,484
Set Back Temperature (2)	3,000	2.7	971	16,030
8. Improve and Maintain Boiler Efficiency	100	.8	225	2,787
9. Install Storm Windows	7,700	3.8	1,671	23,668
10. Insulate Pipes and Tanks	200	2.9	60	921
11. Add Roof Insulation	3,456	2.6	1,143	18,945

Note: The First-Year Energy Cost Reduction figure is the gross amount saved—the "off the top" savings on utilities during the first year. The Ten-Year Savings figure is the projected *net* amount saved over a 10-year period, before taxes. It takes into account the initial implementation expense, annual maintenance costs (if any), estimated rate of inflation, and anticipated increases in energy costs.

FIGURE 15.3

UTILITY CONSUMPTION RECORD

Utility Company _____ Property _____
_____
_____

Billing Period		Billing Date	Area Serviced	Consumption	Cost
From	To				

The property manager also may consider converting from master metering to individual tenant metering. This conversion can be an expensive undertaking. However, according to one study, tenants on master meters use about 30 percent more electricity than do tenants in similar buildings with individual meters.

If the property manager decides to convert to individual meters, tenants undoubtedly will retaliate. Every precaution must be taken to see that the program is accepted and that tenant turnover is minimized. For instance, timing the action is crucial. The conversion should occur in early spring or fall, when utility bills are usually lower, and, therefore, tenants' first utility bills smaller. Management also should consider a rent reduction or rebate so that tenants can share in the economic advantages of individual metering.

Basic to evaluating the success of retrofitting measures is keeping a record of fuel, electricity, and other utility consumption, as well as their costs. A worksheet like the one in figure 15.3 can be helpful in maintaining this record. A comparison of the amounts used will provide an accurate picture of a property's energy consumption.

The alert, professional property manager will become familiar with retrofitting techniques and acquire a reputation for being capable of reducing energy expenses. This manager will be much more successful than the one who ignores the energy problem and fails to recognize its impact on investment real estate.

Mixed-Use Projects

The past two decades have seen the development of suburban neighborhoods and the consequent decline of central business districts. Many efforts have been made to reverse this trend. One of the more successful is the development of *mixed-use projects,* which provide mutually supporting facilities within a single project.

A mixed-use project, according to the Urban Land Institute, meets three criteria: (1) it incorporates at least three income-producing uses (i.e., retail, office, and residential); (2) it is integrated functionally and physically and represents an intensive use of urban land; and (3) it is developed according to a detailed, coherent plan.

There is no single mix of uses that is appropriate for every situation. A review of three notable mixed-use projects will illustrate:

- The Galleria in Houston contains retail space, office space, hotel rooms, parking spaces, an ice-skating rink, indoor tennis courts, a health club, and a medical clinic.
- Water Tower Place in Chicago contains hotel space, office space, condominium units, retail space, movie theatres, a legitimate theatre, and an underground garage.
- Peachtree Center in Atlanta offers office space, retail facilities, hotel rooms, a merchandise mart, and parking facilities.

The management of mixed-use projects presents a special challenge to the professional property manager. A mixed-use project functions like a city within a city, and its operation can differ considerably from single-purpose projects.

Mixed-use projects often will outperform single-purpose properties, both in obtaining higher rental rates and higher occupancy
levels. This results chiefly from the natural interaction among the
space users. For instance, those who live and work in a mixed-use
project are likely to shop in its retail establishments and dine in its
restaurants. Higher rents can be charged if the project ranks as a
prestigious development. This may be achieved through proper planning and marketing.

Most mixed-use projects are large in scale. This may lead to
operational efficiencies not available in smaller, single-use properties.
Operational economies of scale come largely from savings in manpower and maintenance. Having a centralized plant and equipment
and offering centralized management also can result in operating
expense savings.

Summary

The creative property manager establishes a broad base of profitable
business. This often involves undertaking activities related to real
estate management, as well as the exploitation of opportunities in
new and existing properties.

There are several services related to property management for
consideration. Because the techniques needed to appraise real estate
are the same techniques needed to create a management plan, many
property managers become involved in appraisals. For those owners
whose property does not need ongoing management but can benefit
from occasional advice, consultation may be the solution. Potential
clients for consultation include investors who are weighing buy-sell
decisions, developers planning new projects, and owners who wish to
increase returns from their properties.

To stabilize their firms' business, some property managers participate as owners in real estate ventures. One means of doing this is
through a syndication, usually in the form of a limited partnership.
The property manager becomes the general partner and supervises
the real estate investment. Another way of participating in real estate
ownership is a joint venture.

Increasingly, property management's scope of duties is expanding, and property owners are turning their investments over to
managers for complete administration. In the case of a corporation
that owns real estate, the manager may provide fiscal services such as
organizing meetings of the board of directors, handling inquiries

from stockholders, and keeping the corporate records. Property managers also provide tax service and insurance service to investors.

While these collateral activities can make the management business more secure by allowing diversity, they should not be permitted to overshadow opportunties to be found in the management of new and existing properties. New developments in the real estate industry lead to new opportunities for the property manager. For example, the condominium boom has created a management field that did not exist a decade ago.

Five key areas awaiting the attention of the creative property manager are: (1) rehabilitating neglected real estate; (2) recycling real estate to new uses; (3) converting rental properties to condominiums; (4) implementing energy-conservation techniques; and (5) managing mixed-use projects.

Property managers who are sensitive to the real estate market and aware of local and national economic trends will recognize these types of opportunities early and become future leaders.

REVIEW QUESTIONS

1. Why would a property manager wish to offer services collateral to managing real estate?
2. Define *appraisal.* Why is appraisal a natural adjunct to property management?
3. List three situations in which a property manager would be called on to act as a *consultant.*
4. Define *syndication* and *joint venture.* From a management standpoint, what is the advantage of participating in the ownership of a real estate investment? What is the manager's role in a *limited partnership?*
5. What is the duty of the real estate manager, who has complete responsibility for property operation, concerning real estate taxes?
6. List the taxes that a property manager may have to handle. What is the nature of this service?
7. If a property manager wanted to supplement business with insurance brokerage, outline the steps that must be taken.
8. What is an insurance *broker?* What are the broker's duties and responsibilities to clients?
9. Name three developments in the real estate industry in the last decade that have resulted in management opportunities.

10. Define *rehabilitation*. Based on familiarity with the process of preparing a management plan, outline the steps to be taken in handling a rehabilitation project.
11. What factors have created the popularity of *condominium conversions?* What has been the public's response? Why?
12. What impact do energy costs have on the value of real estate? Define *retrofitting*. Give examples of three retrofitting measures for conserving energy.
13. What are the characteristics of a *mixed-use project?* How does its management differ from the management of single-purpose properties? What is the future of mixed-use projects?

Appendix

FIGURE A.1

MANAGEMENT AGREEMENT

OWNER _____

and

AGENT _____

For Property located at

_____
_____

Beginning _____ 19 _____

Ending _____ 19 _____

MANAGEMENT
AGREEMENT

FIGURE A.1—*Continued*

IN CONSIDERATION of the covenants herein contained, ————————————
———————————————————————(hereinafter called "OWNER), and ————
———————————————————————(hereinafter called "AGENT"), agree as
follows:

1.   The OWNER hereby employs the AGENT exclusively to rent and manage the property
(hereinafter called the "Premises") known as ————————————————————————
——

upon the terms and conditions hereinafter set forth, for a term of ——————— beginning on
the ———— day of ———————————, 19———, and ending on the ————
day of ———————————, 19———, and thereafter for yearly periods from
time to time, unless on or before ———————, 19———days prior to the date last above mentioned or on
or before ——————— days prior to the expiration of any such renewal period, either party
hereto shall notify the other in writing that it elects to terminate this Agreement, in which case
this Agreement shall be thereby terminated on said last mentioned date. (See also Paragraph
6.3 below.)

2.   THE AGENT AGREES:

2.1   To accept the management of the Premises, to the extent, for the period, and upon
the terms herein provided and agrees to furnish the services of its organization for the rental
operation and management of the Premises.

2.2   To render a monthly statement of receipts, disbursements, and charges to the
following person(s) at the address(es) shown:

Name	Address

and to remit each month the net proceeds (provided AGENT is not required to make any
mortgage, escrow, or tax payment on the first day of the following month). AGENT will remit
the net proceeds or the balance thereof after making allowance for such payments to the
following persons, in the percentages specified, and at the addresses shown:

Name	Percentage	Address

In case the disbursements and charges shall be in excess of the receipts, the OWNER agrees to
pay such excess promptly, but nothing herein contained shall obligate the AGENT to advance
its own funds on behalf of the OWNER.

2.3   To cause all employees of the AGENT who handle or are responsible for the safe-
keeping of any monies of the OWNER to be covered by a fidelity bond in an amount and with
a company determined by the AGENT———————————————————————

3.   THE OWNER AGREES:

To give the AGENT the following authority and powers (all or any of which may be exercised in the name of the OWNER) and agrees to assume all expenses in connection therewith:

3.1   To advertise the Premises or any part thereof; to display signs thereon and to rent
the same; to cause references of prospective tenants to be investigated; to sign leases for terms
not in excess of ——————— years and to renew and/or cancel the existing leases and prepare
and execute the new leases without additional charge to the OWNER; provided, however, that
the AGENT may collect from tenants all or any of the following: a late rent administrative
charge, a non-negotiable check charge, credit report fee, a subleasing administrative charge
and/or broker's commission and need not account for such charges and/or commission to the
OWNER; to terminate tenancies and to sign and serve such notices as are deemed needful by
the AGENT; to institute and prosecute actions to oust tenants and to recover possession of the
Premises; to sue for and recover rent; and, when expedient, to settle, compromise, and release
such actions or suits, or reinstate such tenancies. OWNER shall reimburse AGENT for all expenses of litigation including attorneys' fees, filing fees, and court costs which AGENT does
not recover from tenants. AGENT may select the attorney of its choice to handle such litigation.

FIGURE A.1—*Continued*

3.2 To hire, discharge, and pay all engineers, janitors, and other employees; to make or cause to be made all ordinary repairs and replacements necessary to preserve the Premises in its present condition and for the operating efficiency thereof and all alterations required to comply with lease requirements, and to do decorating on the Premises; to negotiate contracts for nonrecurring items not exceeding $_____ and to enter into agreements for all necessary repairs, maintenance, minor alterations, and utility services; and to purchase supplies and pay all bills. AGENT shall secure the approval of the OWNER for any alterations of expenditures in excess of $_____ for any one item, except monthly or recurring operating charges and emergency repairs in excess of the maximum, if, in the opinion of the AGENT, such repairs are necessary to protect the property from damage or to maintain services to the tenants as called for by their tenancy.

3.3 To collect rents and/or assessments and other items due or to become due and give receipts therefor and to deposit all funds collected hereunder in the AGENT's custodial account.

3.4 To handle tenants' security deposits and to comply, on the OWNER's behalf, with applicable state or local laws concerning the AGENT's responsibility for security deposits and interest thereon, if any.

3.5 To execute and file all returns and other instruments and do and perform all acts required of the OWNER as an employer with respect to the Premises under the Federal Insurance Contributions Acts, the Federal Unemployment Tax Act, and Subtitle C of the Internal Revenue Code of 1954 with respect to wages paid by the AGENT on behalf of the OWNER and under any similar federal and state law now or hereafter in force (and in connection therewith the OWNER agrees upon request to promptly execute and deliver to the AGENT all necessary powers of attorney, notices of appointment, and the like).

3.6 The AGENT shall not be required to advance any monies for the care or management of said property, and the OWNER agrees to advance all monies necessary therefor. If the AGENT shall elect to advance any money in connection with the property, the OWNER agrees to reimburse the AGENT forthwith and hereby authorizes the AGENT to deduct such advances from any monies due the OWNER. The AGENT shall, upon instruction from the OWNER, impound reserves each month for the payment of real estate taxes, insurance, or any other special expenditure. In addition, the OWNER agrees to establish a permanent Operating Reserve Account with the AGENT in the amount of $_____ .

4. THE OWNER FURTHER AGREES:

4.1 To indemnify, defend, and save the AGENT harmless from all suits in connection with the Premises and from liability for damage to property and injuries to or death of any employee or other person whomsoever, and to carry at his (its) own expense public liability, elevator liability (if elevators are part of the equipment of the Premises), and workmen's compensation insurance naming the OWNER and the AGENT and adequate to protect their interests and in form, substance, and amounts reasonably satisfactory to the AGENT, and to furnish to the AGENT certificates evidencing the existence of such insurance. Unless the OWNER shall provide such insurance and furnish such certificate within_____ days from the date of this Agreement, the AGENT may, but shall not be obligated to, place said insurance and charge the cost thereof to the account of the OWNER. All such insurance policies shall provide that the AGENT shall receive thirty (30) days' written notice prior to cancellation of the policy.

4.2 To pay all expenses incurred by the AGENT, including, but not limited to, reasonable attorneys' fees and AGENT's costs and time in connection with any claim, proceeding, or suit involving an alleged violation by the AGENT or the OWNER, or both, of any law pertaining to fair employment, fair credit reporting, environmental protection, rent control, taxes, or fair housing, including, but not limited to, any law prohibiting, or making illegal, discrimination on the basis of race, sex, creed, color, religion, national origin, or mental or physical handicap, provided, however, that the OWNER shall not be responsible to the AGENT for any such expenses in the event the AGENT is finally adjudicated to have personally, and not in a representative capacity, violated any such law. Nothing contained herein shall obligate the AGENT to employ counsel to represent the OWNER in any such proceeding or suit, and the OWNER may elect to employ counsel to represent the OWNER in any such proceeding or suit. The OWNER also agrees to pay reasonable expenses (or an apportioned amount of such expenses where other employers of AGENT also benefit from the expenditure) incurred by the AGENT in obtaining legal advice regarding compliance with any law affecting the premises or activities related thereto.

FIGURE A.1—*Continued*

4.3　To indemnify, defend, and save the AGENT harmless from all claims, investigations, and suits, or from actions or failures to act of the OWNER, with respect to any alleged or actual violation of state or federal labor laws, it being expressly agreed and understood that as between the OWNER and the AGENT, all persons employed in connection with the Premises are employees of the OWNER, not the AGENT. However, it shall be the responsibility of the AGENT to comply with all applicable state or federal labor laws. The OWNER's obligation under this paragraph 4.3 shall include the payment of all settlements, judgments, damages, liquidated damages, penalties, forfeitures, back pay awards, court costs, litigation expense, and attorneys' fees.

4.4　To give adequate advance written notice to the AGENT if the OWNER desires that the AGENT make payment, out of the proceeds from the premises, of mortgage indebtedness, general taxes, special assessments, or fire, steam boiler, or any other insurance premiums. In no event shall the AGENT be required to advance its own money in payment of any such indebtedness, taxes, assessments, or premiums.

5.　THE OWNER AGREES TO PAY THE AGENT EACH MONTH:

5.1　FOR MANAGEMENT: _____ per month or _____ percent (_____%) of the monthly gross receipts from the operation of the Premises during the period this Agreement remains in full force and effect, whichever is the greater amount. Gross receipts are all amounts received from the operation of the Premises including, but not limited to, rents, parking fees, deposits, laundry income, and fees.

5.2　APARTMENT LEASING _____

5.3　COMMERCIAL LEASING _____

5.4　MODERNIZATION (REHABILITATION/CONSTRUCTION) _____

5.5　FIRE RESTORATION _____

5.6　OTHER ITEMS OF MUTUAL AGREEMENT _____

FIGURE A.1—*Continued*

---

6. IT IS MUTUALLY AGREED THAT:

6.1 The OWNER expressly withholds from the AGENT any power or authority to make any structural changes in any building or to make any other major alterations or additions in or to any such building or equipment therein, or to incur any expense chargeable to the OWNER other than expenses related to exercising the express powers above vested in the AGENT without the prior written direction of the following person:

Name	Address

except such emergency repairs as may be required because of danger to life or property or which are immediately necessary for the preservation and safety of the Premises or the safety of the tenants and occupants thereof or are required to avoid the suspension of any necessary service to the Premises.

6.2 The AGENT does not assume and is given no responsibility for compliance of any building on the Premises or any equipment therein with the requirements of any statute, ordinance, law, or regulation of any governmental body or of any public authority or official thereof having jurisdiction, except to notify the OWNER promptly or forward to the OWNER promptly any complaints, warnings, notices, or summonses received by it relating to such matters. The OWNER represents that to the best of his (its) knowledge the Premises and such equipment comply with all such requirements and authorizes the AGENT to disclose the ownership of the Premises to any such officials and agrees to indemnify and hold harmless the AGENT, its representatives, servants, and employees, of and from all loss, cost, expense, and liability whatsoever which may be imposed on them or any of them by reason of any present or future violation or alleged violation of such laws, ordinances, statutes, or regulations.

6.3 In the event it is alleged or charged that any building on the Premises or any equipment therein or any act or failure to act by the OWNER with respect to the Premises or the sale, rental, or other disposition thereof fails to comply with, or is in violation of, any of the requirements of any constitutional provision, statute, ordinance, law, or regulation of any governmental body or any order or ruling of any public authority or official thereof having or claiming to have jurisdiction thereover, and the AGENT, in its sole and absolute discretion, considers that the action or position of the OWNER or registered managing agent with respect thereto may result in damage or liability to the AGENT, the AGENT shall have the right to cancel this Agreement at any time by written notice to the OWNER of its election so to do, which cancellation shall be effective upon the service of such notice. Such notice may be served personally or by registered mail, on or to the person named to receive the AGENT's monthly statement at the address designated for such person as provided in Paragraph 2.2 above, and if served by mail shall be deemed to have been served when deposited in the mails. Such cancellation shall not release the indemnities of the OWNER set forth in Paragraphs 4 and 6.2 above and shall not terminate any liability or obligation of the OWNER to the AGENT for any payment, reimbursement, or other sum of money then due and payable to the AGENT hereunder.

7. This Agreement may be cancelled by OWNER before the termination date specified in paragraph 1 on not less than ———————— days' prior written notice to the AGENT, provided that such notice is accompanied by payment to the AGENT of a cancellation fee in an amount equal to ————————% of the management fee that would accrue over the remainder of the stated term of the Agreement. For this purpose the monthly management fee for the remainder of the stated term shall be presumed to be the same as that of the last month prior to service of the notice of cancellation.

8. The OWNER shall pay or reimburse the AGENT for any sums of money due it under this Agreement for services for actions prior to termination, notwithstanding any termination of this Agreement. All provisions of this Agreement that require the OWNER to have insured or to defend, reimburse, or indemnify the AGENT (including, but not limited to, Paragraphs 4.1, 4.2, and 4.3) shall survive any termination and, if AGENT is or becomes involved in any proceeding or litigation by reason of having been the OWNER's AGENT, such provisions shall apply as if this Agreement were still in effect. The parties understand and agree that the AGENT may withhold funds for thirty (30) days after the end of the month in which this Agreement is terminated to pay bills previously incurred but not yet invoiced and to close accounts.

FIGURE A.1—*Continued*

This Agreement shall be binding upon the successors and assigns of the AGENT and their heirs, administrators, executors, successors, and assigns of the OWNER.

IN WITNESS WHEREOF, the parties hereto have affixed or caused to be affixed their respective signatures this_____ day of_____ , 19_____ .

WITNESSES: OWNER:

_____   _____

_____   _____

_____   _____

                                              _____

                                        AGENT:

                                        Firm _____

                                        By _____
_____
Submitted by

FIGURE A.1—*Continued*

POWER OF ATTORNEY

KNOW ALL MEN BY THESE PRESENTS, THAT

_____
(Name)

_____ located at
(State whether individual, partnership, corporation, etc.)

_____ has made,
(Address)

constituted, and appointed, and, by these presents does hereby make, constitute,
and appoint, _____ , a resident of
the United States, whose address is _____ (its)
true and lawful attorney for (it) (me) in (its) (my) name, place, and stead to

execute and to file any Tax Returns due on or after _____

_____

under the provisions of the Social Security Act, now in force or future amendments thereto.

Dated at_____this_____day of_____, 19 _____

                                    _____
                                    Signature of Taxpayer

                                    _____
                                    Title

Executed in the presence of: _____
                                    Signature of Taxpayer

                                    _____
                                    Title

_____   _____
Witness   Signature of Taxpayer

_____   _____
Witness   Title

        Acknowledged before me this _____ day of _____, 19 _____
        NOTARIAL
        SEAL

FIGURE A.2

APARTMENT BUILDING INSPECTION REPORT

THE INSTITUTE OF REAL ESTATE MANAGEMENT
of the
NATIONAL ASSOCIATION OF REALTORS"

Form '40A

_____ __ _____ 19____

APARTMENT BUILDING INSPECTION REPORT

Name of Property_____ Address_____

Type of Property_____

No. of Stories_____

Report Submitted by_____

No. of Apts.: 1's _____ 1½'s _____

2's _____ 2½'s _____ 3's_____ 3½'s_____

4's _____ 4½'s_____ 5's _____ 5½'s _____

6's _____ 7's_____ 8's _____Total_____

EXTERIOR

Items	Character and Condition	Needs	Estimated Expense Involved
Grounds			
1. Soil			
2. Grass			
3. Shrubs			
4. Flowers			
5. Trees			
6. Fences			
7. Urns			
8. Walks			
9. Cement flashings			
10. Parking curbs			
Brick and Stone			
11. Front walls			
A. Base			
B. Top			
C. Coping			
D. Tuck pointing			
E. Cleanliness			
12. Court walls			
A. Base			
B. Top			
C. Coping			
D. Tuck pointing			
E. Cleanliness			
13. Side walls			
A. Base			
B. Top			
C. Coping			
D. Tuck pointing			
E. Cleanliness			
14. Rear walls			
A. Base			
B. Top			
C. Coping			
D. Tuck pointing			
E. Cleanliness			
15. Chimneys			

FIGURE A.2—*Continued*

GENERAL INTERIOR

Items	Character and Condition	Needs	Estimated Expense Involved
Vestibules			
1. Steps			
2. Risers			
3. Floors			
4. Marble slabs			
5. Walls			
6. Ceilings			
7. Door mats			
Vestibule Doors			
8. Glass			
9. Transoms			
10. Hinges			
11. Knobs			
12. Door checks			
13. Door finish			
14. Kick plates			
15. Handrails			
Mail Boxes			
16. Glass			
17. Doors			
18. Locks			
19. Name plates			
20. Intercom			
21. Signal buttons and connections			
Stair Halls			
22. Steps			
23. Landings			
24. Handrails			
25. Woodwork			
26. Carpets			
27. Walls			
28. Ceilings			
29. Skylights			
30. Windows			
31. Window coverings			
Rear Halls			
32. Steps			
33. Landings			
34. Walls			
35. Ceilings			
36. Handrails			
37. Garbage cans			
38. Waste-paper receptacles			
39. Windows			
40. Window coverings			

FIGURE A.2—*Continued*

Items	Character and Condition	Needs	Estimated Expense Involved
Elevators			
41. Signal buttons			
42. Doors			
43. Cab floors			
44. Cab walls			
45. Cab ceilings			
46. Control mechanism			
47. Cables			
48. Pulleys			
49. Motor			
50. Shaft walls			
51. Shaft ceiling			
52. Shaft floor			
53. Floor numbers on doors			
Public Light Fixtures			
54. Entrance			
A. Brackets			
B. Fixtures			
C. Bulbs			
D. Switch			
55. Vestibule			
A. Brackets			
B. Fixtures			
C. Bulbs			
D. Switch			
56. Halls			
A. Brackets			
B. Fixtures			
C. Bulbs			
D. Switch			

BASEMENT

Items	Character and Condition	Needs	Estimated Expense Involved
Laundries			
1. Floors			
2. Walls			
3. Ceilings			
4. Washers			
5. Driers			
6. Vending Machines			
7. Tubs & Faucets			
8. Toilet bowls			
9. Lavatories			
10. Drains			
11. Windows			
12. Doors			
13. Window coverings			
Boiler Room			
14. Floor			
15. Pipes			
16. Fuel bin			
17. Fire hazards			

FIGURE A.2—*Continued*

Items	Character and Condition	Needs	Estimated Expense Involved
Boiler Room (cont'd)			
18. Ceiling			
19. Walls			
20. Windows			
21. Doors			
22. Cleanliness			
23. Window coverings			
24. Trash containers			
Boiler			
25. Flues			
26. Tubes			
27. Valves			
28. Diaphragms			
29. Flange unions			
30. Grates			
31. Ash pits			
32. Pointing on brickwork			
33. Motors			
34. Draft controls			
35. Chimney			
36. Thermostats			
37. Hydrostats			
38. Stoker			
39. Insulation			
40. Combustion chambers			
41. Water level			
Hot-Water Heater			
42. Tank			
43. Insulation			
44. Ash pit			
45. Incinerator			
46. Submerged system			
47. Hydrolator			
Pumps			
48. Motors			
49. Sump			
50. Pressure			
51. Circulating			
Lockers			
52. Floors			
53. Walls			
54. Ceilings			
55. Doors			
56. Fire hazards			
57. Aisles			
Central Air Conditioning			
58. Motors			
59. Cleanliness			
60. Accessibility			
General			
61. Plaster			
62. Trash and junk			
63. Screens			

Appendix   *343*

FIGURE A.3

OFFICE BUILDING INTERIOR INSPECTION REPORT

THE INSTITUTE OF REAL ESTATE MANAGEMENT
of the
NATIONAL ASSOCIATION OF REAL ESTATE BOARDS

Form 50B

_____ 19____

OFFICE BUILDING INSPECTION REPORT

Name of Property...Address...

Type of Property...Office Area Rental Rate...

No. of Stores...Store Area Rental Rate...

Report Submitted By...Basement Area Rental Rate...

Owner...

INTERIOR

Items	Character & Condition	Needs	Est. Expenses
Lobby			
1. Ceiling			
2. Walls			
3. Floors			
4. Lighting fixtures			
5. Glass			
6. Directory			
7. Signs			
8. Mail box			
Interior Doors			
9. Type			
10. Glass			
11. Rails			
12. Stiles			
13. Hand rails			
14. Hinges			
15. Locks			
16. Pulls			
17. Push plates			
18. Kick plates			
19. Mail slot			
Stairway			
20. Treads			
21. Risers			
22. Gates			
23. Bannisters			
24. Handrails			
25. Walls			
26. Ceilings			
27. Windows			
28. Skylights			
29. Electric lights			
Corridors			
30. Ceilings			
31. Walls			
32. Wood trim			
33. Floors			
34. Hardware			
35. Doors			
36. Glass			
37. Lighting fixtures			
38. Lighting switches			

FIGURE A.3—*Continued*

GENERAL INTERIOR

Items	Character & Condition	Needs	Est. Expenses
Corridors (Cont'd)			
39. Convenience outlets			
40. Waste paper receptacle			
41. Sand jars			
42. Fire hose			
43. Fire extinguishers			
44. Required signs			
45. Safety code violations			
46. Hopper rooms			
47. Maintenance			
Office Interiors			
48. Ceilings			
49. Walls			
50. Floors			
51. Lighting			
52. Fixtures			
53. Switches			
54. Elec. outlets			
55. Radiators			
56. Air conditioning			
57. Doors			
58. Transoms			
59. Hardware			
60. Baseboards			
Windows			
61. Type			
62. Frames			
63. Sash			
64. Sills			
65. Stops			
66. Weights			
67. Glass			
68. Glazing			
69. Caulking			
70. Weatherstripping			
71. Locks			
72. Screens			
Elevators-Passenger			
73. Permit expiration date			
74. Serviced by			
75. Contract			
76. Full maintenance			
77. Parts, oil, grease contr.			
78. Make			
79. Type			
80. Capacity (weight)			
81. Capacity (passengers)			
82. Lobby door fronts			
83. Corridor door fronts			
84. Operatorless			
85. Pit			
86. Full automatic			
87. Self leveling			
88. Door operator			
89. Electric			
90. Air			
91. Manual			
92. Cab size			
93. Cab trim			

FIGURE A.3—*Continued*

Items	Character & Condition	Needs	Est. Expenses
Elevators-Passenger (Cont'd)			
94. Cab walls			
95. Cab doors			
96. Cab lighting			
97. Cab ceiling			
98. Cab floor			
99. Cab ventilation			
100. Position indicators			
101. Floor indicator			
102. Signal lanterns			
103. Signal buttons			
104. Emergency switches			
105. Telephone			
106. Elevator shafts			
107. Pits			
108. Walls			
109. Guide rails			
110. Hoisting cables			
111. Compensating cables			
112. Governor cables			
113. Sheaves			
114. Motors			
115. Generators			
116. Governors			
117. Signs in shaft			
118. Floor numbers on shaft walls			
119. Floor numbers on door			
120. Miscellaneous			
121. Control panels			
122. Threshold lights			
Elevators - Freight			
123. Permit expiration date Contract			
124. Serviced by			
125. Full maintenance			
126. Parts, oil, grease contr.			
127. Make			
128. Type			
129. Capacity, pounds			
130. Platform size			
131. Platform lighting			
132. Shaft doors			
133. Cab gates			
134. Hoisting cables			
135. Compensating cables			
136. Governor cables			
137. Pit			
138. Motors			
139. Generators			
140. Signal buttons			
141. Signal buzzers			
142. Shaft numbers			
143. Shaft safety signs			
144. Guide rails			
145. Comments			
Public Rest Rooms-Men			
146. Floors			
147. Floor drain			

FIGURE A.3—*Continued*

Items	Character & Condition	Needs	Est. Expenses
Public Rest Rooms-Men			
(Cont'd)			
148. Walls			
149. Wainscote			
150. Ceiling			
151. Watercloset enclosure			
152. Watercloset type			
153. Tank			
154. Flushing valve			
155. Vacuum breaker			
156. Seat			
157. Bowl			
158. Lavatory			
159. Trim			
160. Soap dispensers			
161. Urinal			
162. Type- wall - floor			
163. Flushing valve			
164. Stall panel			
165. Hardware on door			
166. Locks			
167. Deodorants			
168. Ventilation			
169. Light fixtures			
170. Switches			
171. Window			
172. Waste receptacle			
173. Towel Cabinets			
174. Mirrors			
175. Signs			
Public Rest Rooms-Women			
176. Floors			
177. Floor drain			
178. Walls			
179. Wainscote			
180. Ceiling			
181. Watercloset enclosure			
182. Stall doors			
183. Stall doors hardware			
184. Watercloset type			
185. Tank			
186. Flushing valve			
187. Vacuum breaker			
188. Seat			
189. Bowl			
190. Toilet tissue holder			
191. Lavatory			
192. Trim			
193. Soap dispenser			
194. Mirrors			
195. Vanity shelf			
196. Deodorants			
197. Ventilation			
198. Light fixtures			
199. Switches			
200. Windows			
201. Waste receptacle			
202. Sanitary napkin vendors			
203. Signs			

FIGURE A.3—*Continued*

Items	Character & Condition	Needs	Est. Expenses
Basement Stairway			
204. Entrance door			
205. Treads			
206. Risers			
207. Hand rails			
208. Walls			
209. Landings			
210. Ceilings			
211. Light			
Basement Area			
212. Floors			
213. Sump pumps			
214. Walls			
215. Ceilings			
216. Fire doors			
217. No. of exits			
218. Sprinkler system			
219. Lighting			
220. Convenience outlets			
221. Ventilation			
222. Elevator service			
223. Storage space			
224. Heating			
225. Utility space			
226. Carpenter shop			
227. Plumber			
228. Paint shop			
229. Superintendent office			
Men Employees Rest Room			
230. Showers			
231. Watercloset			
232. Type			
233. Lavatory			
234. Urinal			
235. Lavatory trim			
236. Floor			
237. Walls			
238. Ceilings			
239. Lighting			
240. Heating			
241. Ventilating			
Men's Locker Rooms			
242. Floors			
243. Walls			
244. Ceiling			
245. Lighting			
246. Switches			
247. Heating			
248. Ventilation			
249. Doors			
250. Fire hazards			
Women Employees Rest Room			
251. Showers			
252. Watercloset			
253. Type			
254. Lavatory			
255. Trim			
256. Floor			
257. Walls			

FIGURE A.3—*Continued*

Items	Character & Condition	Needs	Est. Expenses
258. Ceiling			
259. Doors			
260. Heating			
261. Ventilation			
262. Lighting			
263. Switches			
Women's Locker Rooms			
264. Floors			
265. Walls			
266. Ceiling			
267. Lighting			
268. Heating			
269. Ventilation			
270. Doors			
271. Fire hazards			
Boiler Room			
272. Floor			
273. Walls			
274. Ceiling			
275. Fire doors			
276. Fire hazards			
277. Ventilation			
278. Lighting			
279. Switches			
Boilers			
280. Type			
281. Pressure, high			
282. Pressure, low			
283. Flues			
284. Tubes			
285. Draft control			
286. Valves			
287. Blow-off pit			
288. Vents			
289. Grates			
290. Fire box			
291. Pointing fire brick			
292. Steam line insulation			
293. Fuel, kind			
294. Storage tanks			
295. Coal chutes			
296. Coal bins			
297. Stokers			
298. Oil burners			
299. Gas burners			
300. Injectors			
301. Low water cutout			
302. Pop-off valves			
303. Gauges, pressure			
304. Gauges, water level			
305. Automatic controls			
306. Diaphragms			
307. Flanges			
308. Gaskets			
309. Packing glands			
310. Draft regulators			
311. Smoke detectors			
312. Steam condensate return			

FIGURE A.3—*Continued*

Items	Character & Condition	Needs	Est. Expenses
Vacuum Pump Make			
313. Storage tank			
314. Control (elec.) make			
315. Control (elec.) voltage			
316. Water level float switch voltage			
317. Combination negative & pressure gauge			
318. Strainer			
319. Motor			
320. Type			
321. Horse power load			
Hot Water Heaters			
322. Inside lining			
323. Steam coils			
324. Insulation			
325. Gaskets			
326. Thermostat			
327. Steam trap			
328. Safety valve			
329. Fire box			
330. Fuel			
331. Burner			
Pumps			
332. Sump			
333. Pressure			
334. Feed water			
335. Circulating			
336. Vacuum			
Water Softeners			
337. Type			
338. Sand filters			
339. Valves			
340. Differential gauges			
341. Tank, filter			
342. Softener			
Salt Tank			
343. Coating			
344. Float valve			
345. Overflow			
346. Tank			
Compressors			
347. Filters			
348. Automatic switch			
349. Safety valve			
350. Drive			
351. Motor H.P.			
352. Tank capacity			
353. Purpose of comp. air			
Vacuum Pump-Cleaning System			
354. Automatic switch controls			
Air Conditioning			
Window Units			
355. Miscellaneous			
a.			
b.			
c.			

FIGURE A.3—*Continued*

Items	Character & Condition	Needs	Est. Expenses
Window Units (Cont'd) d.			
e.			
Central System			
356. Type			
a.			
b.			
c.			
Original Installation			
357. Age			
358. Refrigeration			
359. Unit			
360. Refrigerant			
361. Compressor			
362. Capacity			
363. H.P. connec. load			
364. Performance			
365. Cooling tower			
366. Air distribution			
367. Ducts			
368. Insulation			
369. Grills			
370. Thermostats			
371. Zones			
372. Fans			
373. Performance			
Electric Panel Room			
Electric Energy Service			
374. Transformer capacity			
375. Voltage			
376. Cycle			
377. Power			
378. Lighting			
379. Phase single			
380. Phase three			
Panel Board			
381. Maker			
382. Amperage capacity			
383. Power circuits			
384. Lighting circuits			
385. Emergency circuits			
386. Stand by circuits			
387. Spare circuits			
388. Fuses			
389. Circuit breakers			
390. Meters			
391. Lighting meter			
392. Power meter			
393. Tenants meter			

FIGURE A.4

OFFICE BUILDING EXTERIOR INSPECTION REPORT

THE INSTITUTE OF REAL ESTATE MANAGEMENT
of the
NATIONAL ASSOCIATION OF REALTORS"

Form 50A

_____ 19____

OFFICE BUILDING INSPECTION REPORT

Name of Property...Address...

Type of Property...Office Area Rental Rate...............................

No. of Stores...Store Area Rental Rate.................................

Report Submitted By..Basement Area Rental Rate.........................

Owner..

EXTERIOR

Items	Character & Condition	Needs	Est. Expenses
Roofs			
1. Type			
2. Flashing			
3. Valleys			
4. Drains			
Walls - North			
5. Type			
6. Base			
7. Top			
8. Tuck pointing			
9. Stone sills			
10. Coping			
11. Parapet walls			
12. Terra cotta			
13. Metal trim			
Walls - East			
14. Type			
15. Base			
16. Top			
17. Tuck pointing			
18. Stone sills			
19. Coping			
20. Parapet walls			
21. Terra cotta			
22. Metal trim			
Walls - West			
23. Type			
24. Base			
25. Top			
26. Tuck pointing			
27. Stone sills			
28. Coping			
29. Parapet walls			
30. Terra cotta			
31. Metal trim			
Walls - South			
32. Type			
33. Base			
34. Top			
35. Tuck pointing			
36. Stone sills			
37. Coping			

FIGURE A.4—*Continued*

GENERAL EXTERIOR

Items	Character & Condition	Needs	Est. Expenses
Walls - South (Cont'd)			
38. Parapet walls			
39. Terra cotta			
40. Metal trim			
Walls - Court			
41. Type			
42. Base			
43. Top			
44. Tuck pointing			
45. Stone sills			
46. Coping			
47. Parapet walls			
48. Terra cotta			
49. Metal trim			
Chimney			
50. Type			
51. Comment			
Sidewalk Elevators			
52. Permits - expiration date			
53. Make			
54. Type			
55. Capacity			
56. Parts, oil, grease contr.			
57. Sidewalk doors			
58. Shaft			
59. Platform size			
60. Shaft gates			
61. Motors			
62. Pumps			
63. Tanks			
64. Generator			
65. Signal			
66. Safety locks			
67. Controls			
68. Pits			
69. Signs			
70. Comments			
Bldg. Entrance			
71. Doors			
72. Hinges			
73. Locks			
74. Checks			
75. Side lights			
76. Transoms			
77. Canopy			
78. Signal button			
79. Lighting			
80. Building name			
81. Street numbers			
82. Entry steps			
Exterior Fire Escapes			
83. Signs			
84. Access windows			
85. Access ladders			
86. Maintenance			
87. Ladder treads			
88. Hand rails			
Sidewalks			
89. Comments			

FIGURE A.4—*Continued*

GENERAL EXTERIOR

Items	Character & Condition	Needs	Ext. Expenses
Light Wells			
90. Skylights			
91. Roof			
92. Comments			
Fire Hazards			
93. Defective wiring			
94. Trash and rubbish			
95. Oil, gasoline or paint storage			
96. Gas leaks			
97. Self-closing doors			
98. Breeching and flues			
99. Dumbwaiter enclosures			
100. Hot ash disposal			
101. Defective fire hose			
102. Fire extinguishers			
Windows - Office			
103. Type			
104. Frames			
105. Stops			
106. Sash			
107. Sills			
108. Lintels			
109. Anchor bolts			
110. Glass			
111. Glazing			
112. Caulking			
113. Weather strip			
114. Screens			
115. Locks			
Windows - Store			
116. Frames			
117. Transoms			
118. Sash			
119. Glass			
120. Caulking			
121. Glazing			
122. Screens			
123. Hinges			
124. Sash			
125. Locks			
Penthouse - Elevator			
126. Roof			
127. Walls			
128. Steps			
129. Doors			
130. Windows			
131. Flooring			
132. Fire protection devices			
Other Roof Structures			
Miscellaneous Extras			

Glossary

ACCREDITED MANAGEMENT ORGANIZATION® (AMO®)
A designation conferred by the Institute of Real Estate Management to real estate management firms that are under the direction of a CERTIFIED PROPERTY MANAGER® and comply with stipulated requirements as to accounting procedures, performance, and protection of funds entrusted to them.

ACCREDITED RESIDENT MANAGER (ARM®) A designation conferred by the Institute of Real Estate Management to persons who have qualified as resident on-site managers.

Ad valorem Tax that is levied against property, based on its value.

Affidavit of service A sworn statement that an eviction notice has been served properly.

Agent A person who enters into a legal, fiduciary, and confidential arrangement with a second party and is authorized to act for that party.

Allodial system Form of private landholding in which land is held in absolute ownership.

Alteration The process of changing the function of a property.

Amortization Of assets, a means of gradually reducing the book value of a fixed asset by spreading its depreciation over a period of time; of debt, a means of gradually retiring an obligation by making regular payments of principal and interest over a period of time.

Amplitude The distance on a graph between the height of a wave and the depth of a dip.

Anchor tenant   A key tenant in a shopping center that will attract other businesses as well as consumers.

Appraisal   An estimate of value.

Articles of incorporation   A certificate that establishes a condominium association as a corporation under the laws of the state.

Assessment   Amount charged against each owner or tenant of a property to fund its operation.

Automatic renewal clause   A lease provision that automatically ensures renewal of the lease unless either the tenant or the landlord notifies the other party of a desire to terminate the agreement.

Base-unit-rate approach   A method of establishing rental rates in which a typical unit within a specific submarket is defined and becomes the standard against which all similar units may be measured.

Block grant program   A federal revenue-sharing program that makes direct grants to local governments in developing urban communities.

Board of directors   The official governing body of a corporation, including condominiums and cooperatives.

BOMA standard method   A standardized method of measuring office space developed by BOMA (Building Owners and Managers Association), a national organization of professionals in the office building industry.

Budget   A prediction of income and expenses over a specific time period for a particular property.

Bulk user   A commercial enterprise that utilizes a large quantity of office space.

Bylaws   Regulations that provide specific procedures for handling routine matters in a condominium operation.

Capitalization   The process of converting a property's anticipated future income into value.

Cash flow   The amount of cash available after all payments have been made for operating expenses and mortgage principal and interest.

Cashier   The person in the property management firm who records all income, bills accounts, and draws buildings' payrolls.

CERTIFIED PROPERTY MANAGER® (CPM®)   The professional designation conferred by the Institute of Real Estate

Management on individuals who distinguish themselves in the areas of education, experience, and ethics.

Chit　A receipt issued in lieu of gold.

Classified advertisement　A basic medium for briefly announcing space for rent, which usually appears in a special section of a newspaper.

Commercial paper　Short-term promissory notes issued by reputable business firms.

Common area　Space that is not used and occupied exclusively by tenants, such as lobbies, corridors, and stairways; in a condominium, the property in which a unit owner has an undivided interest.

Common area maintenance clause　A provision in a shopping center lease which states that the tenant must pay a share of the cost of operating and maintaining the center and the manner in which these charges will be assessed.

Common expenses　The costs of operating, managing, maintaining, and repairing a condominium's common areas and administering the condominium association.

Common law　A system of laws, originating in England and based on court decisions, which treat everyone equally, regardless of geographic or social status.

Community development block grant program　A revenue-sharing program that makes direct grants to fund local governments in developing urban communities.

Community shopping center　A retail area, covering approximately 100,000 to 250,000 square feet, which offers convenience items, apparel, and home furnishings, and often features one department or variety store.

Condhotel　A residential building in which seasonal occupants purchase hotel rooms on a contract for one month and sublease them for the remaining 11 months.

Condominium　A form of ownership that combines absolute ownership of an apartment-like unit and joint ownership of areas used in common with others.

Condominium association　A condominium's governing body to which every unit owner automatically belongs.

Condominium unit　A three-dimensional space of air located within the walls, floor, and ceiling of the condominium structure.

Conduit　An ownership vehicle that passes income tax benefits or liabilities directly through to individual investors.

Consultation A service offered to owners whose properties do not require ongoing management but who do need advice on specific problems, such as rehabilitation, modernization, or property conversions.

Consumer price index A figure constructed monthly by the U.S. Bureau of Labor Statistics that weights products by their importance and compares prices to those of a selected base year, expressing current prices as a percentage of prices in the base year.

Consumerism A movement seeking to protect the rights of buyers through government action and controls.

Controllable expense An operating expense over which management has definite responsibility and control.

Cooperative A corporation that owns real estate, usually a multifamily dwelling, including the building and land on which it is built; individual shareholders do not own their units but have the right to live in them.

Corporation A form of business organization created by statute law and which is considered legally as a separate entity.

Corrective maintenance Ongoing repairs that must be made to a building and its equipment.

Cost approach A method of estimating a property's value by determining the value of the land plus the cost of reproducing improvements.

Credit investigating agency A firm that prepares credit checks on prospective tenants for property owners or managers at a fixed fee per report.

Creeping socialism A slogan for increased government involvement in all aspects of the economy.

Custodial maintenance The policing and housekeeping duties associated with a property.

Cycle The time interval during which a regularly repeated series of events occurs; on a graph, the length of time required for a wave to move up from the normal line to its peak, down to the lowest point, and back to normal.

Decentralization The withdrawal from an area of concentration (i.e., urban decentralization).

Declaration A condominium association's constitution which creates the condominium and defines the owners' and association's responsibilities.

Deferred maintenance   Ordinary maintenance that is not performed and negatively affects a property's use and value.

Deflation   An economic condition occurring when money declines in quantity and goods are relatively scarce.

Demised premises   Property covered by a lease agreement.

Deteriorating neighborhood   An area in which buildings have been cut up or converted or are in disrepair and transciency is high.

Developing neighborhood   A growing area, with recently constructed buildings and stable families and social institutions.

Direct financial influence   A factor that increases the housing supply through credit and institutional arrangements, exclusive of providing direct financial aid.

Direct housing subsidy   A financial grant that increases the housing supply available to specified households (i.e., low- and moderate-income, handicapped, elderly).

Direct-mail advertising   A medium of promotion through letters, cards, or brochures, sent by mail to potential customers and which relies heavily on specialized mailing lists.

Director of leasing   The person in a property management firm who prepares the marketing and leasing strategy for a building.

Director of property management   The person in a property management organization who oversees the activities of the firm's property supervisors.

Direct solicitation   A procedure in which a property manager specifically asks an owner for the management of a building.

Display advertisement   A large paid notice designed to attract the public's attention in marketing a new property, especially commercial and industrial space.

Dynamic cycle   A trend illustrated on a graph by the gradual upward movement of the normal horizontal line; the amplitude of each succeeding cycle is higher than the preceding cycle, as building expenses increase, and, likewise, the amplitude of each succeeding cycle's dip is not as great.

Economic life   The period of time for which a building can be used to produce assets or services.

Economic oversupply   Vacancy that occurs entirely because of consumer inability to pay current rents.

Economic rent raise   An increase in rent determined by market shortage and general consumer income level.

Economic shortage   A condition, based on a technical shortage, occurring when there are more able-to-buy consumers than available rental units.

Electronic data processing (EDP) bookkeeping system   A computerized bookkeeping system that issues accurate records and establishes controls over income and expenses.

Employee policy manual   A handbook listing job descriptions, company policies, and rules and regulations, which is given to each new employee.

Energy conservation   Program of reducing energy waste.

Environmental Protection Agency (EPA)   A government agency organized in 1970, operating on all government levels, to regulate air and water pollution, noise abatement, and waste treatment.

Escalation clause   A provision in a lease which guarantees automatic rent adjustments for increased operating expenses.

Established neighborhood   A sound, healthy area in which all the land has been developed and families and social institutions are stable.

Eviction   The legal ejection of tenants and their possessions from the leased premises by the landlord.

Eviction notice   A written notice to a tenant to pay the rent immediately or leave the leased premises within a specified time.

Executive property manager   The person who is directly responsible for all management policies, procedures, and employees in a property management firm.

Fair Credit Reporting Act   Legislation requiring a property manager to advise applicants if a credit information agency is employed to investigate their credit.

Fan-shaped city   A pattern of urban development in which growth is concentrated behind a natural barrier, such as a lake or river.

Farmers Home Administration (FmHA)   A government agency that provides economic assistance to rural communities.

Federal Housing Administration (FHA)   An agency created by the National Housing Act of 1934 to provide a home-financing system through federal mortgage insurance.

Federal housing policy   Legislation that affects government housing agencies and the programs they administer.

Fee simple ownership   The greatest and most absolute ownership of land, subject to the least number of restrictions.

Fenestration   The design and placement of windows in a building.

Feudalism A political and economic system of the ninth to 15th centuries in which the king had supreme right over the land, which then was divided among lords and their vassals based on conditions of homage and service.

Fiat money Currency not backed by gold or silver.

Financial analysis A complete evaluation of real estate as an investment including valuation, depreciation, tax benefits, and cash flow calculations.

Fiscal services Duties other than the management of real property that are assumed by management firms to assist corporations.

Fixed-dollar rental A set rental amount for a retail store; there is no upward or downward adjustment based on volume of business or franchise operation.

Flashing Sheet metal or weather stripping used to reinforce and weatherproof the joints and angles of a roof.

Foreclosure A court action initiated by the mortgagee for the purpose of having the court order the debtor's real estate sold to pay the mortgage.

Franchise rental A type of rental in which the price of the retail location is directly affected by the location of the space and potential consumer traffic.

Frequency On a graph, the number of cycles in a given period of time.

Garden apartment A low-rise building designed for multifamily living, usually located in a suburban area.

General partner The participant in a limited partnership who manages the real estate operation and is liable for all debts.

Gold standard A guarantee that for each currency unit issued a certain weight of gold could be redeemed on demand.

Government National Mortgage Association (Ginnie Mae or GNMA) A federal government-owned corporation formed in 1968 to invest in mortgages for government-subsidized housing.

Gross floor area The total floor area in a shopping center, including the common area, or space that is not used exclusively by tenants.

Gross leasable area (GLA) A measurement of the total floor area designed for the occupancy and exclusive use by tenants in a shopping center.

Gross lease An agreement in which the tenant pays a fixed rental and the owner pays all the expenses associated with operating the property.

Hand-posted bookkeeping system   An accounting system in which collections are posted by hand on ledger cards and operating reports are prepared manually with a calculator.

Heating, ventilating, and air-conditioning (HVAC) system   The unit regulating the even distribution of heat and fresh air throughout a building.

Highest and best use   The most productive use to which real property may be put for the most desirable period of time considering all economic factors.

High-rise apartment   A multifamily structure averaging 25 stories and 300 units, usually located in a major metropolitan area where space is at a premium.

Home Owners Loan Corporation (HOLC)   An agency established in 1933, that provided long-term, self-amortizing emergency loans to families threatened by foreclosure during the depression.

Household   All persons, related or not, who occupy a housing unit.

Housekeeping   The regular duties involved in keeping a property clean and in good order.

Housing and Community Development Act of 1974   Legislation that authorized the Section 8 and community development block grant programs.

Housing and Urban Development Act of 1965   Legislation that created the U.S. Department of Housing and Urban Development (HUD).

Housing finance agency (HFA)   A state agency that provides construction and mortgage loans to a wide range of income groups by issuing tax-exempt bonds.

Housing unit   Any residential arrangement that constitutes separate living quarters.

Income approach   A method of estimating a property's value by capitalizing the flow of income that can be expected from the property during its remaining useful life.

Index escalation clause   A provision ensuring rent adjustments in an amount equal to the annual change in a specified index, usually the Consumer Price Index.

Indirect influence   An impact on housing as a result of monetary, fiscal, and credit policies.

Individual meter   A utility-measuring device for each tenant in a multiunit building.

Industrial park   A subdivision designed to accommodate light manufacturing and comparatively small land users.

Industrial real estate   Property that is used for the processing and manufacture of goods.

Inflation   An economic condition occurring when the money supply increases in relation to goods and is associated with rising wages and costs and decreasing purchasing power.

Institute of Real Estate Management (IREM)   A professional association affiliated with the NATIONAL ASSOCIATION OF REALTORS® for persons who meet standards of experience, education, and ethics with the objective of continually improving their respective managerial skills by mutual education and exchange of ideas and experiences.

Institutional advertising   A technique designed to raise the prestige of the property management firm or building through some promotional medium, such as billboards or wall displays.

Insurance   An agreement in which one party promises to pay a sum of money to another if the latter suffers a particular loss in exchange for a premium paid by the insured.

Insurance broker   One who, for compensation, places an order for insurance on behalf of the client.

Interest-only loan   A loan for which no amortization is required and the entire principal is due at maturity.

Jobber   One who buys merchandise from a manufacturer and sells it to a retailer.

Job description   A written outline of how a job is to be performed, its meaning, and its importance.

Job specification   A written outline of the specific duties and requirements for each position in a company.

Joint venture   An association of two or more persons or legal entities conducting a single business enterprise for profit.

Laissez-faire   An economic philosophy stating that government should not interfere with commerce and economic affairs.

Landlord   One who owns property and leases it to a tenant.

Land-use planning   The formation of all-inclusive plans for large-scale improvements, usually in urban areas.

Lease   A contract given by the landlord to the tenant for use or possession of real property, for a specified time, and in exchange for fixed payments.

Leasing agent   The person in a management firm directly responsible for renting space in assigned properties.

Lessee   In a lease, the tenant.

Lessor   In a lease, the landlord.

Life-support systems   The safety and security procedures that are adopted by a property's management.

Limited liability   Responsibility for the debts of a business that is restricted to the size of one's investment in it.

Limited partner   A participant in a limited partnership whose liability is confined to his investment and who does not have a voice in the management of the partnership.

Limited partnership   A business arrangement which allows certain partners to invest, take no part in the management, and assume limited liability.

Listing clerk   The person in a property management firm who distributes leads to rental agents.

Location   A reference to the comparative advantages of one site in consideration of factors such as transportation, convenience, and social benefits.

Loft building   A structure of two or more stories designed for industrial use.

Management agreement   A written contract in which a property owner contracts the management of a property to an individual manager or firm and which details all rights and obligations of both parties.

Management fee   Monetary consideration paid monthly or otherwise for the performance of management duties.

Management plan   An outline of a property's physical and fiscal management that is directed toward achieving the owner's goals.

Market   A meeting of people for the purpose of private purchase or sale.

Market analysis   The process of placing a property in a specific space market and then evaluating it by those market standards.

Market approach   A method of estimating a property's value by comparing it with similar properties that have been sold recently.

Marketing   All business activity involved in moving goods and services from producers to consumers.

Market survey The process of gathering information about specific comparable properties and comparing it to data concerning the subject property in order to weigh its advantages and disadvantages.

Mart building A multistory, finished-interior property that is a cross between a retail arcade and a loft building, used by wholesalers and jobbers to display sample merchandise.

Mechanized bookkeeping system An accounting system that relies on a bookkeeping machine to post accounts and uses one trust fund account with a subsidiary ledger for each property.

Merchandising An aspect of marketing that creates a desire for a particular article that people use almost universally by pointing out features in the item that will appeal to the buyer.

Merchants' association An organization that advances the common interests of shopping center tenants in planning advertisements, promotions, decorations, etc.

Mid-rise apartment A multifamily structure that ranges from six to nine stories and is found in both cities and suburbs.

Miniwarehouse A facility that provides self-storage units to private individuals and businesses on a rental basis.

Mixed-use project A planned development that provides at least three income uses (e.g., retail, office, and residential) within a single project.

Mobile home A factory-manufactured dwelling that often is located on a fixed lot and connected to local utilities.

Modernization The process of replacing original equipment with similar features of up-to-date design.

Money A universally valued commodity, used as a medium of exchange.

Money supply The total amount of currency outstanding plus the total number of demand deposits in all the nation's banks.

Mortgage A conditional pledge of property to a creditor as security against a debt.

Municipal Bankruptcy Act Legislation passed in 1975 to assist cities facing financial disaster.

Narrative operating report A letter enclosed with the monthly statement to an owner describing a property's condition and potential.

National Housing Act of 1934 The first significant housing legislation; created the Federal Housing Administration.

Negotiation   Dealings between two parties, especially tenant and owner, in order to reach an agreement on price, quantity, quality, or other terms.

Neighborhood   An area within which there are common characteristics of population and land use.

Neighborhood analysis   A study of a neighborhood and comparison of it with the broader economic and geographic area of which it is a part to determine why individuals and businesses are attracted to it.

Neighborhood conservation   Large-scale plan to improve a neighborhood, including the buildings and economic conditions.

Neighborhood shopping center   A relatively small retail district, approximately 25,000 to 75,000 square feet, designed to provide convenience shopping for day-to-day consumer needs.

Net (single-net) lease   An agreement in which the tenant pays the rent and also certain expenses connected with the leased premises.

Net-net lease   An agreement in which the tenant pays all maintenance and operating expenses plus property taxes.

Net-net-net (triple-net) lease   An agreement in which the tenant pays maintenance and operating expenses, property taxes, and insurance.

Noncontrollable expenses   Items such as real estate taxes, insurance, and labor-union wages over which the property management has no control.

Nuisance rent raise   The rent raise a tenant will pay to avoid the expense, discomfort, and inconvenience of moving.

Occupancy agreement   A residential lease.

Office building   A single-story or multistory structure where business is carried out or services provided, usually divided into individual offices and offering space for rent or lease.

Office landscaping   A technique in space planning that utilizes floor space in an open manner.

Open-space planning   An office design that eliminates fixed partitions and permits the tenant to rearrange work stations as needs require.

Parking index   The number of parking spaces per 1,000 square feet of a shopping center's gross leasable area.

Pass-through fund   A financial arrangement in which single-family house mortgages are pooled to back real estate investment securities.

Percentage lease   An agreement used for retail properties in which the rental is based on a percentage of gross sales or net income made on the premises or a minimum fixed rent, whichever is greater.

Percentage-of-gross fee   A property manager's regular compensation based on a given percentage of monthly gross collections.

Percentage rent   Rent that is based on a percentage of the gross sales or net income of the tenant, often against a guaranteed minimum.

Personalty   Personal property.

Physical life   The length of time for which a building is a sound structure, which depends on the quality of maintenance.

Policy   Management guideline within which decisions are to be made.

Prestige   In real estate, the status that individuals or a firm acquire from a property's desirable location and tenancy.

Preventive maintenance   A program of regular inspection and care that allows potential problems to be prevented or at least detected and solved before major repairs are needed.

Primary goods   Merchandise of the first priority, such as food and clothing.

Primary housing unit   A dwelling unit that is the basic home of its occupants.

Principal   In property management, the property owner who authorizes an agent to act for him.

Private limited partnership   An arrangement designed for modest-sized projects, which has less than 35 investors and usually does not require federal or state registration.

Procedure   The steps for implementing a particular policy.

Profession   An occupation that requires considerable education and specialized training.

Professional reputation   The overall opinion of the business community as to the character and capability of a property manager.

Property analysis   A complete description of a piece of real estate, including its accommodations, architectural design, and physical condition.

Property management   A service profession in which someone other than the owner supervises a property's operation, according to the owner's objectives.

Property manager　A professional who administers real estate according to the owner's objectives.

Property supervisor　The person who has direct responsibility for specific properties, including tenant, owner, and personnel contact.

Proprietary lease　A document which gives a shareholder in a cooperative the right to occupy a unit under certain conditions.

Prospect　A potential customer.

Prospectus　A formal summary of a proposed commercial venture.

Public housing program　The principal form of federal housing assistance for low-income families.

Public limited partnership　A legal organization with a large number of limited partners, which must be registered under state and federal securities laws.

Public relations　The activities employed by a firm to promote a favorable relationship with the public in order to meet marketing objectives.

Purchasing agent　The person in the management firm who supervises the purchase of goods and services.

Qualification　The process of judging a prospective tenant's acceptability.

Quebec Act　This Act stated in 1774 that only the Crown could grant lands in the western territories, which interfered with westward movement and precipitated the Revolutionary War.

Radius clause　A provision in a shopping center lease under which a tenant agrees not to own or operate another outlet within a specified distance of the center.

Real estate　The land and any improvements found on it; the term often is applied to nonagricultural property, which accommodates individuals, business, and industry.

Real estate cycle　A period of time in the real estate industry that experiences regular and recurring economic changes.

Real estate investment trust (REIT)　A single-tax entity set up to sell shares to investors and use the funds to purchase real estate investments.

Real estate security　A form of personal property (stocks, bonds) secured by real property and which is evidence of real estate ownership or indebtedness.

Recommendation　The process of obtaining referrals from satisfied clients.

Recruitment   The active process of obtaining new employees.

Rectangular city   A pattern of urban development in which geographical conditions prevent growth in two directions but permit it in the other two.

Recycling   The process of reclaiming old buildings for adaptive uses.

Referral   A technique of obtaining new management business by recommendations from satisfied clients.

Regional analysis   Identification of the general economic and demographic conditions and physical aspects of the area surrounding a property and determining which trends affect it.

Regional shopping center   A large retail district, approximately 300,000 to 1,000,000 square feet, that offers a wide selection of merchandise and serves a large residential sector.

Rehabilitation   The process of lengthening a building's economic life within its present design by restoring it to a well-maintained condition.

Reminder notice   A notice sent to tenants when rent is delinquent.

Rent   Periodic payment made for the use of a property over a period of time.

Rental inquiry card   A record of all prospects who call or visit a property for future reference when other units become available.

Rental ledger   A written record noting tenants' names, units, phone numbers, rents, security deposits, and other leasing information.

Rental price level   An indicator that moves up or down in response to supply and demand and reveals the economic strength of the real estate market.

Rental schedule   A listing of rental rates for units or space in a given building.

Rent bill   An invoice sent to tenants just before the rent is due.

Rent control   Government regulation imposed on rents to prevent them from being increased.

Rent receipt   A record of a payment (i.e., rent) received.

Rent roll   A balance sheet for the account of each rental area, listing tenants' names and their unit numbers, along with all income payable and paid.

Resident manager   The person responsible for general administration and maintenance of a property and supervising its personnel and resources.

Retail properties   Establishments in which goods and services are sold directly to individuals and households.

Retrofitting The replacement of some fixtures or facilities in a building with more energy-efficient fittings.

Rider An amendment to a lease, signed by both the lessor and lessee.

Rules and regulations Guidelines for personal behavior in any property; measures that affect relations among neighbors also may be included.

Sale The transfer from one person to another for a consideration of the possession and right of use of some particular article of value to both parties.

Savings and loan association An institution that provides funds for financing home mortgages.

Secondary goods Merchandise such as furniture and appliances, usually offered in regional shopping centers.

Second-home condominium A condominium that is occupied for a part of the resort season.

Section 8 The federal government's principal medium for housing assistance, authorized by the Housing and Community Development Act of 1974, which provides for new construction and rehabilitation.

Security deposit Money advanced by a tenant and held by an owner or manager for a specific period of time to cover possible damages and ensure faithful performance of the lease by the tenant.

Service request clerk Member of the property management firm who arranges for all maintenance requests to be handled.

Sheridan-Karkow formula A method of applying a rental schedule to office space which was devised by two Chicago building managers.

Sherman Antitrust Act An Act passed in 1890 that declared trusts and monopolies illegal and provided for fines and imprisonment of violators.

Sign restriction clause A provision in a shopping center lease that limits the use of outdoor and indoor advertisements and other graphic displays.

Slum A core area of a city in which overcrowding and deterioration are evident.

Slum clearance The process of razing urban real estate when it has deteriorated to a point at which salvage is impossible.

Social obsolescence A loss in value brought about by social condition; i.e., a condition occurring in neighborhoods with desirable locations but in which homes are too large for present-day families.

Sole proprietorship   A form of business organization in which an individual owns and manages the entire enterprise.

Sound, aging neighborhood   An area in which most of the land is improved and buildings are used as originally intended.

Space   In real estate, an area providing for residential, commercial, or industrial occupancy.

Space planning   The process of combining functional efficiency and effectiveness with a pleasing appearance in creating office interiors.

Space rental   A method of establishing rental rates on retail space by calculating the costs of land, construction, and projected maintenance.

Special-purpose building   A structure designed for the particular needs of its occupants, such as a medical or dental building.

Specialty center   A small retail district, approximately 250,000 square feet, that offers specialized merchandise, atmospheric restaurants, and attracts shoppers from a wide business area.

Split mortgage   A financing method of the 1920s that broke loans into small denomination bonds for sale to the investing public through investment bankers.

Spot zoning   A change in the use of an individual property which may be inconsistent with an area's classification.

Square city   A pattern of urban development with approximately equal growth in each direction.

Standard tenant improvement allowance   An allowance for items that may be installed on the leased premises of an office building at no extra charge to the tenant.

Statement of disbursements   A listing of all expenses incurred by a property during a specific operating period.

Statement of operations   The primary record produced by the management firm's accounting department for the owner; a statement of money received and money paid out.

Strip development   A retail center in an outlying area designed as a straight line of stores, usually very narrow in proportion to its length.

Summary of operations   A brief description of income and expenses relative to a property for a specific period, usually one month.

Super-regional shopping center   A retail center covering more than 750,000 square feet.

Syndicate An association of persons or firms to accomplish a joint venture of mutual financial interest.

Syndicator The entity that organizes a syndicate and oversees its operation.

Tax A government levy usually made on a regular basis and based in principle on the relative value of the object being levied.

Taxable income Income for a given period of time against which there is an income tax liability to a municipal, state, or federal income tax agency.

Technical oversupply A condition arising when there are more property units in a given community than there are consumers for them.

Technical shortage A condition existing when there are more consumers than units.

Tenant One who pays rent to occupy or gain possession of real estate.

Tenant mix The wide representation of businesses and services that comprise a shopping center or office building; of households that comprise a multifamily development.

Tenant union An organization that represents tenant interests.

Term lease A binding landlord/tenant agreement for a specified time.

Topping off A ceremony marking the completion of the structural frame of a building.

Townhouse A type of single-family home built as attached or semi-detached row houses.

Trade inception A decentralization trend that refers to locating new, convenient retail centers between the consumer and existing centers.

Trading area The people and facilities within specified limits of a shopping center.

Traffic report A record of the factors that lead prospects to visit or make inquiries at a property.

Tuck-pointing The cement repair of mortar joints on brick and stone walls.

Uniform Residential Landlord and Tenant Act Legislation designed to regulate and standardize the relationship between residential landlords and tenants.

Unit deed A document that legally transfers the title of a condominium unit and its undivided portion of the common areas to the owner.

Unit make-ready report A maintenance checklist for defects in a newly vacated unit.

Urban Land Institute An independent, nonprofit research and educational organization founded in 1936 to improve the quality and standards of land use and development.

Urban renewal A complete program for clearing slum areas and designing redevelopment projects.

U.S. Dept. of Housing and Urban Development (HUD) A government agency established in 1965 that provides federal assistance in planning, developing, and managing public housing.

Use clause A provision in a shopping center lease that explicitly states how the area leased will be used.

U.S. Housing Act of 1937 Legislation that established the public housing program to be administered by the U.S. Public Housing Authority.

U.S. Housing Act of 1949 An act providing for federal assistance for slum clearance and urban development, construction of low-rent public housing, and rural housing.

Utility A public service, such as gas, water, or electricity.

Value The worth or usefulness of a good or service expressed in terms of a specific sum of money.

Zoning Any restriction on the use of real property within a given area.

Index